"The idea of making friends with helpful!" –BW, Professional Pianist

"Loved! My hypothesis was this would be helpful for high-level competitors. True, but more! It also applies to regular, routine life. Incredibly empowering. A book for the masses." –ML, three time 1st Place Dance Collegiate National Champion, 1st Place International Title, Choreographer

"I was asked to review this book while adding certification to my helicopter pilot license. I didn't think I had time. Reading saved me time! The info cut down study time for the exam and expensive flight time learning maneuvers. Highly recommend." –CR, Commercial Helicopter Pilot

"Good insight into body and brain functions under stressful situations and how to navigate the brain through barriers in daily life. Very insightful." –CH, Education Administrator

"Valuable reinforcement! Recognizing patterns that drag down energy and performance is valuable not just to players but also coaches and parents." –SD, Sports Team Manager, Parent of Cal Ripken World Series athlete

"This book changed how I look at and empower myself. The questions and case studies were helpful in analyzing a deeper look. It's too good to skim!" –PH, Business Banker

"I definitely needed to read this! I realized most of my stress comes from outcome anxiety. I learned awesome skills that I hope will also help my children." –SM, Student, Parent

"Finding fear is a friend was a tad insightful. I never considered overcoming anxiety a whole-body approach. Short, sweet chapters engage personal connections. Oh that all can have this confidence, especially worried teens!" –MM, Teacher, Musician, Parent of champion athletes

"What an amazing book! I found it to be engaging, insightful, practical, universally applicable, and full of life-changing concepts. I do not know a single person who would not benefit. Well done."–KB, Top 1% Scholar

Boost Core Power
And Bust Anxiety:
Learn to Eliminate Outcome Anxieties

Like Performance, Test, Sports, Public Speaking, Appearance,
Technology, Stage, Finance, Business or Relationship Anxiety

How to find Peak Ability and Flow in the Zone

———————

By Mariann R. Adams, MS, NCTM

———————

To give feedback, receive private coaching
See other books by Mariann R. Adams
Schedule a lecture, enjoy tips, or
Other information see:

www.aplusperformingarts.com

BOOST CORE POWER AND BUST ANXIETY

Editorial supervision: Alison Parker
Illustrations: Kamryn Brockbank
Photo: Teresa Lynn Anderson

Adams, Mariann R.
Boost Core Power and Bust Anxiety: How to find peak flow in the zone /
Includes bibliographical references
ISBN-13: 978-1-7326959-0-0
ISBN-10: 1-7326959-0-3
1. Performance, Test, Sports Anxiety—psychological, neurological, physiological
2. Stress management
3. Self-help techniques

To Bart

Thank you for believing that I am now
The person I someday hope to be.

Preface

Research shows that clear, fun info is easier to understand and apply. But let me translate that last sentence into academia to show you:

Peer-reviewed journal documentation indicates strong positive correlations between accessible cognitive constructs associated with positive affect and concrete comprehension, resulting in effective concept coherence, implementation, and improved psychological and behavioral modulation.

See what I mean?

This book isn't just fluffy ideas. It's solid research that works. But it's deliberately written in a light style because everything in this book is designed to support you and build core power.

Let's *bust* anxiety.

Table of Contents

1
Rickety Bridges

Whether you're a kid taking a spelling test or a neurosurgeon operating on a tough case, there are huge benefits in understanding anxiety. Eliminating fear starts with understanding core safety.

Fear *never* happens without safety concerns. Brains and bodies are hardwired for safety, and this is good. But it also means it's impossible to ignore safety. Physical safety is usually guarded, but internal core safety is treated downright recklessly. Is it any wonder that hard-wired fear responses take over?

Imagine crossing a narrow rope bridge swinging above a deep ravine. Suddenly twine snaps and a few rotted boards plummet earthward. As you precariously grab the rails and grope for stability, is your concentration on the day's tasks and beautiful view or are you riveted on the disintegrating bridge?

Now imagine yourself crossing the same ravine on a massive bridge reinforced with ample steel and cement. Where is your concentration now? Does safety affect focus, enjoyment, and the ability to accomplish tasks? You bet! The bridge is your core. It matters if you're safe.

But core safety is neglected and even mocked. Have you heard, "Why are you afraid of performing? No one is pointing a gun. There's no *real* threat."

No threat, really? Consider the boss's reaction after the important business proposal; the disappointment of blanking when meeting "mister right"; the junior high kids' ridicule in speech class; the lost opportunity from a low exam score; the director's threats and clamoring replacement competition; the result of a bad job interview; the humiliating game mistake and decades of national TV replays. No threats?

It's ridiculous to say there are no threats! Maybe you won't land in the hospital or morgue, but the threats are real nonetheless. A *lot* can be at stake like jobs, quality of life, health, and personal dignity. But forget the big stuff, even tiny losses add up. Daily confidence and competence is important.

Core safety matters. Subconscious and conscious concerns affect ability whether a performance is known only seconds in advance (like answering a phone) or months in advance (like a competition or ACT test). Performance anxiety, test, sports, interview, reading, public speaking, math, business, new technology anxiety—even appearance anxiety or fixing-a-flat-tire anxiety, are the same thing. They come from being unsure of successfully handling the situation. A more accurate name for these anxieties is "unsure-of-coming-out-okay-anxiety," or *outcome anxiety*. The other names distract from solving the problem.

Outcome anxiety also surfaces as procrastination, imposter syndrome, hesitancy, frustration, insecurity, and indecision. They're all from being unsure of coming out okay. Any of these outcome anxieties can hamper ability.

A "performance" is anytime ability is demonstrated. It can be a test, sports competition, phone conversation, business evaluation, concert, job interview, media broadcast, question response, social media post, theater production, technology share, or even parenting in public. Any of these can produce "unsure-of-coming-out-okay" feelings. And if you agree with Shakespeare that "all the world's a stage," the application is even wider.

Everyone has outcome anxiety at some time. Have you ever felt unsure, fearful, frustrated, or apprehensive about coming out okay? Have you felt anxious regarding finances, managing a schedule, or a bad hair day? If anxiety causes problems with big stuff it also causes problems with little stuff.

Understanding anxiety eliminates problems and unleashes peak "flow in the zone" or flow/zone. This is effortless, pleasurable, maximum ability. The brain and body work optimally. Peak ability isn't just for Olympic athletes, exceptional celebrities, honors students, business CEOs, or other top performers. Anyone can enjoy it anytime. It's learned. Skills can improve ability in seconds.

Incapacitating anxiety and fleeting inconsistency are the same problem. The core psychological and emotional causes are the same—just different ends of the spectrum. So the skills that *decrease* anxiety also *increase* peak flow in the zone.

The solution to anxiety becomes clear when the cause is known. The solution isn't to minimize, suppress, deny, lean on addictive crutches, or avoid. The solution to high performance is to build a strong core! Fear disappears when the core is safe just like fear on a bridge disappears when safe. Core safety demands attention just as physical safety does.

It's almost impossible to override internal fear responses; but it's fairly easy to boost core power. If you were on a rickety bridge would you want to stay, hide fear and convince yourself there was no problem or step onto a strong bridge and move on?

The one-size-fits-all fear strategies don't work because they don't address core safety and they overlook the unique differences between people. The result is failure, frustration, limitations, missed opportunities, embarrassment, stress-related health issues, shame, injuries, and discouragement.

Inaccurate information increases problems. The only way to eliminate outcome anxiety is to *meet core needs*. Individual needs vary. But when core needs are met, *it can be felt*. Self-consciousness melts, anxiety is eliminated, stress is reduced, ability expands, and self-respect increases.

Anxiety is more noticeable in high-stakes situations like a performance, test, competition, or important meeting. Of course! There's greater concern about coming out okay! But those who have anxiety in high-stakes situations *are also limited daily* in low-stakes situations. The information in this book definitely improves high-stakes performance. But the bigger benefit is improved *everyday* ability, including an improved capacity to prepare, grow and enjoy life.

Some say, "I don't have anxiety; I don't need anxiety information." But stress-related issues are an occupational hazard for performers—and everyone performs in some way. Knowledge makes a difference. Electricians, doctors, and police officers are specially trained to avoid specific occupational hazards. This training prevents many problems and prepares them when difficulties can't be prevented. Anxiety information does the same for you.

Anxiety information is especially important for leaders. Coaches, teachers, directors, administrators, and executives *affect others*. The information in this book improves ability in individuals. It also improves ability in groups like athletic teams, businesses branches, performance troupes, and school classes. Parents are anxiety coaches by default, and their impact lasts a lifetime.

Most anxiety information manages fear *symptoms*. But isn't it better to get rid of the *causes* of fear? Managing fear symptoms is like weeding by flicking leaves instead of yanking roots. This information removes anxiety roots. Simple strategies work,

3

whether the goal is to eliminate anxiety, prevent anxiety, or mentor others through anxiety.

So, those with anxiety, get ready to eliminate it. Those without anxiety, get ready to unlock new peak ability. And those who are leaders get ready to make a difference on a whole new level. Are you in?

2
Measly Monsters

To eliminate outcome anxiety, you'll need to know the difference between managing *symptoms* and addressing *causes*. It's illustrated in these two scenarios of a little girl and her mother handling a nighttime "monster" under the bed. See if you can discern the difference between managing symptoms and addressing causes.

"Mommy, there's a *MONSTER* under my bed! I can hear him and see him, and I'm afraid he's going to eat me!"

"Goodness! You've got an increased pulse, rapid breathing, tense muscles, problems concentrating, tummy distress, and catastrophic thoughts of bad things happening—all preventing sleep. Don't worry. I know just what to do! Let's do a pre-sleep routine, think safe thoughts, breathe deeply, systematically relax, submerge in a mental protective bubble, focus your senses, and visualize sleep. And whatever you do, DON'T think about a monster pouncing and eating you! Sweet dreams! See you in the morning…"

Will this work? Isn't it crazy to ask Suzie to sleep when she thinks a monster is lurking beneath her? Imagine her at breakfast the next morning, "Thanks Mom! Wow, that worked great! It didn't bother me at all to have a monster—fangs, claws, and all—just six inches below me!"

It's ridiculous. But essentially this is expected when anxiety is managed by addressing *symptoms* instead of *causes*. Discouragement results when this doesn't work; but actually, something would be wrong if it did work!

No matter how sincerely Suzie tries, if she addresses the problem this way, it's likely to get worse. Her self-esteem and confidence may plummet from repeated failure. Others may even think something is wrong with *her*, adding embarrassment, isolation, frustration, and shame to the problem.

5

Does this sound familiar? It's found every day in the testing center, the conference room, the field, the court, the stage, the gym, the school classroom, and the concert hall. Symptoms are targeted instead of causes and it doesn't work. The problem isn't the *person*, it's the *method*! Suzie needs to get rid of the monster, not learn to cope with him. So, let's redo this scenario and address causes instead:

"Mommy, there's a *MONSTER* under my bed! I can hear him and see him, and I'm afraid he's going to eat me!"

"Sweetheart, I know you're afraid and it can be scary at night, so let's turn on the light and look...Is there a monster under the bed? No. See? The noise you heard isn't a monster; it's the tree kissing the sky in the wind. And the light you saw isn't a blinking monster's eye; it's the street lamp peeking through the leaves and shining on the wall to say goodnight. Come to the window. Isn't that funny? See, you're safe; there's nothing to be afraid of. Hugs and kisses. Sweet dreams. See you in the morning..."

Suzie's fear *automatically* dissipated when she understood the causes. Similarly, anxiety automatically dissipates when the causes are understood. There are *always* reasons for feeling unsure of an outcome. The mind and body naturally react. If causes are ignored, it's like trying to cope with a monster inside. The result is rapid breathing, increased pulse rate, inability to concentrate, shaking, terrifying thoughts and an inability to do one's best. (And later you'll learn about asymptomatic fear that can affect even talented individuals. So expect benefits even if fear symptoms aren't generally a problem.)

Managing symptoms has its place. For example, things like a pre-performance routine, focusing on senses, breathing deeply, redirecting fear, systematically relaxing, thinking safe thoughts, cocooning in a protective bubble, reframing, or other management methods can reduce symptoms; and certainly do what helps. But ultimately, isn't it better to eliminate the problem and not deal with it anymore? That's the goal: Build core power to *eliminate* anxiety. This is done through understanding core concepts.

The right core things must be strengthened for anxiety to melt. Individuals are unique. The concepts that strengthen your core will be unique and speak to you. But not all concepts will speak to everyone. So it's important to be aware of this. Don't be put off by things that are perfect for someone else and then miss the gems that are perfect for you. Understand your uniqueness. Also realize that some benefits may not be recognized until examined closely. All the information is valuable, especially for leaders who work with diverse personalities.

Each chapter includes five elements: 1) new chapter concepts to build core understanding; 2) chapter summaries to increase core comprehension; 3) case studies to clarify core concepts; 4) "empower yourself" paradigm thumbnails to encapsulate core power; 5) Fast-Track ReflACTION questions to apply core skills. ReflACTION = Reflection + Action; the last half is capitalized because the benefits gather momentum.

Many have commented on the particular value of the case studies and ReflACTION questions. These clarify and focus. What if Suzie stayed in bed fearfully ruminating (reflection) or looked down the hall instead of under her bed (action)? She'd still have problems. Suzie's anxiety melted because reflection and action were *focused in the right direction*. That's the job of ReflACTION. It strengthens core power through focused application. The *Core Power Pro-Launch Pad*, a companion workbook to this book, maximizes focused application.

Whether using this companion tool or not, writing honest responses to ReflACTION questions with a curious attitude is more effective than simply thinking responses. So write if you can. It helps the subconscious brain process to the conscious brain. When this happens, new insight melts a piece of anxiety (similar to Suzie looking under the bed and out the window). Insight strengthens the core. And watch out, there can be unexpected benefits! Perhaps anxiety isn't a problem in routine activities, but are there uncomfortable things that are avoided? Discomfort and avoidance are symptoms of anxiety. So ability and comfortable competence may improve in unexpected ways.

If you experience any degree of anxiety, the solution is different than you think or you'd have taken care of it already. Right? Simple things made a difference for Suzie. Simple things can make a difference for you—like reading and ReflACTION. Strengthen your core by considering the power of focusing in the right direction.

Next up, it's time to unlearn...

Summary

To strengthen the core and eliminate anxiety, the focus must shift from managing *symptoms* to eliminating *causes*. Discouragement results when working on the wrong thing. Problems are usually due to the method, not the person. The idea is to eliminate problems, not cope with them. You are a VIP with a unique history, so the specific things that eliminate your anxiety will be unique. ReflACTION (reflection + action, building momentum) focuses effort in the right direction and takes into account your uniqueness. Insight comes through subconscious and conscious processing. Processing is enhanced by written, honest, curious reflection in personal notes or using *The Core Power Pro-Launch Pad*. Problems dissipate when thoroughly understood. Solutions to problems are usually different than realized or the problems would already be solved. Little things make a big difference.

Case Study

Brent's love of the game decreased as the pressure increased. If not for his scholarship he would have quit already. He felt like a fraud, despite solid stats and interested scouts. He churned inside and hid the problem. Then, in a special interview, a respected pro player admitted to having performance anxiety and explained how he dealt with it. This was a ray of hope. Brent was determined to figure this problem out. He actually loved the sport; it was the anxiety he hated.

Empower Yourself

Dodge problems, or...determine solutions.

Fast-Track ReflACTION

1) How does anxiety affect your ability (or those you mentor)? What could be gained by performing better? Do you ever hide or suppress anxiety?
2) Do you experience this outcome anxiety: inconsistency, frustration, agitation, insecurity, dread, avoidance, irritability, procrastination, or apprehension; how could addressing anxiety improve relationships and health?
3) In the past have you addressed *causes*, targeted *symptoms*, or *avoided* situations? What was the result? What insights have surfaced and how do they affect your perspective, motivation and hope?

3
Ready, Set—Unlearn!

Whether you are gifted and managing well or struggling and desperate, there are benefits in understanding outcome anxiety and how a strong core increases ability. In fact, understanding anxiety is not optional for optimal output. Awareness of the impact of conscious and subconscious concerns is the foundation for peak flow in the zone.

It's common to believe that outcome anxiety (such as performance anxiety, procrastination, indecision, or "choking" and inconsistent flow/zone) is a personal defect. This is not true. Anxiety is a learned reaction—that can be "unlearned". So, if you've got any form of outcome anxiety, give yourself a break. This problem can be eliminated. Most likely the things that caused it were completely out of your control.

A common form of outcome anxiety is performance anxiety, so let's talk about it for a minute. Full-blown performance anxiety is so common that if a person *doesn't* have it, they're the odd one! A high school coach said 100% of his athletes had it. A study showed 70% of top professional orchestra musicians were significantly limited by it. A middle school principal confided, "It's amazing how many kids get sick the day of mandatory speeches." And have you heard of NFL players or Olympic athletes concerned about it? You bet! Statistically, if you walk into a stadium, the *majority* of the people you see have some type of full-blown performance anxiety—even the professionals you came to watch. And many of those who are limited by it don't recognize it, especially if anxieties are in unexpected areas.

Usually activities are avoided when there is an anxiety, or anxiety is hidden because of embarrassment, fear, or discouragement. Anxiety frequently affects athletes, performing artists, students, sales personnel, and executives to the point that ability and choices are limited. Believing that others manage better can increase the problem. Some even start to believe that *they* are the problem. DON'T believe this! Despite these common difficulties, pretty much *no one* starts life out with any type of anxiety. Zip, nada, zero, none! Surprised?

Children as young as age three produce slightly higher cortisol when performing, but problematic performance anxiety is basically unheard of in preschoolers. In fact, almost all little children run around saying, "WATCH ME!" It doesn't matter how badly they mishandle a ball, mess words up, pound the piano, bobble a twirl, slaughter a song, or fall on their face; they unabashedly bask in the sheer joy of learning, exploring, and sharing! Even if you now have extreme anxiety, you were once an embrace-the-world-kid and part of that kid is still inside.

Various forms of outcome anxiety usually begin in the early to mid-elementary grades and anxiety peaks or continues to grow after junior high. There are usually fewer problems when children are raised in secure environments. This is because high emotions, unexpected difficulties, or unpredictable circumstances can cause feelings that children are not capable of resolving. This affects core development and strength and may result in long-term anxiety.

Even if love was predominant, times of anger, confusion, instability, financial distress, or other incidental situations can leave pockets of negative impact here and there. So outcome anxiety is common. Unaddressed anxiety can grow, so it's important to identify it. But it's also important to avoid guilt or blame because these slow progress. Awareness of the past is used to move forward. The past isn't a problem. Issues can be overcome when understood.

Outcome anxiety develops from: 1) *experiencing* a negative situation; 2) *observing* someone in a negative situation; 3) *imprinting*. Anxiety is usually the result of multiple negative experiences, but it can emerge from a single *very* bad experience. Flow/zone problems emerge from milder situations that might not even be considered "negative" (as you'll see documented later). Personality plays into the picture and all contributing factors intertwine. Most people understand what it means to experience or observe a negative situation, but what's imprinting?

Just as a baby duck bonds to the first moving object after hatching, the emotion a person has when first learning a skill imprints on that skill. Then this imprint affects all future learning of that skill unless there is specific intervention. For example, Sandy and Jack wanted to sing. Both sounded awful. Sandy's teacher cheered her, resulting in positive feelings; Jack's teacher cringed, resulting in negative feelings. Sandy was imprinted with a positive emotion toward singing which made it easier and she became good at it; Jack was imprinted with a negative emotion, which made it difficult even though he had more innate talent.

In other words, if a person has a great experience when first learning to read, future reading will be easier; if a person has a bad experience when first learning to read, future reading will be harder. Of course, this is a simplification because many factors can be involved in a single skill, but as a general rule, most people permanently imprint with the positive or negative emotion they have when first exposed to something. Do you see how this can affect your core power?

Also, the age-old nature/nurture question factors in. It is now believed that genes affect more than how tall you are and the color of your eyes. There are correlations between genetic markers and other things, including anxiety and depression. Also, certain gene alterations have been found in those experiencing extreme trauma, like Holocaust victims. Additionally, the offspring of mice who have learned a maze pick it up faster than the offspring of those who haven't.

So initial tests point to a very real possibility that memories may be coded and passed through genes. These may then activate to interplay with life-experiences. If genes can change for the worse they can also change for the better. So your decisions may affect more than just your future. Whatever extent that ancestors' memories and genes may or may not affect you, it is certain that your choices alter your life. Gene bars don't account for choices in purposeful lifestyle and coping strategies. So no matter what you may have inherited or experienced, you can move forward. You can build core power.

The result of experiences, observation, imprinting, and nurture/nature is that most people have at least some hang-ups. Pigeon-hole thinking sets in. Abilities are believed to be set... "I'm good at this" or "I'm not good at this" or "This is just my personality." Most people don't know that experiences and environment shape perceptions let alone how to reverse a negative impact and shape positive outcomes.

So how does all this relate to outcome anxiety? These factors make a big difference in how aptitude plays out. Little pockets of core inadequacies can interfere in an otherwise competent person. Core inadequacies feel like wading through mud. If you've ever felt their effects, it's likely you have more ability and can progress faster than you realize. Noticing things that influence the core, increasing knowledge, and improving skills result in significant, positive changes.

Change involves awareness of *thoughts* and *feelings* and attending to them. Uncomfortable feelings result in giving up sooner and not reaching potential. Comfortable feelings result in increased effort. Striving for flow/zone without understanding the things that affect it (like past experiences, imprinting, or other factors) is like having one foot on the gas and the other on the brake. Mixed feelings and this inner fight of wills impedes progress. In a rush to move past limitations, many people force themselves forward. But force doesn't ease the brake pedal off, self-understanding does.

It's a hassle to have a limitation like anxiety, but could there be unforeseen benefits? Limitations tend to develop specialized qualities like courage, resilience, patience, tenacity, self-awareness, and compassion. No one *wants* a limitation, but there can be benefits *because* of a limitation. In fact, research shows that approaching limitations with a positive attitude *increases* mental and physical resources, problem-solving skills, overall skills, and even happiness. So working through a limitation may ultimately put you ahead, not behind. Understanding the potential benefits of a limitation strengthens the core.

Handel's greatest work, *The Messiah* (esteemed by generations as one of the greatest pieces of music ever written, and certainly the most performed) was created after a severe limitation. A stroke left him devastated and paralyzed for months. These overwhelming difficulties fostered the internal qualities that eventually immortalized him. Ironically, after his stroke he no longer wanted to *impress* but rather to *inspire*. He ended up impressing *and* inspiring. Do you see how the struggle changed his core?

Similarly, Beethoven experienced an inner struggle and musical transformation after going deaf. Inspiration is abundant. Serious injuries have preceded Olympic medals. Years of rejection have preceded unprecedented business success. Tragedy has preceded triumph everywhere. Prominent people periodically share that anxiety or other problems made them kinder, more motivated, and even grounded and protected them. In fact, sometimes the very reason a person is highly respected is *because* of conquering limitations. Limitations may be uncontrollable, but they do not control success or failure! Limitations do not determine your future.

Difficulty can propel a person forward. There is *always* the potential of unexpected benefits. Limitations are not handicaps, they are opportunities. Every person's life includes easy stuff and hard stuff. Outcome anxiety just happens to be the hard stuff for some people. Did Suzie move massively forward when she understood her fear? Yes!

Knowledge—*deep, awesome knowledge*—is the most powerful weapon to eliminate outcome anxiety and increase flow/zone. Knowledge strengthens the core. That knowledge includes an understanding that limitations are not handicaps. They are opportunities with benefits attached. Strengthen your core by considering that common anxieties may be uncommon opportunities.

Next up, what's the "primary" problem?

Summary

Whether a person is gifted and managing well or struggling and desperate, there are benefits in understanding outcome anxiety and its affect on output. Outcome anxiety is common, especially performance anxiety. Anxiety is hidden due to embarrassment, fear, or discouragement. Thinking that others are doing better, or that you're the problem, increases outcome anxiety. Everyone's life has hard stuff and easy stuff; outcome anxiety and flow/zone issues are the hard stuff for some people. Anxieties are learned reactions that can be "unlearned." Young children don't have performance anxiety. It develops from a combination of experiences, observations, imprinting, genes, and personality. Loving environments are usually imperfect so most people have hang-ups and "pigeon-hole". Identifying contributing environmental factors speeds progress in eliminating anxiety; blame and guilt slow progress. Limitations may be uncontrollable, but they do not control success or failure. Limitations are not handicaps; they are opportunities with benefits attached. Limitations can be used to strengthen the core and propel a person forward. Moving forward is facilitated by knowledge.

Case Study

Abam felt he wasn't good at technology. This limited his ability to share his areas of expertise. After he learned about imprinting, Abam reconsidered his abilities. Whenever frustrated, he asked himself, "Why am I unsure? What about this is too hard for me? Why do I feel incapable of handling this situation?" It seemed a mental door widened enabling him to learn things he had struggled with. He was better at technology than he thought.

Empower Yourself

Take a detour, or...get to the core.

Fast-Track ReflACTION

1) What possible limitations do you sense; what may have caused them?

2) What factors determine whether limitations propel or hamper? What can you do to ensure benefits?

3) What is easy for you; how can you use these strengths to overcome limitations?

4
Performance Anxiety Doesn't Exist

It's tough to solve a problem without knowing what it is. Anxiety is complicated. It has many different names, and if that's not confusing enough, there are positive and negative types. But despite this, there's actually no such thing as "performance anxiety" or similar anxieties. But *something's* going on, so what is it? It is an anxiety. But it doesn't have anything to do with performance or similar tasks. We've touched on this, but let's go deeper.

Anxiety never happens without feeling incapable to some degree. That's why the brain and body react. Names like "performance anxiety" or "test anxiety" mislead and point down a dead-end path. The name "*outcome anxiety*" is more accurate. Outcome anxieties are *always* due to feeling unsure of coming out okay.

A name is a BIG deal. Names help define problems. Choosing a definition is like choosing a fork in a road. Different definitions lead down different paths. The right definition provides clear direction, while the wrong definition leads away from the solution. Remember, I said that those with anxiety get discouraged, isolated, and give up. It all starts right here with the definition.

There's a greater *fear of not coming out okay* when performing, so more fear surfaces then. But a person can feel incapable anywhere, anytime, doing anything. Outcome anxiety can even start several months before a big performance. Yes, incapable feelings can surface *waaay* before a test, tournament, recital, competition, audition, or business meeting! It's even possible to feel incapable *after* a performance—have you ever rehashed or ruminated? This is also outcome anxiety.

Fear limits ability—whether during performance or not. In fact, unsure feelings can even affect whether things are attempted.

So attention to feelings is important. Unsure feelings can surface in something as small as answering a phone to as big as an international TV broadcast. Flow/zone is often affected by *very subtle* unsure feelings. Even so, these core concerns can be sensed.

Some performance problems are due to a lack of performance skill. But ongoing performance problems are different. They're usually due to primary fears. Primary fears are insecurities about feeling loved, accepted, appreciated, secure, valued, and capable. If performance skills are addressed, but the problem is a primary fear, performance problems continue. This is frustrating. Discouragement surfaces when the wrong thing is addressed. Everyone has primary fears surface periodically. So everyone should be aware of them.

Primary fears increase when interpersonal support is in question. A person can manage, even if a performance bombs, as long as he/she still feels loved, accepted, appreciated, secure, valued, and capable. And a person will struggle, even if a performance shines, if he/she doesn't feel loved, accepted, appreciated, secure, valued, and capable. Support matters.

Performance support is strongest when others are kind and knowledgeable regarding anxiety. Some people are kind but not knowledgeable. They may respond with inappropriate reactions or advice. Others may be knowledgeable but not kind. They may respond brashly or indifferently. If kindness or knowledge is missing, there can be uncertainty.

Feeling loved is so important that there's a tendency to hide "unlovable" stuff. However this compounds problems. Unlovable things are hidden from self through suppression or denial. This disconnects the person from their core. It also disconnects the person from others. Of course, unbridled disclosure of unlovable things isn't wise. It leaves the person vulnerable to those who are unkind or unknowledgeable. But it is also unwise to disconnect from those who genuinely care. It's wise to support yourself and seek appropriate support from others. Be aware of disconnection.

How is internal disconnection overcome? Notice thoughts and feelings. Don't be afraid of what is found when looking inside yourself. There will be positive and negative things. That's okay. The core has "perfect imperfections." When given permission the conscious and subconscious parts of the brain team up to increase awareness. Sometimes childhood coping strategies block the ability to receive support. Awareness helps reprogram them. This results in an ability to receive greater internal and external support. Core safety increases.

Core awareness increases confidence. Confidence is the greatest protector against anxiety. Coaches and parents try to build confidence. This is good. But it doesn't work if it just distributes positive fluff. Awareness and knowledge are needed. Without knowledge it's easy to feel at the mercy of anxiety. Knowledge helps to change this. Knowledge increases core power which results in improved confidence and performance.

Improved confidence and performance is nice, but it's not the most important reason to address anxiety. The most important reason is to improve health and quality of life. Anxiety causes stress. Daily stress is so common that it's considered normal. When performance demands are added on top...yikes! Anxiety stress is a major occupational hazard for performers—whether you're a student performing on tests or a professional performing in your career. Have you ever felt stress wear on you?

Continual stress can cause physical problems like immune suppression, systemic inflammation, respiratory issues, hormone imbalance, digestive problems, insomnia, arthritis, heart disease, and even permanent brain damage. It can also cause disrupted concentration, impeded memory, suppressed creativity, drug use, alcoholism, depression, and even suicide. Additionally, stress can cause interpersonal problems like work-place conflict and familial discord. Why are these higher among CEOs, performers, students, and athletes? Some say it's from "type A personalities," "artistic temperaments" or "sports egos." But this ignores the occupational hazards of performing. Performance is hard. Reducing stress is important.

Who wants stress-related problems? Nobody! There's good news for performers. The skills that decrease anxiety and increase flow/zone are also the tools that reduce stress and improve enjoyment in life. So get ready for a lot of benefits. Addressing outcome anxiety improves learning rates, relationships, stamina, health, *and* performance ability. (I'm not just saying this; it's strongly supported in the research.) Would you like these benefits? Strengthen your core by becoming aware of primary needs.

Next up, what's often neglected in practice?

Summary

Outcome anxiety is feeling unsure of coming out okay. The mind and body react to feeling unsure. Names define problems. An accurate name provides a laser-beam direction. An inaccurate name limits progress and can result in discouragement. There's greater fear of not coming out okay when there's an audience. Fear immediately causes limitations in practice and performance. Usually unsure feelings are a symptom of primary fears like feeling loved, accepted, appreciated, secure, valued, and capable. Everyone experiences primary needs and fears at times. Even if a performance bombs, a person will be okay if feeling loved, good enough, understood, accepted, appreciated, important, capable, or valued. Conversely, even when a performance shines, a person will not be okay if not feeling loved, good enough, understood, accepted, appreciated, important, capable, or valued. Unsure feelings are compounded by being unsure of support. "Unlovable" things tend to be hidden from self and others. A person who is kind is not necessarily knowledgeable; a knowledgeable person is not necessarily kind. Optimally, supportive people are both kind and knowledgeable. Disconnection clogs subconscious and conscious problem solving and impedes confidence. Disclosure is not always wise. Connection to one's core is always wise. Performing well is not the most important reason for addressing anxiety. Stress is an occupational hazard for performers. Stress has serious physical, mental, and interpersonal consequences. The skills that decrease anxiety also reduce stress. These skills also improve enjoyment, relationships, learning rates, stamina, health, and performance ability. This is strongly supported the in research.

Case Study

Terrie was churning inside. She decided to leave the exhibition hall and pace in the lobby until her turn. As she prepared to exit, her friend, Midgett, gently teased, "Relax! There's no need for performance anxiety." Terrie felt defensive. This was just extra energy, and certainly to be expected! After all, she couldn't be sure she would handle everything well until she was done. Peeved, she snapped, "Seriously! I just want to walk. I'm *fine!*" Midgett knew that anxiety could change personalities and responded, "Good idea. I'll come for you a couple of minutes before. You'll do great." [Terrie disconnected from herself and others by not understanding or acknowledging anxiety and not being aware.]

Empower Yourself

Disconnected core, or...distinguished core.

Fast-Track ReflACTION

1) How does the name "outcome anxiety" affect anxiety-elimination tactics? How could having anxiety when rehearsing or alone impact a performance?

2) What primary fears speak more strongly to you; why? (Consider the impact of nature/nurture.)

3) What unlovable things do you hide from yourself or others? What are the advantages and disadvantages of hiding things? How can you use awareness to better support yourself?

5
The Inseparables

Anxiety management and performance are *inseparable*. They go together *every* performance, *every* time. Waiting until a performance to manage anxiety is like waiting until the test to hit the books, the game to practice the kick, the concert to practice the music, or the meeting to check the presentation. Ignoring anxiety leaves a person vulnerable. Some performances are not known in advance—like pop quizzes or unexpected phone calls. But most preparation can include anxiety management.

If anxiety isn't managed, the other preparation doesn't matter. You'll hear that a person is going to the library to study for the test, the gym to work on the game, the practice room to work on the music, or the bathroom mirror to work on the speech. But have you heard, "I'm heading out to work on anxiety management"? No! Anxiety is ignored unless it's extreme. However, even miniscule anxiety affects ability.

Performers commonly possess tenacity and perseverance. These qualities help when *facing* problems and hurt when *ignoring* problems. So, ignored problems can get pretty big before they're addressed. (This is not just true regarding anxiety; performers are also notorious for ignoring injuries, fatigue, thirst, etc.)

Ignoring anxiety is common. Why? The importance of anxiety management is underestimated, the need is not admitted, or past effort has failed. I get it! But no more excuses. Anxiety management must be prepared *as much as* other things to enjoy peak ability. The two parts of preparation can happen simultaneously, but it doesn't happen automatically. Effort must be deliberate.

I'm not talking about practicing the usual anxiety management strategies. Rehearsed breathing, trained relaxation, practice tests/events, etc. can be helpful, and helpful things should not be overlooked. But to *eliminate* anxiety the strategies must be different. Practice is a time to improve the quality of the performance (skills/study) and the quality of thoughts and feelings (anxiety management). Essentially, anxiety management is attending to your core.

This doesn't mean to become bogged down or distracted. It's being mindful and curious. When preparing a performance, thoughts and feelings are also "practiced". These influence outcomes. If practice thoughts include "I can't do this" or "I can hardly wait to quit," these become embedded with the skill. Other things can be embedded like the emotional effects of injuries. Additionally, some don't feel they deserve success or they don't feel qualified. Practice is a time to notice these things that affect core power. Core concerns can then be processed. The quality of thought improves.

Quality practice includes quality thoughts and feelings. Things that feel unsure in performance are a *little unsure* in practice (or personal life). Hone in on these. Consider their origins. If enormous effort yields little improvement then it's clear that the skill is affected by other factors. Scanning for unsure feelings helps determine those factors. (Scanning can also improve ability in those who perform well.)

Unsure feelings can be directly, indirectly, or unrelated to performance. For example, a person might be unsure of a ball grip. If the unsure feeling is directly related, practice the grip. If the unsure feeling is indirectly related, look for fear associated with the task like concern about repeating a grip mistake that cost the championship last year; examine variables on and off the field. If the unsure feeling is unrelated, look for deeper fears like a childhood experience that caused a fear of trying, which now affects the grip and other things; examine patterns and review core concerns. Also, look for primary fears.

What controls the body? The brain does (and also the heart, as you'll see later). Can you see that it doesn't matter how much time is spent practicing if the brain and heart short-circuit the effort? Many individuals become stuck because attention is not paid to things beyond the actual task. All unsure feelings limit ability to some degree. This can be taken care of. But improvement doesn't happen until core feelings are recognized.

Does this seem overwhelming? Remember Suzie, little things make a big difference. Insights aren't hard. *Insights come to you.* Your mind and body *want* to support you. Even unexpected insights can improve ability. For example a common anxiety is "there isn't enough time." Since everyone has the same amount of time, this "unrelated" anxiety can reveal core belief patterns and insights. (For example, often those who don't feel there's enough time also don't feel there's enough money, friendships, etc.) Curiosity draws core safety concerns to the surface. Curiosity isn't hard. It's interesting. It's okay to feel what you feel and find what you find.

Only you can access your core thoughts and feelings, so you are your own VIP detective! Whether decreasing anxiety or increasing peak flow/zone, the process is the same. Notice fleeting thoughts and feelings in order to *collect data*. Unsure feelings aren't a big deal, but they do provide valuable core insights. And that's a big deal.

Just as performance ability increases or decreases depending on things like injury or extra practice, anxiety increases or decreases depending on things like emotional injury or core awareness. Anxiety is fluid. What wasn't a problem may become one. And what was a problem may dissipate. So continual awareness is needed.

It's important to note that there's a difference between *self-awareness* and *self-consciousness*. Self-awareness increases ability; self-consciousness decreases it. This is discussed in depth later, but it's mentioned here as a heads-up. The goal is to enjoy self-awareness without self-consciousness. Curious self-awareness is a big part of anxiety management.

There are *always* reasons for unsure feelings. The subconscious and conscious brain is able to uncover them. Most people only consider direct connections between unsure feelings and skills. This can limit their ability to improve. Your brain now knows there can be direct, indirect, and unrelated factors. This automatically puts the subconscious brain in "scan mode" and the conscious brain in "reception mode." Yes, it's that straight forward. Strengthen your core through deeper awareness.

Next up, how fear is your friend...

Summary
Performance and anxiety management are inseparable. Performance preparation should include anxiety management. Anxiety management is neglected because the importance is underestimated, the need is not admitted, or past effort has failed. Anxiety management can be practiced with skill development, but it doesn't happen automatically. Preparation strategies are different when eliminating anxiety. Lack of awareness can result in

difficulty moving forward. Awareness does not mean to become bogged down or distracted. Awareness involves being mindful and curious. Practice is a time to improve the quality of the performance (skills/study) and the quality of thoughts and feelings (anxiety management). Thoughts and feelings during practice bond with the skill and affect performance. Unsure feelings can be fleeting or overwhelming. Unsure feelings can be directly, indirectly, or unrelated to performance. You are the only person with access to your thoughts and feelings, so you are the only one who can collect data. Unsure feelings aren't a big deal, but the associated insights are. Anxiety changes so it's always good to be aware. There are always reasons for unsure feelings, and the subconscious and conscious brain is able to uncover them. Awareness puts the subconscious brain on scan mode and the conscious brain on reception mode. Anxiety management is straightforward.

Case Study

Klon was overwhelmed. How could he succeed when his college classes were filled with smart students who came from neighborhoods that were night-and-day different from his own gang-and-drug-filled one? Self-doubt grew and rattled him as a big test neared. It was the first he'd really become aware of his feelings. He confided his concerns to his roommate, TJ, who responded, "Look, if you don't deserve to be here, nobody deserves to be here. Just because no one at home has done this doesn't mean you can't. You made it this far, who says you can't take it all the way?" Klon's doubts subsided enough that he was able to work again. He studied fiercely and aced the test.

Empower Yourself:

Insufficient preparation, or...invincible preparation.

Fast-Track ReflACTION

1) What might have happened if Klon *didn't* explore unsure feelings; what if Terrie in the last chapter *did* explore unsure feelings? Are unsure feelings affecting you?
2) How can you improve the quality of thoughts and feelings during study or practice; what could be the impact beyond improved performance?
3) How does noticing unsure feelings increase the ability to trust and support yourself, accept support from others, and give support to others?

6
Fear Is Your Friend

Fear can actually be a good friend. When challenges arise, the body kicks in adrenal support to help out—and that's pretty cool! Adrenaline enhances ability, sharpens thinking, and strengthens muscles. This edgy fear prepares you to succeed. In fact, things like the pre-game shout, "Go team!" deliberately corrals and positively directs this good, edgy fear. Positive edgy fear isn't talked about much because it isn't a problem.

But edgy fear can turn into over-edgy fear. That's when too much "assistance" kicks in. This uncomfortable feeling can cause a "fear of fear", which can cause more adrenaline, then more fear...and soon there's an out-of-control "fear cycle." There can actually be more fear of fear than fear of the performance. But research shows that fear is easier to manage when it's understood. So let's look at adrenal function more closely. (Actually the adrenals work in conjunction with the hypothalamus, pituitary, pancreas, and other response glands and there are numerous hormones involved in both edgy and over-edgy support. But the adrenals are key players and so they're referred to here for simplicity.)

The adrenals are there to help you. If there was an accident and you suddenly needed to lift a car off of a loved one, you'd be grateful for the influx of adrenaline. But forget extreme situations. Even in daily life, the adrenals and other response glands are faithful friends.

They kick in to help avoid an accident when another driver does something stupid; they give an extra boost to finish the gym workout; they allow for missing a meal when running late; they compensate when you're up late but should have called it a night. In short, the adrenals and associated glands help compensate for unusual physical, emotional, or mental stress.

Daily life can produce stress and the adrenals are happy to cover. Can you see that the adrenals are constantly on call to provide support? Understanding this actually helps them provide less adrenaline when it's not needed and plenty when it is.

The adrenals respond to fear. Fear is usually initiated by built-in safety reactions. Then fear is perpetuated by thoughts. Initial safety reactions are usually automatic, so you can't really control them. But you can control thoughts. Automatic safety reactions and fearful thoughts release hormones into the blood. Healthy core thoughts can stop more hormones from being released, but they can't do anything about the hormones already in the blood. Those must run their cycle. After they run their cycle, the fear sensation stops. It doesn't take long, but it is long enough to think that fear can't be influenced. If that happens, new fearful thoughts may dump more hormones into the blood. But understanding the interplay can automatically help reduce the problem. There's more control over fear than most people realize.

The adrenal system is amazing. But there are more amazing things about it. Too much fear causes fear symptoms. These can be used to track the *cause* of anxiety and flow/zone problems. As the saying goes: where there's smoke, there's fire. If a fear response has kicked in, *something* caused it. Fear is a protection indicating a safety concern. The source is either due to an automatic response or a thought. Thoughts are often tied to core concerns and primary fears. So fear encourages addressing problems. It's good to be able to spot fear.

It's helpful when others, like parents, coaches, or teachers can spot it, but there's no substitute for spotting your own fear. Why? Maximum ability starts inside. You are the only person who can access your thoughts and feelings. Some fear is never visible. Other fear can be addressed before it escalates enough to become visible. So spotting your own fear has huge advantages.

Fear causes symptoms, whether it's fleeting apprehension or incapacitating dread. Common symptoms are usually recognized. But less common symptoms are often missed. It's important to be able to identify all symptoms because fear is like cancer; it can grow if not detected and early detection makes treatment more effective. Some people think that they don't have fear. But it's as unlikely that a person never has any fear as it is to always have maximum fear. So whether or not fear seems to be a problem, it's wise to pay attention.

Most people identify fear by the physical symptoms, but there are physical, mental, emotional, and behavioral symptoms.

Additionally, most people only look for symptoms during performance, but symptoms can appear any time. Here's what to look for:

Physical symptoms include varying degrees of things like dry mouth, loose bowels, throwing up, shaking, increased heart rate, faster breathing, insomnia, nightmares, increased fidgeting, rashes, paleness, semi-fetal positions, pacing, wringing hands, tapping, hair twisting, rocking, nervous movement, feeling light-headed, passing out, etc. The intensity of physical symptoms can range from so slight they are barely noticeable to absolutely incapacitating. You've probably noticed some of these in performance. Are they present any other times?

Mental symptoms include things like catastrophic thoughts (thinking of major or minor things that could go wrong), worry, confusion, inability to focus on a task (whether in personal life, practice, or performance, and not necessarily performance-related), doubt, indecision, rehashing, fussing, low confidence, low self-belief in a positive outcome, thinking problems (crunching, fogging, blanking), perfectionism (all or nothing extremes, self-pressure, flawless expectations), rumination, etc. An individual might mentally over-engage by obsessing about the performance or other things; they might under-engage as evidenced by difficulty focusing. It's even possible to go back and forth between over- and under-engagement. Mental symptoms can start long before a performance, like "what if I _____." And they can continue long after the performance with thoughts like "If I did/didn't do _____, what would have happened?" Do your thoughts ever get in the way?

Emotional symptoms include things like irritability, impatience, intolerance, clinginess, vulnerability, anger, guilt, talkativeness, extra interaction, higher positive or negative emotion, etc. In other words, personalities change when experiencing anxiety. A person who is shy might become more shy or more talkative; a person who is outgoing might become shy or more talkative. A calm person might become agitated or excited. The increase in energy before a show or game is an emotional symptom of fear. Have you noticed this? Emotional symptoms can cause excitement and bonding, or short tempers and conflict. This doesn't just happen before shows or games. When a person behaves differently in daily life there's often a hidden anxiety. Do you see how common this is?

Behavioral symptoms include such things as avoidance, procrastination, tardiness, cancelling commitments, missing engagements, "paralysis by analysis," self-sabotage, assurance seeking, leaving early, taking excessive breaks, failing to prepare, inappropriate or "stiff" laughter, verbal protests, misplaced items, avoidance of challenging material or situations, hostility toward self or others, seeking too much or too little help, pronounced apathy (appear not to care but actually care deeply and cannot manage), grudging effort, or quitting. Often people don't understand their own behavior. When behavioral improvement is attempted without addressing anxiety, problems usually increase. Have you experienced behavioral symptoms?

It's valuable to be able to identify fear symptoms, but not all symptoms indicate anxiety. It's more complicated. It's important to consider the reason behind a symptom. Appropriate responses can be the exact opposite when anxiety is involved. Laziness needs a push forward; anxiety needs a pull back before moving forward. Sometimes preparation is *impossible* without addressing anxiety first (see chapter 28 case study). Individuals either can't start preparations or they start and are ineffective. Also, the same person may need different responses in different situations (see this chapter's case study).

Improper responses decrease preparation, decrease output, and increase dropout. Appropriate responses reduce anxiety, increase preparation, and increase ability (at astonishing rates). Even taking only a couple of minutes to address anxiety can immediately improve test scores without more study or instruction. This phenomenon has also been seen in musicians who immediately improve without additional practice. Productivity increases when fear symptoms are noticed and addressed, particularly when this is done *in the moment*. The brain literally functions differently (as you'll see later).

It's possible to spot symptoms in the moment. Fear looks different. Fear feels different. Any activity can be hampered by conscious or subconscious nervousness. It's easier to reverse problems when understanding that fear is a friend. It kicks in edgy fear to give support. And it leaves a symptom trail to track down the causes of over-edgy fear. Strengthen your core by recognizing fear and realizing it is your friend.

Next up, move from defense to offense...

Summary

Edgy fear prepares you to succeed. Adrenalin enhances ability, sharpens thinking, and strengthens muscles. Fear can be a good friend in personal life, practice or performance. Over-edgy fear produces physical, mental, emotional, and behavioral symptoms. Some fear is common, other fear is uncommon and often unrecognized. It's important to be able to spot all fear. Maximum ability starts inside. Individuals are as unlikely to have all fear symptoms as to have none. Fear is unique to the individual. Fear changes behavior and personalities, and these changes are often seen right before a performance. There can be bonding or conflict. Fear can cause a person to over-engage or under-engage. Taking a few minutes to address anxiety saves time. Test scores and ability immediately increase after addressing anxiety. Over-edgy fear can be used to track and eliminate the causes of anxiety. Fear is your friend.

Case Study

Latt was initially excited to solo, but now he wasn't so sure. He loved playing his oboe but his mouth was so parched that he was worried about being able to play. Did he eat the wrong food for lunch? He drank more water but his mouth was still dry. He was afraid if he drank more he'd have to go to the restroom in the middle of the performance. He didn't know what was wrong or what to do. This made him more nervous than ever.

Case Study

LaNara asked her daughter to clean her room, a job that was *long* overdue. LaNara checked in several minutes later. Her daughter had hardly moved. In the past LaNara might have burst out in anger, but now she knew better. She recognized the overwhelmed look. She gently asked, "Do you feel capable of doing this?" Her daughter burst into tears. LaNara gently broke the big job into little tasks. Her daughter progressed quickly and was almost done when a favorite novel surfaced. She stopped cleaning and began to read. LaNara checked and insisted the room be finished first. Soon her daughter was reading in a completely clean room. LaNara smiled. It wouldn't be long until her daughter could work independently. [Do you see the difference between anxiety-based procrastination and non-anxiety-based procrastination? When there's anxiety, it's most effective to pull back before pushing forward. When there isn't anxiety, push forward. This may be necessary when assigning tasks to employees, students, etc. If a task seems too hard, leaders or individuals can break big jobs into smaller tasks. LaNara and her daughter would have saved even more time if this was done immediately.]

Empower Yourself:
Ignore symptoms, or...identify symptoms.

Fast-Track ReflACTION
1) How have your adrenals helped you in positive ways this week?
2) What physical, mental, emotional and/or behavioral fear symptoms have you seen in yourself; what subtle fear symptoms might be missed that may be impacting you?
3) What could keep you from noticing fear *in the moment*; why is noticing fear in the moment particularly important?

7
Fix Quick
Without Quick Fix

Most people avoid negative feelings like fear, depression, anger, etc. Why? Duh, they're *negative*. Right? But negative feelings are actually positively helpful. They indicate core safety concerns. They are *always* warnings. So are negative feelings "bad" from this perspective? Let's take a look.

How often is a threat so ominous it requires incapacitating performance anxiety, an obstacle so insurmountable it requires debilitating depression, or a danger so extreme it requires explosive anger? Negative emotions tend to go overboard. But did you ever wonder why?

The mind and body are hard-wired for safety. Any potential threat sets off the sympathetic nervous system. An internal "negative emotion alarm" goes off and the volume often increases, demanding to be heard. But are negative feelings listened to? It depends on whether the alarm is about physical safety or emotional safety.

Physical safety is usually attended to. If fear surges because a car crosses the line and is headed straight for you, action is taken. There's no debate about whether swerving might hurt the other driver's feelings, or if a jostle will upset people in the car. Physical safety is clear so it's easy to respond to. There's no internal or external debate; rather, there's internal and external support to immediately address issues.

Emotional safety is different. Emotional concerns can be confusing, uncomfortable, and intimidating. Problems are harder to discern and understand. So what happens? There's second guessing. Internal or external support is undependable and safety is unreliable. So instead of listening to fear and attending to issues, quick-fix responses take over that side-step core issues.

"Quick fix" reactions include blame, anger, excuses, aggression, evasion, denial, running away, repression, explosion, suppression, minimization, intimidation, avoidance, projection, cowering, accusations, stuffing, yelling, denial, enabling, pretending, withdrawal, abusing, ignoring, etc. I know you've done some of this and so have I. Brilliantly mature, aren't we? Do these "quick fixes" solve problems? No. These types of fight, flight, freeze impulses compound them.

Quick fixes maneuver past immediate distress. But, they don't address the problems that initiated the emotional alarms. So the subconscious or conscious safety concerns are still there. Then what happens? The next time there's a similar situation both the current *and* past alarms sound.

A wave of inappropriately strong emotion crashes through. This is a trigger. Triggers seem to come out of nowhere, but they're actually past issues resurfacing. So, what seems like "unreasonable" anxiety (or anger, etc.) actually has reasonable origins. But when emotion resurfaces it's usually pushed aside again with more quick fixes.

As this cycle repeats the emotion gets stronger. Situations become rough as issues compound and relationships struggle. To relieve discomfort, triggers are often directed toward certain people or certain things (like performing). This side-tracking draws attention away from the real issues and complicates attempts to resolve problems. Triggers from different individuals can clash and cause unwarranted negativity. Triggers immobilize thinking and make solvable situations feel unsolvable. How many office problems, neighborhood disputes, or divorces could be avoided if triggers were understood? How many people would perform better?

Triggers are common. They can develop anytime, but most start in childhood. Children have difficulty processing challenging situations because they're inexperienced and powerless. Additionally, the needed brain structures don't fully develop until the mid-twenties. So even in ideal childhoods triggers can develop. Triggers surge when thoughts and feelings are too difficult to process.

Most parents and caregivers do their best but fall short. (Have you ever met a perfect parent?) The resulting problems can also cause triggers. Triggers must be recognized to be addressed. But shame and blame slow progress. So it's helpful to respond to those who may have caused you triggers in the way you would want the next generation to respond to triggers you may inadvertently cause. Be grateful for honest effort. Learn. Move on. Identify triggers and resolve issues.

Quick fixes and triggers indicate where better core support is needed. But there's a problem. Instead of listening to these feelings and using them to resolve problems and strengthen the core, most people try to stop the negative feeling (like fear). If they can't stop the negative feeling, they ignore or repress it. This is like turning off a fire alarm instead of putting out the fire. The problem isn't solved so the alarm reoccurs (like reoccurring fear). The answer is to listen to the alarm and take care of problems. In other words: become aware.

This doesn't mean to dredge up the past; it simply means to sense how the past affects now. Awareness is not terribly difficult, but it doesn't happen overnight. Problems build up in layers, and though they dismantle more quickly, they're still dismantled in layers. Progress is a process.

But excessive fear can impede progress. Just as a person may be so emotional they can't provide an address when calling 911, individuals can become so stirred by negative emotion that they can't respond appropriately. Then quick fixes and triggers loop. So in order to move forward there has to be a way to get past negative emotion (like fear, anger, etc.). Fortunately there is.

"Sit" with the negative emotion. Negative emotions are uncomfortable and tend to grow, so there are three important ground rules that keep negative emotions from taking over: Acknowledge or "hear" the emotion 1) without further arousal, 2) without judging it as bad or good, and 3) without acting on it—especially no quick fixes.

"Sitting" with emotion has different names like "going neutral," "suspension," "floating with," "not judging," "refusal to worry," "observing," "releasing concern" (especially regarding what others think), "mindfulness," "clearing," "power awareness," "energy awareness," "finding one's core," "allowing things to go *through* you rather than stay *with* you" (like audience stares), "surrendering," "being in the moment," "centering," "grounding," etc. If you're afraid, you're doing fear anyway; you might as well acknowledge that you can.

Sitting with emotion is awareness on steroids! It's an immediate switch from defense to offense. Do you see how it's turning *toward* the problem instead of evading? Emotion is deliberately faced in order to learn from it. Sitting with emotion doesn't solve all problems, but it's a *huge* start. That said, facing strong emotion head-on is scary, especially without quick-fix fight, flight, or freeze crutches. But it's just emotion. Even intense emotion can't hurt you. It's okay to face it. It can even be helpful to say

"I can do fear. It's okay to be nervous." And then just sit with it. Feel it. Sense it. Keep the three ground rules while examining it.

Negative emotion loses power when heard. If you sit with fear and you're still afraid, you haven't completely faced it yet. When faced, there's peace. It sounds weird, but it makes sense once experienced. With practice it takes only seconds (and it does take practice). But even if done imperfectly, sitting with negative emotion starts peeling away triggers and quick fixes.

Difficult situations are easier without triggers. Conversely, easy situations can seem overwhelmingly hard when years (or generations) of quick fixes and triggers complicate things. Focusing on the present reduces strong emotional surges. Dealing only with current problems provides protection. It avoids trigger and quick fix overload. If a trigger or quick fix sneaks in, just reboot. "Sit" again.

Sitting with fear (or other negative emotions) is mega-empowering. Fear is no longer in charge. It seems a little thing to deliberately face emotion without being roused or reacting, but actually it's big. It's similar to extinction exposure therapy used for phobias like fear of critters or heights. Sitting with emotion strengthens the core. Conditioned fear responses are disrupted. It's no small feat to take down layers of quick fixes and trigger villains.

You've already started fixing problems just by reading. Knowledge automatically engages the subconscious brain to notice triggers. The subconscious and conscious brain engages even more when sitting with emotion. Awareness increases. Triggers and anxiety both indicate conscious or subconscious concerns about coming out okay. Issues may be directly, indirectly, or unrelated to the activity at hand. There are many possible reasons a person might feel unsure.

Two basketball players feel unsure; one's concerned about lighting, the other about an injury. Two salesmen feel unsure doing identical presentations; the rookie's concerned about proving himself, the veteran about paying a medical bill. Two pianists feel unsure playing the same piece; one's concerned about making parents proud, the other about memorization. Two runners feel unsure; one's concerned about a personal tragedy, the other about the temperature.

And this is the first level of awareness. Why is lighting or injury a concern? Why does the rookie need to prove himself or the experienced person worry about success? Answers surface. It's tuning *in* not tuning *out* that solves anxiety and/or trigger problems.

Many anxiety-management techniques advocate variations of sitting with fear (like deep breathing, quiet mind, cocooning, relaxation, etc.) So what's the difference between sitting with fear to *manage* it versus sitting with fear to *eliminate* it? Sitting with fear to managing it is done to *calm*. It's repeated whenever afraid. Sitting with fear to eliminating it is done to *understand* (which also happens to calm). Managing fear is turning off the fire alarm. Eliminating fear is putting out the fire. The goal is *waaay* deeper.

You deserve to take control. Sitting with emotion not only helps take down quick fixes and triggers, it enhances understanding. Switch from defense to offense. Strengthen your core by recognizing the positives of negative emotion.

Next up, how to track progress...

Summary

Negative feelings initiate protection. Negative feelings signal conscious or subconscious safety concerns and increase until heard. The intensity of a negative feeling is not always justified. Quick fixes are used when emotion is overwhelming. Quick fixes are used instead of exploring why an emotion sends an alarm. Quick fixes compound problems and combine with triggers. Triggers are past and present emotion combined. They are stronger than the situation merits but have logical origins. Triggers and anxiety indicate a conscious or subconscious concern. "Hearing the alarm" is solved by sitting with emotion and focusing on the present. It's possible to leave intergenerational triggers behind and move forward. Negative emotion loses power when confronted. Sitting with emotion (without further arousal, judging, or acting on the emotion) changes the situation from defense to offense. It unlocks mega awareness. There can be good reasons for unsure feelings. Facing fear opens the door to recognizing those reasons. There are positives to negative emotion.

Case Study

Cameron patted his horse's flanks and thought, *Okay, this is ridiculous, it's not my first rodeo.* He had been underneath razor-sharp hooves before, why was he suddenly so afraid? Earlier, his sister had teased that perhaps his fear wasn't about the injury at all; maybe it was because he didn't know what he'd do when it was time to retire from the rodeo. He had to admit that the injury brought this concern to the forefront, and the thought of giving up the rodeo scared him almost as much as being trampled by a bull...but was *that* his real concern? Honestly, he couldn't see himself doing anything but rodeo. Emotion surged when he thought about quitting. The surge seemed irrational. Was this something more? His dad passed away a couple of years ago and it still seemed that he watched from the stands. In fact, when Cameron was in the arena he felt closer to his dad than at any other time. It seemed that leaving the rodeo would also mean letting go of this special connection. But then a new thought hit Cameron. His dad had quit the rodeo, too! Cameron let the thought wash over him, and in an instant felt a new connection with his dad. He swung into the saddle and moved forward. [Cameron faced his fear and discovered layers. Uncovering this type of layered awareness usually takes a few days.]

Case Study

Drannon had bad experiences the first three grades of school. His mother hired a tutor because he was so far behind. The tutor had him work on spelling to increase his reading and writing skills. He became proficient at learning words above his grade level, but still struggled with certain easier words. His tutor explained that this was common in children with backgrounds similar to his and said, "You just have some little 'trigger critters'. Keep scrunching them with 'sure power'. When the trigger critters are all gone your brain will think easy words are easy! Sure power reprograms your brain! It won't replace hard work, but it will help your hard work pay off faster."

Empower Yourself:

Ignore layers, or...explore layers.

Fast-Track ReflACTION

1) What negative emotions have you experienced in the last week; what was the warning about?
2) What quick fixes do you commonly use/see? What are the negative side-effects?
3) When could you benefit by sitting with emotion? Do you side-track, what situation or person is blamed?

8
Progress!

Many performers use recorded data to track progress. Videos, stop watches, statistics, journals, weight scales, exercise repetitions, test grades, sales records, music recordings, and written observations are all used to evaluate and improve. Imagine a skier without a stopwatch or a long jumper without a tape measure! Observed, measured, recorded information is helpful—even essential for some types of improvement.

Records track progress, identify patterns, assist adjustments, and systematically improve performance. Records also increase enjoyment and sustain motivation. Aspiring *pro*fessionals, who are serious about *pro*gressing and *pro*ducing, use *pro*ficient *pro*grams to *pro*fusely *pro*fit, *pro*gressively *pro*ceed, and *pro*foundly *pro*pel themselves forward toward being *pro*digious, *pro*lific *pro*-formers! (I couldn't resist. :)

Records strengthen the core. They provide a framework to evaluate progress. They're helpful in overcoming anxiety. But maybe you're worried about time. Research shows that addressing anxiety *saves time*. Remember Suzie in chapter two; how long did it take to look under the bed and out the window? Her core was strengthened in seconds. Yours can be, too.

Records make other efforts more productive. But if you're uncomfortable keeping a record, don't feel guilty! The information in this chapter is helpful whether or not a record is kept. It will show you what to be aware of. And awareness is everything in overcoming anxiety.

"Record" has two meanings—1) to write, and 2) to break a phenomenal landmark. Both meanings are applicable to overcoming anxiety: track data to break personal landmarks! There are many ways to record insights, but haphazard data is not very helpful. So the companion workbook to this book, *The Core Power Pro-Launch Pad [CPPro-LP]* was developed to maximize benefits and track data quickly. Its use is optional (unless this is for a class, then we'll both defer to your teacher.) But the data it collects is *critical*. Appendix A is from the *CPPro-LP*. The information in this chapter, the next chapter and Appendix A helps in honing in on the things that eliminate anxiety.

There are *always* reasons for anxiety. Additionally, there are *always* reasons for performance improvement or decline. You can speed progress by spotting key factors, especially when reversing a slump. For example, each element on the form in Appendix A addresses specific anxiety factors, many of which are overlooked. So take a note of these whether or not the *CPPro-LP* is used to systematically track. Each item on the form will make more sense as you read further. But introducing them now gets the conscious and subconscious process started toward eliminating problems.

How long are observations recorded? Typically benefits are experienced in just five minutes, once or twice a week, for six weeks—or about an hour total! How's that for fast, mega data? Five minutes of regular, honest, sincere reflection *does* make a difference. After six weeks the record can be continued, or revisited as needed. Text-style writing is recommended (unless a teacher indicates otherwise.) This reduces writer's block and puts the focus on insights. Think deeply. Write simply.

Observations are noted after performance *and* practice. Why? Improved performance starts with improved practice. ("Practice" means a study session, rehearsal, lesson, business preparation, team workout, etc.) Benefits are usually experienced immediately and increase over time. The goal is not just to write. It's to gain insight. It's helpful to consider: *what, when, where, why and how much* anxiety—whether the anxiety is a fleeting thought or total incapacitation. Any anxiety limits ability to a degree and awareness helps in eliminating it.

What anxiety surfaced (or didn't surface)? Were there physical, mental, emotional or behavioral fear symptoms? Symptoms are a big deal. They are secret tracking devices to spy on anxiety and eradicate it. Also what happened *right before* any positive or negative change?

When does anxiety happen? Do symptoms occur only during performance or also during practice or personal time? Are there reactions when *thinking* about specific situations or people? Also, do changes occur during routine or unusual situations?

Where does anxiety happen? Are symptoms tied to specific locations or events? Also, where are you *mentally* when a symptom occurs? (Do symptoms happen in performance, practice, or at odd times like thinking in bed?)

Why does anxiety happen? Notice whether symptoms change when variables change such as the people performed for, audience size, event importance, equipment used, lighting, food, quality of sleep, or other details. Notice small things (especially when working on flow/zone).

How Much does anxiety happen? Notice the *intensity, frequency,* and *effect.* The *CPPro-LP* uses 1-10 scales so specific data can be recorded quickly and consistently. These types of observations yield a wealth of data.

Don't become bogged down, but don't work superficially. Quick, deep reflection goes a long way. Look for what's behind the obvious. You are the only person who can collect your data! Show up for yourself and do a good job. Strengthen your core.

Performance quality changes when variables change. Variables provide clues. Anxiety is linked to specific things. For example, it's usually highest right before a performance (walking in and starting), but can be high as much as months before (ask anyone taking the ACT). Knowing these things can reduce anxiety and improve preparation. Records reveal a bigger picture.

Let me elaborate. How did you feel about keeping a record? (Don't worry. This isn't a trick question or a guilt trip.) The brain is hardwired to conserve energy. Did you feel this? Avoidance, irritation, hesitation, sighs, impatience, or frustration are common when initiating tasks. *Resistance is often a form of low-level, low-stakes anxiety.* Did you know that? Records can reveal small patterns like this and get to deeper issues which release the drag.

Tracking big things is valuable, but not the whole picture. Fleeting, seemingly insignificant things also limit ability. A "film" slides over the brain (the brain literally functions differently). Tasks feel hard. But in reality, anxiety is hard. Noting it can reveal patterns, making elimination easier. It's relatively easy to fix anxiety, but not without being aware of it. Do you see how anxiety awareness and records can team up?

All anxiety affects performance. This chapter started the process of looking for "awareness gems." The next chapter hones these "treasure hunting" skills. A record helps in identifying anxiety patterns. Initially only big things are noticed. But soon even fleeting things are spotted. Earlier I backed off on keeping records. Now I want to plug them again. But this isn't a pep talk, it's based on neuroscience. There are solid reasons to use "record keeping awareness." Use them to your advantage! Strengthen your core with "record progress."

Next up, avoid problems before they happen...

Summary
Most performers use records. Records track progress and enhance skill development. Anxiety records help, as well. Haphazard records yield haphazard data. The *CPPro-LP* can assist in tracking data. No matter how anxiety is tracked, think deeply; record simply. It's helpful to track what, when, where, why, and how much anxiety. Look beyond the obvious. Data reveals patterns. Records don't have to take a lot of time to be beneficial. You are the only person who can collect your data. Show up for yourself. The brain is hardwired to conserve energy. Resistance is a form of anxiety. It dampens ability and enjoyment. Tasks aren't hard; anxiety is hard. As awareness grows, even fleeting anxiety is spotted—and that's where the magic is.

Case Study
Kollin shoved the anxiety record in his duffle. Was his coach serious about keeping an anxiety record? Good thing it was only 5 minutes, a couple of times a week, for 6 weeks. And why did his coach insist that records include both practice and games! Who cares about practice? It's the game that counts! Kollin dutifully wrote in the record. *Boring.* But, after three weeks he noticed a pattern. He did well until he made a major mistake. It was downhill after that. This happened in practice and games. Also, he belittled himself a lot. But when he objectively rated his performance, he did well in both practice and games. Wow, he had no idea how much he focused on his mistakes! Knowing this made it easier to work on self-improvement without self-criticism. He became more consistent. Crashes became rare. How weird was that? Okay, maybe his coach wasn't completely crazy about keeping the record!

Empower Yourself.
Guess about data, or...gather good data.

Fast-Track ReflACTION
1) When do you experience resistance anxiety? How can you reduce the drag? (Resistance is common when getting up in the morning, resuming a task, etc.)

2) How does anxiety awareness give you an edge; why is aware-ness in the moment an even bigger edge?

3) What anxiety patterns do you suspect/observe; how can rec-ognizing patterns reduce anxiety?

9
Treasure Hunt

It usually takes a catastrophe before anxiety is attended to. Why wait until disaster? It's better to be proactive. This chapter helps in becoming more proactive. It's approached as if an anxiety record is kept. But even if it's not, the information establishes a proactive mindset. Awareness produces insights that become "hidden treasures" toward being proactive.

Conscious and subconscious concerns surface more quickly when actively looking for relevant factors and patterns. Paying attention to *what, when, where, why, and how much* is a big deal in gaining insights. Each insight helps. So a choice to accelerate awareness is a choice to accelerate progress. But it's easy to miss important information. So this chapter focuses on what to look for. It was developed after analyzing extensive research. This information puts you years ahead of trial-and-error observation.

Most observation is too superficial. Here's a case study to illustrate both superficial and deep observation. Joyce recently graduated and found a job teaching children's musical theater. She was proficient on the piano and had won high school competitions. But now she had difficulty, especially when observed. She didn't know if she had anxiety or if she was overloaded since her job required her to play the piano, listen to the singing, and check choreography.

This is a superficial observation of Joyce's situation: *What* happens: she chokes; *when:* playing piano; *where:* at work; *why:* anxiety or overload; *how much:* she circled a number 2 on her record because she doesn't feel nervous. Done! Did this reveal any helpful treasures? Nada zip! She's got to go deeper if she's going to solve the problem. So let's try again.

This is deep observation: *What* happens: she has difficulty doing all her responsibilities; *when:* playing piano. But wait, her mind fluctuates between the kids, piano, and parent/boss perceptions, especially when she questions her adequacy. *Where:* mostly in class when her boss or parents are present, but not always. Oh wait, it also happens when they're gone but she's thinking about their reactions. *Why:* she feels overloaded. But is the overload from playing the piano? She feels a heavy responsibility to keep her job, positively impact the kids, and give parents "their money's worth." *How much:* she doesn't feel particularly nervous, so she doesn't think there's much anxiety. Oh wait, could her occasional tummy upset, sleepless nights, and new aches and pains be physical symptoms of anxiety? Maybe her confusion when doing class plans, insecurity when talking to parents, and increased irritations with her husband are mental, emotional, and behavioral symptoms. It appears her anxiety is actually an 8 or 9.

Joyce has rather severe anxiety. Where is it coming from? She feels that past piano competitions were for fun. But now the kids' development and her job are on the line. These *private* rehearsals are higher stakes than past *public* competitions. And in reality, when her boss or the parents are present, it is a performance for her. Additionally, she had higher expectations of herself than her boss, the other teachers, or the parents. She put this extra pressure on herself!

She thought the problem was overload or anxiety. But the problem was actually unrealistic expectations of herself. She also had unrealistic expectations of her husband. The record helped in identifying the problem and then in developing more appropriate expectations. Do you see the benefits of looking for *patterns*? As her perspective changed, her ability improved, enjoyment increased, stomach settled, sleep increased, and her relationship with her husband improved. She was no longer overwhelmed. Decisions became easier and confusion dissipated. The problem was relatively easy to solve once she understood. That's the power of insight. What if she tried to calm her piano anxiety instead of looking for insights? Anxiety comes from core concerns. Anxiety leaves when concerns resolve.

Awareness is not just performance changing, it's life changing. Anxiety is specific to the individual. A superficial record is not very helpful. But a thoughtful record uncovers insight and strengthens the core. Anxiety is always caused by *something*. These things may affect anxiety: preparation, environment, audience size, specific people in the audience, thoughts, injuries, sleep, food, support from others, personal distress, distractions, who is in the vicinity (or in thoughts), or unusual circumstances. Look for increases or decreases in performance quality. These indicate anxiety skills or problems. Notice patterns.

Anxiety is *specific* to certain activities or even specific skills within an activity. It's possible to have lots of anxiety in one situation and absolutely no anxiety in another. For example—when singing but not dancing, when playing one instrument but not another, when using technology but not when lecturing, when throwing a ball down the field but not laterally. Outcome anxiety and inconsistent flow/zone is very specific and is affected by anything that contributes to feeling unsure of coming out okay *for that person*. Those who generally do not have anxiety may miss small situations when they are hampered by isolated anxiety at very specific times.

Anxiety is tied to *specific* conscious or subconscious concerns. General performance concerns might be fear of memory slips, completing team requirements, keeping a position, fulfilling responsibilities, missing an opportunity, or an inadequate skill. Personal concerns might be fear of not looking good, meeting expectations, or improving enough. Interpersonal concerns might be fear of not being accepted by friends or not pleasing someone like a teacher, coach, judge, parent, scout, or famous guest. Unusual concerns might be a room that's too cold or too hot, arriving too early or late, delayed food allergy, keeping personal belongings secure during performance, having the wrong glasses, an unfamiliar city, room change, or new equipment.

Anxiety is tied to *specific* situations and high stakes. Performance might go well at home but not for a small audience, for a small audience but not a large audience, any live audience but not when televised or recorded, for millions on TV but not for one certain person. Other situations might include performing well in a season game, but not in a tournament—or vice versa. Common difficulties include high-stakes situations like applying for a job, senior recitals, keeping scholarships, competitions, auditions, being observed by a scout, entrance exams, licensing tests, prestigious events, or even just when someone better is present. Some situations are high stakes only to the performer, such as a special grandparent in the audience who has traveled a long distance.

Anxiety patterns can be seen. Anxiety is more common in the *least* gifted and the *most* gifted performers. Gifted performers cover better, but crash longer and harder when overwhelmed. So, gifted students, athletes or artists may suddenly falter. Immediate support and attention to anxiety can prevent total collapse.

Females have more problematic anxiety than males, but it's amply found in both genders. The older generation tends to have anxiety handling new technology. The younger generation has more anxiety in face-to-face interaction. If parents have anxiety, children are typically more susceptible.

Anxiety can grow inside a person or between people. An athlete may be consistent in every situation but one. But insecurity in one thing can cause insecurity in other things. One person can spread insecurity to others by saying things like, "I don't think we're going to win" or "it's going to be a hard test." Careful self-talk and positive interpersonal talk is important. Problems can be reduced by deliberately countering negativity. Genuine positivity counters unsure feelings.

Anxiety awareness surfaces in layers. It's a "peel and heal" process. Joyce didn't recognize her anxiety immediately. In fact, initially she didn't think she had anxiety because it manifested in unexpected ways. But her anxiety was actually severe. Awareness is a "treasure" that unlocks solutions. There are common anxiety factors and patterns that affect ability. Awareness of patterns strengthens the core. It decreases the possibility of catastrophes and proactively empowers. Strengthen your core by uncovering VIP treasures that reveal VIP solutions.

Next up, spot when brain power fluctuates...

Summary

A proactive stance can minimize performance problems and help avoid performance disasters. Outcome anxiety is very specific to certain situations, people, conditions or skills. Anxiety is common in high-stakes situations, females, and the most and least capable. The most capable hide anxiety better but crash worse when overwhelmed. Reoccurring problems allow patterns to be identified. Insights usually come in layers. Identifying patterns helps in eliminating problems. Records maximize awareness. Awareness allows a person to react proactively.

Case Study

Naddie was a news reporter. She had absolutely no performance anxiety in front of the camera and didn't think a record would be beneficial. But she kept one on a whim. To her surprise she found a pattern. She was uncomfortable reading names. At times the insecurities about names affected other parts of her job. This reduced when she became aware. She then proactively

46

adjusted her preparation to include attention to names and phonetic spelling. She wasn't going to take a chance on disaster! She felt much more secure. Her record helped to identify and reverse the one thing that held her back. [The record helped improve performance and preparation. Her core was strengthened.]

Empower Yourself

Reactively respond, or...proactively prevent.

Fast-track ReflACTION

1) Do you experience apprehensions during some activities or school subjects and not others?

2) Do you experience apprehensions in parts of an activity and not other parts; which parts, why? (For example, a baseball player might feel more comfortable catching a fly verses a ground ball; it might be because of a lack of practice, a bad experience, or an injury.)

3) Scan the chapter and list the categories you fit in (younger vs. older; female vs. male, gifted vs. struggling, anxiety in all activities vs. isolated parts of some activities, etc.) What factors or patterns emerge?

Note: The Chapter 9 endnotes contain a more comprehensive list of anxiety factors and patterns than presented in this chapter.

10
Got Your Brain?

Many people try to perform without their brain. It's hard. Most don't realize that brain *function* can fluctuate. This is different than brain focus. The concept of brain function and thought construction is very new and was developed from synthesized neurological, physiological, psychological, and educational research. Attention to thought construction immediately improves learning rates and performance, which is why this is one of my most requested workshops. It's a new way of thinking about brain use and thoughts.

The concept of addressing thoughts to minimize anxiety is not new. In fact, most interventions address thoughts in some way—like the importance of avoiding catastrophic thinking and increasing positive thinking. However, those approaches focus on the *content* of the thought; but this approach focuses on *construction* of thought. It's a layer deeper. So this isn't what a thought is about, but how thought feels when produced. Quality thought construction flows effortlessly. It feels different than inconsistent, laborious thought. By recognizing quality construction, a person can learn to create thought flow. This is important. Peak performance flow is impossible without quality thought flow. Brain support, through consistent thought flow, is an important part of feeling core strength.

When adrenaline hits the bloodstream it changes the way the body functions, but this same blood goes to the brain. Did you ever consider how it might change brain function? High adrenaline and high emotion go hand in hand. Research shows that high emotion, like stress or anxiety, causes the learning and processing centers of the brain to slow or even stop. The reasons are still being pinpointed, but it is well documented that *brain function changes under pressure*. Performance (and practice) pressure can cause elevated emotion, which affects thinking. The processing parts of the brain slow or shut down for micro intervals. This explains a lot, doesn't it? A high percent of anxiety is due to this problem. Most people experiencing it have no idea.

During a brain micro-shutdown, the person flies solo without needed brain support. I call this problem "brain shorting" and it's like trying to work on a computer with fluctuating power; even small inconsistencies wreak havoc. Brain shorting is responsible for a lot of outcome anxiety and flow/zone problems because many people unknowingly *lack continuous thought.* I'm not talking about psychologically losing focus. I'm talking about physiologically *losing the ability to think* for micro intervals. There's a big difference!

When problems arise, "losing focus" is typically blamed instead of brain shorting. While there may be times when focus shifts, most of the time this isn't the problem at all. Can you see that trying to fix the wrong thing doesn't work? But even if focus is the problem, focus is more easily fixed when paying attention to brain shorting. Why? Brain shorting is a deeper fix. It fixes focus and function problems simultaneously. It's hard to focus if you don't have function. Fixing brain shutdowns fixes other things, too. In this chapter you'll learn to identify brain shorting and the next chapter you'll learn what to do about it.

There are three types of brain shorting:

Crunching. Brain crunching is more common in exuberant, extroverted personalities (but is found in all personality types). It feels like a mental clawing or gripping in the front of the brain. It comes in spurts of short duration, usually during the harder parts of a task or when something unexpected requires quick high-pressure processing. The mental tension is often accompanied by physical tension—a stiffening of muscles, flicker of fear, breathing change, or visible hesitation like a micro lunge or a tiny tremor. It typically lasts only a microsecond to a couple of seconds at a time. During the "crunch" the flow of thought is uncomfortably forced. Crunching is like a mental "fight" to power through the problem.

Fogging. Brain fogging is more common in shy, introverted personalities (but is found in all personality types). Brain fogging is a nebulous uncertainty, lingering insecurity, pulled-back hesitancy, and/or significantly impaired confidence. Brain fogging occurs when a person feels particularly incapable and "in over their head." It usually happens when there is inaccurate understanding or insufficient skill. It often happens when something new is introduced. Extreme insecurity causes flat, diffused, less-active thinking. It can happen briefly but is usually longer. In fact, once this nebulous thinking pattern starts, it can increase to the point that ability regresses. A capable person can become incapable. The person "forgets" what was known, and then a fear of regression can cause even more fogginess. Over time the person may look mentally or physically deficient. In reality there may be ability, but it is inaccessible due to a lack of brain support. So brain fogging can linger, grow, and even take over. Also, a person can perform well in some skills but have difficulty in others, which can make the problem confusing and hard to identify. Fogging can become a constant way of thinking toward a subject or situation. Fogging is like a mental "flight" away from the problem.

Blanking. Brain blanking is like hitting a mental brick wall. The difference between brain crunching and brain blanking is that crunching is a mental gripping *through* difficulty. Brain blanking is a *stop* of thought. Crunching is uncomfortable. Blanking has little or no sensation. For a moment the person cannot retrieve things they know—a best friend's name, a game play, a memorized speech, a musical phrase, a test question, or a statistic. A blank can last from a microsecond to a few seconds. It's like the brain momentarily "freezes" and stops working when faced with a problem. Most people think that blanking is an inability to *remember,* but it's actually an inability to *process*—which then causes an inability to remember. Do you see the difference?

There are other variations of blanking. A person may hear but not see—common in musicians, such as playing by ear without realizing that touch and/or sight are not being registered. A person may see and not hear—common in dancers, such as dancing by muscle and music memory without realizing that the music isn't actually heard. A person may mentally disconnect—such as a teammate missing a ball when a play is plainly evident or a speaker missing part of a question when the inquiry was clearly communicated.

Many times blanking is not recognized because other highly-refined skills takeover without the person realizing it, such as muscle memory. (Note that both "blanking" and "overthinking" involve muscle memory, but they are different. Using muscle memory during "blanking" decreases ability because there is a *stop* in mental processing. Using muscle memory during "overthinking" increases ability because it prevents a *shift* in mental processing—more on this later.)

Sometimes blanking is accompanied by a breathing change or small wave of fear, but often there is no fear sensation. If the blank is long enough to notice, it's easy to spot; but if the blank is a microsecond, it is difficult to identify without extra-sharp awareness. Micro shorting is *very* common and *hard* to spot, so take time to consider this. It's often an unrecognized cause of performance anxiety and usually a culprit in flow/zone problems. In my experience, fixing the thought sensations involved with crunching, fogging, and blanking fixes the majority of thought-based performance problems. Attention to brain shorting is also preventative.

There are additional ways to identify brain shorting. If ability plateaus or is inconsistent despite diligent practice, brain shorting is probably involved. Other signs include musicians who have difficulty sight reading, dancers who have difficulty learning new material quickly, actors who have difficulty in cold auditions, business personnel who have difficulty during open question/answer sessions, and athletes who have difficulty with spontaneous game changes or interviews. And brain shorting not only affects performance, it affects learning rates.

If any of these describe you, pay special attention. Brain shorting probably affects *more than just these situations*. One last note, brain shorting can also occur in very capable individuals who do not show signs of problems due to 1) no fear sensation, 2) quick recovery, and 3) exceptional ability. However, even gifted performers experience an increase in outcomes when thinking patterns improve. Brain support increases core confidence. So whether you struggle or strut, consider how increased brain support can make a positive difference for you. Strengthen your core by recognizing the power of thought formation sensations.

Now more brain support...

Summary
Trying to perform without the brain is hard. Anxiety management usually focuses on the *content* of thoughts. Functional brain support focuses on thought *construction*. Functional thought construction immediately increases learning rates during practice and quality output during performance. Attention to thought sensations produces immediate benefits that increase over time. Thinking problems are easy to miss. Brain micro-shutdowns are responsible for a lot of performance anxiety and flow/zone problems. Adrenaline in the blood not only goes to the body, it goes to the brain. High emotion slows and even stops the learning centers of the brain. Performance and practice pressure can elevate emotion and affect brain function. Brain shorting is a

lack of continuous brain function, resulting in a lack of continuous thought. This is not a loss of *focus*; it's a loss of *function*. There are three types of brain shorting: crunching—fight, fogging—flight, blanking—freeze. They correlate to mentally pushing through, pulling back, and the inability to process. All three hamper the ability to think. Micro blanks can be almost undetectable, especially if other highly-refined skills compensate. Plateaus in ability are often due to brain shorting. Brain micro-shorting can occur in very capable individuals who have no fear sensation, recover quickly, and compensate well. Even capable individuals experience improved outcomes when thinking improves.

Case Study

All these years, Jadley thought her brain processed music notes so quickly that she simply skimmed them. What a shock to learn that she wasn't reading the notes at all—she was playing by ear! Honestly, it was a relief to finally understand why she had difficulty sight reading and what to do about it. She changed her practice strategy. Instead of focusing on the notes, she focused on brain sensations and continually considered, "How does my brain feel? Is it processing?" She learned to sense how her brain felt when actually reading versus playing by ear. She was surprised that sometimes she crunched and sometimes she fogged. She expected that her sight reading would improve, but did not expect that *everything* would improve. Wow! Who would have thought that focusing on brain sensations instead of notes would cause such a breakthrough! (Jadley told two college friends, who then had similar success applying brain awareness to volleyball and test taking.)

Empower Yourself

Disregard brain function, or...recognize brain function.

Fast-Track ReflACTION

1) When have you experienced (or observed) crunching, fogging, or blanking?
2) In what subjects or activities do you "struggle," and how could better brain function benefit you?
3) In what subjects or activities do you "strut," and how could better brain function benefit you?

11
Bring Your Brain

In order for the brain to respond better during performance, it must be used better during practice. It is impossible to eliminate anxiety if brain support fluctuates. Mistakes usually happen where brain shorts have occurred. Performance flow starts with practice flow, and flow is basically impossible if there is mental crunching, fogging or blanking. Eliminating these things is good mental hygiene. It improves performance flow.

Crunching. Crunching is due to an overactive brain. The natural reaction is to push harder through the gripping feeling. Why? There is a tendency to equate increased mental tension with increased ability. But this is not true. If you're a quarterback, a tense mental stance won't reveal a receiver or keep the pocket from collapsing. If you're in an interview, a tense mental stance won't improve intellect or keep unexpected questions at bay. Overactive mental tension is counterproductive.

Decreasing mental tension doesn't mean to decrease focus or determination. These actually increase, but in a *comfortable* way. Mental discomfort is a warning that mental support is *not* flowing. It is possible to feel the difference between tense, mental distress and solid, comfortable focus. These sensations are felt in the upper front and near front/top part of the brain. Usually crunching happens during the hardest part of a task, so deliberately work toward a consistent, focused, relaxed mental stance between the hard and easy parts. This encourages thought to flow fluidly. Most people practice until they can do a task. But material should be practiced until the task can be done *without a change in mental or physical tension.*

A good mental stance teaches the brain how to work. Mental flow becomes a habit. Peak mental ability is comfortable, energetic, focused and satisfying. When thought flows fluidly the performance immediately improves. Why? The person now performs with the brain. Attention to brain sensations solves problems deeply and quickly. That's why there are reports of noticeable improvement overnight. Attention to brain sensations rapidly increases peak performance levels.

Fogging. Fogging is due to an underactive brain. (Underactive fogging is the opposite of overactive crunching.) To fix fogging thought is encouraged to move forward instead of retreat. This doesn't mean to go overboard and crunch. It means to strongly engage. Deliberately and aggressively address foggy things. A foggy brain feels like "I don't know if I can ever figure this out, maybe I should sit this one out." Addressing the problem feels like "This is NOT too hard for me, bring it on! What *exactly* is the problem? Watch me take it down!"

Tasks should be practiced until they can be completed *without a nebulous feeling*. A nebulous response increases the problem. When I work with students, I tell them, "Never do anything with a 'question mark'"—like play weakly, speak timidly, or gesture half-heartedly. Similarly, choral directors commonly say, "If you're going to make a mistake, make a BIG one; it's easier to fix." This isn't just because a big mistake is easier to hear. The brain functions differently when pushing forward versus pulling back. Mentally retreating in the face of uncertainty is detrimental. It's a bad habit and poor mental hygiene.

Once fogging starts it often expands. This can happen in the moment or over time. For example, a tough test question can cause second guessing on the rest of the test. Or a difficult math concept (like percentages or long division) can cause kids to foggily regress until 2 + 2 can feel hard. Similarly, third or fourth year piano students who are unsure about a challenging new piece may regress until they are unsure of middle C. Adults are not immune to this phenomenon. Fogging is not just difficulty learning new material. It's associated with confusion, indecision and discomfort moving forward.

Some people use distraction, avoidance, coyness or jokes to hide foggy uncertainty. This increases problems. It's okay to be a kind, fun person. It's not okay to train the brain to retreat when it's needed. It's also not okay to evade the problem by covering it with a laugh. Nebulous brain sensations must be addressed or fogging worsens. Students who are clowns, belligerent, or apathetic usually have some degree of brain fogging problems. Similar reactions can be found in athletes or employees.

I tutored a girl who was behind several grade levels and used shrugs and coyness to cover inadequacies. She was so unsure that even the answers she absolutely knew were delivered with "question inflections." The first session I insisted that she stop shrugging and fishing for validation, especially when reading. Her mother intervened. After I explained the neuroscience behind fogging this wonderful mom gave great support to me and her daughter. I taught this girl to counter fogging and to be kind, but firm, with herself. I said that eliminating fogging would immediately improve grades. Two and a half weeks later the girls' school teacher contacted the mother. The teacher wondered what caused the girl's new confidence, smiles, and full grade jump. Yes, it's that effective. This immediate grade jump was likely due to countering brain fog because it was the only core skill I had taught her at that point.

Ability improves when nebulous thinking is replaced with clear, focused thinking. Fogging is a bad mental habit. When it is eliminated (or being eliminated) there is an immediate jump in ability. Why? It's easier to do things with a brain.

Blanking. Blanking is due to a non-functional brain. It is common. It's often the culprit when there is little improvement despite hard work. Some blanking is accompanied by a sense of discomfort or panic, like when forgetting a name during introductions or a section of memorized material during performance. Panic makes the situation worse. Panic is a high emotion and high emotion slows and/or stops the processing centers of the brain. Thinking can't happen without blood flow, chemical reactions, and electrical impulses in the brain. So to reverse blanking be calm. (Also avoid reacting with fogging or crunching.) Blanking diminishes as the brain is trained to stay calm.

This works if you know about the blank, but what about the nearly undetectable micro blanking? It's hard to spot, but not possible. Learn to spot it. The last chapter gave several clues, and here are more. Micro blanks can be "seen" in dancers, athletes, public speakers, actors, and musicians—suspect one if there is a non-productive, hesitant, subtle break in smooth movement. Micro blanks can be "heard" in musicians and speakers—suspect one if there is an unintended difference in volume, tempo, or quality of sound. Micro blanks can be "felt"—suspect one if there is a sudden change in breathing, mental comfort, or physical tension, even if a change is only a split second. It's almost certain a blank has occurred if there is also a flicker of fear or tension.

There are two reasons that micro blanking isn't spotted: some types are nearly undetectable—but still cause problems, and other skills can be used to compensate—like playing by ear or re-lying on muscle memory.

Performance mistakes usually happen during a brain short. This is why crunching, fogging, or blanking should be attended to during practice. Attentive practice can feel slow, but it's actually a huge fast track to success. To improve brain ability, progressively go from easy skills and low pressure to difficult skills and high pressure. Use care that no brain shorting creeps in. *Ever.* One musician started with beginning level music and slowly worked up to advanced music, paying attention to brain sensations. Though she had been a professional for years she described new confidence. She found she could rely on skills instead of pharmaceuticals to handle anxiety. Her core was stronger.

Sometimes fears build up at "that hard part". It's not enough to be able to do a task. Mental discomfort is an indication that there is still room to grow, even if the task can be executed well. Consistent brain comfort is *essential* for consistent quality. Brain skills can be developed and are cumulative. Persistence pays off.

The brain is amazing. Athletes who deal with high speeds—from downhill skiers to baseball players—can attest to the brain's ability to process. Things zipping by at 100 miles/hour can feel like slow motion. The brain can do *waaay* more than is typically expected. Just as a muscle develops through specific use, the brain develops through specific use. Brains can support. So, why does brain shorting happen? The person is *unsure* of successfully handling the situation to some degree. Sound familiar? However, there's no reason to feel unsure of the brain's ability.

Spotting brain sensations works. Why? It's more than working on brain flow. It's noticing where you are unsure—did you see that coming? Anxiety elimination is unsure feeling elimination. Addressing brain shorting address unsure feelings, before a thought even occurs. *This means that anxiety is addressed before it happens.* Can you see that addressing unsure feelings is not touchy-feely, emotional-boggy-down stuff? It's just powerful awareness and productive focus. It's developing core skills.

You will likely get *waaay* more than you bargained for when paying attention to brain shorting. One student said that she progressed "10 years in 10 months". Perhaps you will, too. However, notice that she didn't say ten minutes or even ten days. Consistent skills are *developed.* But it is possible to discern brain shorting and do something about it. Recognize overactive crunching; detect underactive fogging; discern non-functional blanking;

demolish brain shorting. Performance flow is impossible without thought flow. No matter how smart or talented you are, you can't perform without your brain. Strengthen your core with flow during thought construction.

Next up, shape the brain...

Summary
Better performance starts with better brain support during practice. It's impossible to eliminate performance anxiety if brain support fluctuates. Brain shorting disrupts flow. Crunching, fogging, and blanking can be fixed: *Crunching:* The brain is overactive. Release mental tension. Realize that increased mental discomfort does not equate with increased ability. Released tension does not mean to diminish focus or determination—these increase with comfortable flow. Mental tension is counterproductive. Practice until a task can be done comfortably without a change in mental sensation. *Fogging:* The brain is underactive. Stimulate the brain. Counter uncertainty. Don't mask uncertainty with coyness or jokes. Fogging tends to expand and cause uncertainty in mastered things. Students who flounder almost always have brain fogging. Grades and ability shoot up when it is addressed. It's easier to do things with the brain. *Blanking:* The brain is not processing. Develop the habit of being calm. Tension shuts down the brain. Spot micro blanks through breathing changes and micro performance differences. Mistakes usually happen during brain shorting. Watch for compensating skills. Build brain support. Start low pressure and low difficulty, and then increase to high pressure and high difficulty *while maintaining mental flow*. Eliminating brain shorts initially feels slow, but it's actually fast. Notice brain support; zero in on unsure feelings. Addressing unsure feelings is not touchy-feely, boggy-down stuff. It's awareness and new focus. Brain function can be discerned. No matter how smart or talented you are, you can't perform without your brain.

Case Study
Kenna had performed all her life. She was very successful, and never had stage fright. When she learned about brain shorting she was curious and on a whim decided to check brain sensations and breathing. To her amazement, she realized she did have performance anxiety, but *only* during practice and *only* when memorizing new material! Her brain was taking "micro coffee breaks" that slowed memorization. She said, "A great performance

starts with confidence in practice. My confidence went up when I discovered I had performance anxiety! How ironic is that! I thought I didn't have a good memory, but actually, I didn't have good mental flow. Everything has been better since I learned I had performance anxiety and worked on it. Who'd have thought!" (And then she giggled realizing that the problem *was* thought!)

Case Study

Lulee was constantly applauded for her skills. But walking in her office you'd think she was inept! When asked about the piles she said she didn't have time for sorting papers. But when she learned about brain fogging she recognized it in herself. She hated making decisions and paperwork was replete with them. She decided to use her office as a "brain-training boot camp". Each day she spent only fifteen minutes (so as not to become overwhelmed) and sorted a small stack of papers. She was especially mindful of brain sensations and countered any frustration or nebulous feelings. Within a few weeks her office was pristine, but more importantly, the clarity carried over into how she approached life. As she addressed the things she had avoided her life became more balanced and enjoyable.

Empower Yourself

Neglect your brain, or...train your brain.

Fast-Track ReflACTION

1) Do you experience crunching, fogging, or blanking? Consider both performance and non-performance situations. What is a helpful intervention?

2) Name a skill would you like to improve, outline a low skill/low pressure to high skill/high pressure plan to increase flow.

3) What short-term and long-term problems have you experienced that may be eliminated by paying attention to brain shorting *sensations* and thought *flow*?

12
Plan a
Neuroplasticity Party!

Let's take brain support a step further. How about reshaping the brain to what is needed? One great thing from brain research is the discovery of neuroplasticity. It's just a fancy way of saying that your brain is happy to adapt to what is needed! Researchers thought that the brain was doomed to decline. But now they know that what is used improves, and what is not used is pruned away. So the exercise motto "use it or lose it" is true of the brain. Just as muscles can be built and shaped, the brain can be built and shaped.

Theodor Erismann and Ivo Kohler were early pioneers in this research. They used glasses that flipped images upside down or left to right. Within days the subjects could function. Within weeks they had completely adapted. Additional research found that it takes about three weeks wearing upside-down glasses for the brain to mentally flip visual images right side up. Other research involved brain scans. Measurable brain changes appear within a week of starting a new skill. It was previously believed that brain changes were just increased synapses between nerve cells. But neuroscientists now know that both synapses and grey matter increase. How's that for adaptation!

What does this have to do with outcome anxiety? Everything! The research provides hope and a time frame for improvements. Anytime something is improved, there are new neural pathways (and grey matter). And anytime something is neglected, old neural pathways are pruned away. Building or removing brain pathways, is possible. And it will take about three weeks of consistent effort. It's that straightforward.

So why doesn't positive change happen more often? It's usually due to inconsistency, level of belief, unclear goals, or too many goals. When starting a new goal, the brain says, "Oh, you want a new neural pathway! No problem, just give me a few days!" But then, if the effort is inconsistent or unclear the brain says, "Oh, you don't need the new neural pathway after all? Ok, anything you want! I'm happy to go back." And there's regression.

Inconsistency can be so frustrating that improvement might seem impossible. But ironically, the things that make it *hard* to improve are also the things that make it *possible* to improve. The fact that it takes effort to change is a protection. Otherwise the brain would flutter around, influenced by every weird thing that came along. It's *good* that it takes effort. And it's good that change is possible.

Positive improvement may involve physical, mental, emotional, or behavioral changes. Neuroplasticity can help with all. Improvements might include better muscle memory, memorization skills, interpersonal reactions, mental hygiene, emotional regulation, self-esteem, or practice methods. Sometimes the neural processes involved are complex. Complicated visual, aural, and memory elements must interface for some skills. But no matter the complexity, improvement is possible. The brain is happy to change.

It's easy to miss how powerful this is. Have you noticed that difficult things become easier with consistent effort? Have you also noticed that ability regresses without consistent effort? For example, when students, speakers, athletes, musicians, or dancers return after a break, ability is usually diminished. But with effort skills can usually be restored. Typically the brain and muscles are built at the same time, so it's easy to attribute improvement to the muscle being rebuilt. But the brain is also rebuilt.

One teacher deliberately brought attention to neuroplasticity when students struggled with a new movement. She told them that their brain was just figuring out how to tell their body how to work. Later, when the movement became easy, she pointed out that they'd developed a new neural pathway. She felt that neural awareness increased the speed of skill mastery.

Neuroplasticity enables physical, mental, and emotional improvement. A lot of people think that emotional regulation (like managing anxiety) doesn't have much to do with the brain, but this is incorrect. Certain structures in the brain regulate emotion. They are larger and show more activity in people with a lot of anxieties (and depression). But don't worry. Even brain structure can be progressively changed. Amazed?

Practice and repeated patterns develop high functioning neural pathways. Neglect and deliberate avoidance prune neural pathways. Physical action and vivid imagining can create neural changes. Do you want positive change? There are tips below. These things enhance neuroplasticity in actual and virtual practice. So *do* these things to *build* neural pathways (and *don't* do them to *prune* away neural pathways):

Try hard so the brain change is bigger. *Practice* so lots of neural connections are made. *Keep learning* so interconnections increase. *Develop habits* so the brain develops a predictable flow. *Pay attention* so chemicals release in the brain to help you. *Repeat effort* so the brain shifts material from short-term to long-term memory for permanent use (this includes muscle memory). *Rehearse mentally* so improvement is faster without wear and tear. *Use* all types of sensory input (especially in virtual practice). Deliberately hear, see, feel, and even smell and taste so more parts of the brain connect toward the goal. *Think and do quality work* so the brain reinforces your best material.

It's easy to "develop" unwanted neural pathways. If you worry or engage in catastrophic thinking, you "practice" this and actually "develop" undesirable neural pathways. Problematic results are usually attributed to fear cycles. But there's more to it. Negative thinking reinforces negative neural pathways. The probability of problems increases. Who wants that? Worriers might learn this and worry even more. Instead, set an improvement goal, let negative thoughts go, and focus *only* on the positive improvement goal. Do you see how this supports your core?

Neuroplasticity doesn't decide what to strengthen or weaken. You do. Neuroplasticity only follows your lead according to what is engaged in or avoided. (Addictions involve maladaptive neuroplasticity; overcoming them involves reshaping the brain.) Good mental hygiene and careful practice are important. Do you see why exceptional teachers and coaches are sticklers regarding these things? But ultimately, no one knows your thoughts but you. You coach yourself in this.

Habits are a result of neuroplasticity. Highly developed neural pathways are strong and up to 100 times faster than regular neural pathways. That's why habits are hard to break. An engrained habit has a mega neural-highway attached. So slip-ups are common when pruning. Similarly, new habits don't have strong neural pathways yet. So improvement may also involve slips. Don't get discouraged. Slips indicate that your brain is normal. Jump back in. Neuroplasticity will follow.

Some fear management increases unwanted neural pathways which are already strong due to internal safety mechanisms. Countering this can be done by imagining the situation that's feared, immediately "shrinking" it away from you to the size of a quarter, and blinking it in black and white. This proactively disrupts old neural pathways and increases power over fear. (Who's afraid of a situation shrinkable and quarter-sized?)

Neuroplasticity can also be improved by imagery, visualization, and mental practice. These are all slightly different forms of mentally engaging. They can be used to improve skills, goals, self-efficacy, injury recovery, muscle enhancement, motivation, artistry, weight loss, and emotional, mental or physical reactions. To improve most quickly, focus on the *kinesthetic production* of a task—*the sensations, feelings, and energy.* Fully experience. Sense how the muscles feel rippling through movements. Sense how the brain feels. (This is essentially how brain shorting is also overcome.) Sports research indicates that a focus on *kinesthetic energy sensations* maximizes both virtual *and* actual practice. This doesn't just work for athletes. It works for anyone.

There are two possible viewpoints when visualizing: first person (also called internal)—which is imagining a situation as if looking out *through your own eyes*; and third person (also called external)—which is imagining a situation as if looking at yourself *through someone else's eyes.* Basically it's "doing" versus "watching." As a general rule, to *decrease* something, don't visualize at all; to *increase* something, vividly visualize using a first person/internal viewpoint; to stay neutral in order to observe and learn, visualize using a third person/external viewpoint. (Third person is good for "sitting with" negative emotion to *observe* without additional arousal.)

An acronym was developed to maximize skill visualization: PETTLEP. It stands for physical—visualize the actual performance; environment—in the actual environment or a close proximity; task—closely imagining the real task; timing—using real-time speed; learning—practicing at current ability (which may involve initially slowing things down, but keeping them in the context of real time); emotion—with the same emotion as during performance (except replace any negative with positive); and perspective—imagine using a first person stance. It works. The parts of the brain that coordinate motor action also activate during imagined action.

Is mental practice effective? A world-class organist related that while working on a PhD in Europe, his teacher mentioned the benefits of mental practice away from the organ. So that week, the student split time equally between practicing at the organ and practicing in his mind. The next lesson, his teacher was astounded by the progress and asked what had been done differently.

Do you see the benefits of mental practice? Also, when fatigued, visualization can be used to continue practice without the risk of injury. Research shows that when *imagined activity is vivid*, ability improves about as much as actual practice. It even builds muscle mass and elevates heart and respiration. But there are more benefits.

Mental practice before (and during) performance warms up the body and brain. Have you seen a basketball player motion as if shooting the free throw before actually shooting? It's like a practice shot and warms up neural pathways. Actors call this neural pathway warm-up "getting into character"; speakers call it "mental preparation"; skiers call it "visualizing the run." It's why musicians are taught to think the first phrase before performing. In reality, these are just neuroplasticity parties! Can a neuroplasticity party benefit you?

You don't need to know about neurotransmitters, dendrites, and axons to maximize neuroplasticity. You just need to know that the brain is happy to support you. What would you like? Plan a party. Be consistent and watch the improvement. Strengthen your core through focused neuroplasticity.

Next up, when *not* to think...

Summary
The brain can be shaped. Neural pathways can be developed or pruned. It takes about three weeks of consistent effort. The fact that it takes effort to change is a protection that makes change possible. Some tasks require new brain structures and need extra persistence. Neural pathways do not discern good or bad quality. They reinforce what they're given. Negative things develop negative connections, so use care to reinforce positive connections. Deliberately shrinking problems and good habits can propel a person forward. Mental practice/visualization improves ability. Kinesthetic visualization is the most powerful type of visualization. First person and third person visualization have different uses and benefits. Anything can improve through neuroplasticity—plan a party and watch the improvement.

Case Study

This case study happened to me. I was the director of a play when an actress dropped out 2 ½ weeks before the show. No replacement could be found so I jumped in. I wasn't worried because I was a seasoned performer before becoming a director and choreographer. But as I attempted to memorize, nothing stuck and I definitely became unsure of coming out okay. I persisted. In the end, the first half-page took over two weeks and the last half-page took only a few minutes. At the time, I thought that I had finally put in enough time. But later I realized that the timeline coincided with neuroplasticity research, and that neural pathways were probably involved to some extent. (I also realized that directing and acting are as different as conducting an orchestra and playing an instrument. This would also be true of an athlete switching team positions or a business person being promoted, etc. Even when activities are related, the mental skills may be different, hence the need for neuroplasticity.)

Empower Yourself

Accept what you have, or...build what you need.

Fast-Track ReflACTION

1) If you had a neuroplasticity party, what would you like to change and how would you do it?
2) Imagine doing a task "first person" and again "third person;" how could you use each to improve your ability?
3) When might mental practice be more beneficial for you than physical practice?

Please note: Habits involving substance abuse or other addictions that alter normal hormonal or neurotransmitter patterns are complicated by these influences. Trained professionals should supervise these types of changes to provide additional emotional support and maintain physical safety if withdrawal is involved

13
When Not to Think

Just as it is important to learn to think, it is also important to learn when not to think. Why? Conscious thought comes from a part of the brain that can interfere with rehearsed tasks. So, if a performance is primarily drawn from memory (including muscle memory), there is a benefit in "not thinking". Or stated differently, don't "overthink".

It's obvious that things like musical pieces, verbatim business presentations, tests, or theater scripts are built on memory. However, a "spontaneous" performance, like an athletic game, is also built on memory—muscle memory. As you know, well-established neural pathways are developed through repetition. Performances are solidified through mental and muscle memory.

When practice goes well but a performer "chokes," there's a tendency to think that the preparation was inadequate. Sometimes it is. But more often choking has nothing to do with preparation. So, trying to solve choking with extra preparation is like changing a car battery to fix the fuel pump—the battery might be stronger but the car still doesn't function. The right thing must be fixed. Choking usually isn't a personality or preparation problem. It's a brain shift problem. It's not using the right part of the brain (literally).

When learning a skill, the left frontal lobe engages. This part of the brain evaluates and critiques the process so improvement can be made. Once a skill has been learned, it shifts to the brain's right hemisphere. The right hemisphere then executes the skill automatically. When skills are shifted to the right hemisphere, the left frontal lobe is then free to learn new things.

This shifting process is what makes learning possible. Otherwise the learning centers would be stuck executing basic tasks. There would be little brain power to tackle new things. For example, a baby exerts enormous concentration to learn to walk, but an adult hardly thinks about it. The complex task of walking has become automatic. So an adult can engage in other activities while walking, like reading or talking. (In fact, reading and talking have also been automated and shifted, which allows the person to focus on the content of what is read and heard!)

The conscious left frontal lobe can only focus on one thing at a time. So if a previous skill hasn't fully shifted to the subconscious right hemisphere and a new skill is introduced, the previous skill will regress. Teachers and coaches see this when new skills are introduced and previous skills slightly falter. But with practice, both the new and previous skills solidly shift to the right hemisphere.

What happens if these skills are re-analyzed? The mastered material shifts from the right hemisphere back to the conscious left frontal lobe. This is okay and necessary when further refining a skill. But it can throw off the things that were automatic. (That's why words you know seem weird if you think about them—like when writing on a chalkboard.) When a task shifts back to the left frontal lobe, it feels different. So, a brain shift can potentially cause problems in practice, and always causes problems in performance.

Additionally, the short-term working memory can only handle a certain amount before it has to shift things to long-term memory or falter. It takes time and exposure to shift things over (which is good, otherwise there would be no filter on unwanted stuff). But if too many things are in the working memory (like when cramming for a test), ability can be hampered.

Additionally, self-conscious worry can occupy part of the prefrontal cortex and working memory, which can also contribute to overload. There's a tendency to be more attentive and self-conscious when performing. So shifting from the right hemisphere back to the left frontal lobe, taxing the prefrontal cortex, and overloading working memory can be a problem during performance.

Since a "brain switch" feels different, the resulting *unsure* feeling can increase self-consciousness. Also, as the conscious mind imposes judgments and "improvements," muscle memory can be thrown off further. As this detrimental "unsure shifting cycle" repeats, the performance goes downhill. Do you see how brain shifts and working-memory overload can be responsible for performance anxiety, choking, and difficulty with flow/zone?

Pleasurable peak performance is usually due to an optimal use of the right hemisphere. Experienced performers usually perform better than inexperienced ones. It's not so much a difference in ability as a difference in brain use. An inexperienced performer can boost ability by adopting the mental skills of experienced performers. Ability increases with optimal brain use.

How can brain shifting be detected? The right hemisphere isn't consciously aware. So, if you're aware, evaluating, worrying, judging or critiquing, the left frontal lobe is engaged. A common reaction to a brain shift is extra determination in an attempt to force improvement. This usually backfires. The answer is a mental stance similar to "sitting with emotion". Observe.

A "drop" in ability between practice and performance isn't a drop at all. Ability is the same. Performing is just harder. And it's especially hard if the wrong mental tools are used. This isn't surprising. If others use the wrong tools their "ability" drops, too. Imagine a carpenter using a hammer when a drill is needed; or a race car driver in a minivan. Similarly, ability is hampered if the left frontal lobe is used when the right hemisphere is needed, or vice versa. The different parts of the brain are good at their jobs. The use of optimal mental skills can be developed.

During practice it is *important* to use the left frontal lobe. Some people mindlessly practice. They are sloppy and make a lot of mistakes. What's happening? A bad performance is programmed into muscle memory and put in the right hemisphere. Whoa, bad idea! That's why good teachers and coaches encourage as much perfection as possible during practice. They may also break complex tasks down or advise executing skills in slow motion to train precision into the body and mind.

The left frontal lobe discerns between good and bad quality, but the right hemisphere doesn't. The right hemisphere will accept whatever is handed over—whether it's quality or not. So, practice *exactly* the way you want to perform—the same gestures, stance, tone, attitude, eye movements, etc. Even *thoughts* become "rehearsed" and pass to the right hemisphere. Things like "I'm not very good at this" or "I can do this!" are also programmed in.

So, is the old saying "practice makes perfect" true? Nope! A noted professor corrected this to: "Practice makes permanent. Only perfect practice makes perfect." If practice is imperfect, imperfect material is shipped over to the right hemisphere. Then in performance the brain either spits out the imperfect right hemisphere version, or the left frontal lobe takes over and tries to fix things during performance. Either way there's usually trouble! Do you see how this weakens core power?

Usually choking is from trying to improve at the wrong time or in the wrong way. Some think there's something wrong when choking occurs. But the left frontal lobe and right hemisphere are actually working the way they are *supposed* to work. Trying harder during performance isn't always the answer.

One teacher told students to never improve during performance and *always* perform what was rehearsed. She also said to practice the improvement later and implement it in the next performance. What's really advocated? *Stay in the right hemisphere!* This is not to say there's never an exception. Brain functions do overlap during performance; in fact, it takes the left frontal lobe to determine if more right hemisphere is needed! The core is stronger when you know what's going on and take charge.

In practice do small things well—like small sections of music or small amounts of material for a test—then methodically add more material while maintaining quality output. One person joked, "I might not get it all right, but I'll get what I worked on right." A variation is, "My beginning-level skills will look like a pro." Master the material at your level. For example, a beginning musician can sound like an advanced musician playing an easy song. This concept can be applied to any skill.

Careful practice results in additional benefits. Not only is a "good right hemisphere package prepared", the left frontal lobe becomes more proficient. It learns to learn. Careful preparation feels slow. But it's actually a turbo boost to learning, quality, and confidence. On the other hand, practicing poorly is a form of "I'll-fix-it-later procrastination," which trains the neural pathways to function at that lower level. So it can dumb down ability. This problem can be reversed, and it takes about 3 weeks! Careful preparation puts you ahead. It can be done creatively.

One teacher told students that their fingers were factory workers and they were the boss. The boss's job was to supervise but not to do the work. Students used this in practice and performance when they wanted the brain to "attend" but not take over. She intuitively found a way to reduce the left frontal lobe interference. You may find your own ingenious ways.

One athlete chanted a mantra immediately before and during games, "Now is the time to just do." Research found another way to increase right hemisphere function—squeeze a ball in the left hand or clench the left fist just before a task. Oh and students, gum chewing has been shown to raise test scores—who knows, perhaps it helps engage better brain use!

Performance isn't the only time to deliberately back off thinking. Brains need breaks! Even brains that are highly trained to sustain concentration will work better with a couple of minutes off every 40 to 90 minutes. If the brain gets too tired, it spits poor quality into the right hemisphere. A break allows the brain to rejuvenate. So it's not lazy to get a drink or stretch legs during practice, long classes, or extended business meetings. It's also not lazy to build in performance breaks. For example, athletes not only benefit from quarter/halftime breaks, but also time on the bench and timeouts.

Developing brain support strengthens the core. There are several ways to maximize brain support in practice and performance. Strengthen your core by knowing when to think and not think.

Next up, power the brain...

Summary

Conscious improvement comes from the left frontal lobe in the brain; this is helpful in practice. Automated responses and memory (including muscle memory) come from the right hemisphere in the brain; this is helpful in performance. Learned skills shift from the left frontal lobe to the right hemisphere. Brain shifts are good and make complex tasks possible. Memory-based performance relies heavily on right hemisphere automation. Shifting back to the left frontal lobe in performance can be detrimental. Self-consciousness is more likely during performance and is a left frontal lobe function. "Choking" is often caused by a brain shift. Shifting lessens with experience. The left frontal lobe discerns quality, and the right hemisphere accepts what's put in. Imperfect practice puts an imperfect performance into the right hemisphere. This is either spit out as is, or the frontal lobe attempts to correct during performance. Either way, there's trouble. Practicing poorly is "fix-it-later procrastination." Performing as you have practiced encourages quality practice and develops the ability to use desired brain functions on command. Only perfect practice makes perfect. Practice quality. A beginner should look like a professional doing easy skills. Quality practice increases learning ability and confidence. There are quirky things that can engage the right hemisphere and improve performance. Brains need breaks. Quality performance involves optimal use of the left frontal lobe and the right hemisphere during practice and performance.

Case Study

Brach was a defensive lineman and loved reading the offense. He was very diligent about developing skills during practice;

71

but then, in games he felt torn between technique and his gut instinct. One day he missed a couple of tackles, and in frustration he just went with his gut. Suddenly he was nailing everything. He laughed inside—he'd never considered that thinking less could improve his game. He prepared carefully. But in games he seemed to do better if he trusted his gut.

Case Study

Nerves were building. It was understandable, this audition was important. Charie said to herself, "Okay, just sing like you're in the shower! Time for autopilot." She stepped up and went straight for the familiar sensations from practice.

Empower Yourself

Think and sink, or...release the think.

Fast-Track ReflACTION

1) What mental or muscle memory does your type of performances require?
2) What practice changes would send a better performance package to your right hemisphere?
3) What can you do to maximize performing what you practiced?

14
Glucose and Grudge Busting

It's easy to neglect the brain's basic needs. The past chapters considered brain *function* and *use*. This chapter considers how the brain is *powered* and sustained. So, the past brain chapters were like tuning up a car and this chapter puts gas in the engine. Are you ready to power up the brain and take off?

Your brain averages about 60,000 thoughts a day and has about 10 billion brain nerve cells, all linked by about 10 trillion connections. It's estimated that a single scalp EEG electrode provides synaptic feedback for between 10 million and 1 billion neurons. And the neurons all communicate chemically through neurotransmitters. What fuels neurons? Glucose. The brain uses about 20% of the glucose from the food you eat. It makes neurotransmitters with it. Neurotransmitters are essential for mental function because brain pathways can't communicate without them.

Glucose doesn't always burn at the same rate. Attitude affects the speed that glucose is used. When a person is engaged, interested, and enjoying an activity, glucose burns slower and focus widens. When a person is forced (by self or others), uninterested, or detesting an activity, glucose burns faster and conscious focus narrows. Stress also increases glucose consumption.

Maximum mental output requires sufficient glucose. But before you stock up on candy bars, not all glucose is the same. (And more glucose won't help if you already have enough.) Highly-refined foods (like sugar) release glucose very quickly during digestion without adding nutrients. Refined sugar spikes the blood glucose, followed by a crash. This isn't particularly good for the brain or body. It can also create cravings. Ideally glucose is obtained naturally through balanced meals and snacks, like fresh or dried fruits. These release energy in a more sustained way and provide needed nutrients. So, got fruit?

Productive people are notorious for ignoring personal needs and "powering through." Sometimes high-output cultures even support neglectful attitudes. They may portray those who deny personal needs as more committed and amazing. So let's just call this type of attitude what it is—sick. I'm not saying to pull back on commitment, sacrifice, or determination. I'm saying give your body what it needs so it can give full effort! What happens as glucose gets low? Thinking and willpower erode. There's such a strong connection between glucose and willpower that researchers now say "glucose = willpower." So, to keep determination up, maintain glucose! (This also applies to those who are dieting, and as you'll see, attitude impacts glucose, too.)

The effect of food in the gut goes even deeper. Research indicates that the brain doesn't just send signals to the gut, the gut influences the brain—the gut-brain axis. The balance of healthy versus unhealthy gut bacteria has been shown to influence anxiety and depression. Additionally, the bacterium present in young mice appears to affect brain development and can permanently alter emotional responses and brain function. This research indicates that it may be important to eat healthy to eliminate anxiety (and depression), and that to prevent anxiety it may be wise to consider the effect of antibiotics, probiotics, other healthy bacteria (theorized on garden fresh vegetables), and the importance of feeding children healthy food as the brain develops.

Additionally, those with food sensitivities may need to consider the effect of possible allergies. Healthy food is not just about brain-glucose fuel, it's about whole-body fuel. Healthy eating encompasses things like watching out for personal needs. Outcomes can be affected by things like delayed food sensitivities. You should feel energized after eating. Fatigue is often an overlooked sensitivity or allergy. One performer noticed a pattern of fatigue about two hours after eating certain foods. He learned to avoid that food, especially when high performance and mental clarity was needed.

Dehydration also affects the brain. It can spark a chain reaction of stress responses. The brain is only 2% of the body mass, but takes 15% of the blood supply. Dehydration affects the blood and may manifest as anxiety, anger, lower attention, irritation, impatience and depression. Do you think this would affect performance output? You bet! So along with grabbing glucose, grab some quality water!

But what usually happens? Needs are ignored, glucose and hydration become depleted, willpower slackens, and individuals struggle. Then this causes feelings of being incapable and weak, which burns glucose faster. And the cycle repeats. Have you ever seen this? What would happen if an individual got a good breakfast after fasting all night, a little glucose while working, studying, or practicing, and a little more glucose before test taking, a performance, challenging work, or a game? Could that affect outcome and feeling *sure?* You bet! The core does better when powered.

Let's talk a little more about how attitude affects glucose. A grudging attitude burns glucose faster. Does this mean to slack on anything unpleasant? No, it means to develop the art of cheerful engagement. Let's face it, whether you're a student, athlete, performing artist, business person, or parent, there are times when you just have to suck it up and get the job done. But there's a difference between mindlessly powering through and mindfully choosing to be cheerful.

Viktor Frankl, a prisoner in the Nazi concentration camps, stated that even when every other freedom is denied, there is always the freedom to choose one's response to circumstances. In our society it has become an epidemic to respond grudgingly: I *have* to go study, I *have* to go to practice, I *have* to go to work...But is this true? Individuals can choose not to, can't they? Truthfully, these things are choices. It's time to take responsibility. The reality is: I *choose* to study, I *choose* to practice, I *choose* to go to work. And since these represent opportunities, it's even more accurate to say: I *get* to study, I *get* to practice, I *get* to go to work! Taking responsibility immediately reduces anxiety because it is empowering.

Why do grudging attitudes slip in? The brain comes preprogrammed to pull back. So it's easy for grudges to take over. But if something unpleasant must be completed, why not mindfully choose a good attitude and reduce the glucose wear and tear? Face it, life takes effort if only to get dinner. So "grudge bust"! Mindfully choose cheerfulness (as opposed to mindlessly, grudgingly powering through). Cheerfulness results in more enjoyment and energy...and maximizes glucose.

But there are even more important reasons to never do things grudgingly. It's a safety valve. Grudges usually surface from overextension, duty, manipulation, lack of organization, etc. Pulling back can sometimes be a good idea, like when exhausted, overextended, or sick. So "grudge busting" isn't just being cheerful; it's showing up for yourself and paying attention when you need self-care. Grudge busting expands skill in taking responsibility, exercising wisdom, balancing activities, choosing cheerful reactions, and living self-aware. Can this reduce anxiety? You bet! These little decisions significantly strengthen core power.

It's easy to fool oneself and think that pushing forward grudgingly is more productive. But it's counterproductive. Not only is it not fun (for you or those around you), it's not good for you! You already know it increases glucose consumption, but it also changes brain-learning pathways. There are two learning pathways: traumatic (or low road) and transformational (or high road). Transformational/high road learning includes more prefrontal engagement and the ability to place current memories in the context of past wisdom and memories. This learning is deep and rich.

Traumatic/low-road learning happens when negative emotion causes brain functions to re-route to less prefrontal cortex and less memory interconnection. Grudges are negative, so experiences are stored in the memory as a "lump" without rich connections to other experiences. Learning and retrieving becomes more difficult. Who wants that? Does this mean to cut out everything you don't want to do? No, it means to do things cheerfully and to choose activities mindfully. These choices route neural activity through the richest parts of your brain. Do you think this would affect performance? Absolutely! It also strengthens the core. Being cheerful and mindful is good for you and those you interact with.

A choice to maintain glucose, hydration, and cheerfulness is really a choice to live life more purposefully and effectively. So go ahead, take care of your brain! Strengthen your core with cheerful, mindful choices.

Next up, engage the heart...

Summary
It's easy to neglect basic needs that affect the brain. The trillions of cells and connections communicate through neurotransmitters. The brain uses about 20% of consumed glucose. Glucose doesn't always burn at the same rate. Unpleasant activities burn more glucose, pleasant ones burn less. Refined glucose causes blood sugar spikes and lows. Powering through is counterproductive. Self-nourishment enables more effective engagement. Glucose equals willpower. Doing things grudgingly burns glucose faster. When every other freedom is denied, there is still a choice

about attitude. Engaging while mindfully and cheerfully aware of choice is different than pushing through mindlessly unaware. The brain is preprogrammed to protect. It instinctively pulls back and leans toward grudges. "Grudge busting" is a safety valve. This choice involves evaluation of what can and can't be done. There are two learning pathways in the brain. Negative emotions engage the traumatic/low-road pathway while positive emotions engage the transformational/high-road pathway. Transformational learning results in quality learning. A choice to be cheerful and mindful is a choice to use the brain effectively.

Case Study

Catherin was tired of being ineffective. She made a spreadsheet of everything she wanted to accomplish in the month. Each morning she noticed her "protective brain" pulling her away from her new goals and healthy habits. She said to herself, "I can only omit things if I really don't want the benefits. And if I want the benefits I have to start *immediately* and complete each item quickly and cheerfully!" Her energy improved and productivity soared. She confessed that sometimes she did omit things or rearrange her schedule. But she felt that the reason she was so effective was that she switched from "unplanned, irritable, default mode" to "pre-planned, upbeat, choices mode".

Case Study

Ruth had a lot to memorize in a short time and doubted she could. Initially she didn't recognize her doubt. But a friend said she was good at memorizing. Ruth decided to focus on that thought, "I'll be okay. I'm good at memorizing." Wow, retention was *immediately* easier! Shortly afterward she learned about low-level and high-level thinking. Suddenly it all made sense! She told her friend that when she doubted herself the memorized material actually felt like a tense lump in her brain. But her brain seemed to relax and the material "spread out" when she believed in herself and stopped feeling stupid for procrastinating. There were definite brain sensations she hadn't noticed before.

Empower Yourself

Mindless default, or...mindful choice.

ReflACTION

1)   How have glucose levels and hydration affected you today?

2) How could you more mindfully and cheerfully engage; what would be the benefits? Are there things you should respectfully disengage from; what would be the benefits?

3) When do you experience low-level thinking; how can you maximize high-level thinking, and what would be the benefits?

15

Heart Attacking

Most people believe that thinking is just done by the brain, but it comes from the whole body. If it didn't, you couldn't even walk. The brain computes from all the senses, and the motor system helps to organize input. But this body-brain link may be more than sensory. The body may store "memories" that affect ability. One of the most researched body-brain links is the heart-brain link.

Traditionally it was thought that the brain controlled the heart. While the brain obviously does send information to the heart, studies show some unexpected things. The heart sends more information to the brain than the brain to the heart. The heart can anticipate and override the brain. The heart modulates much systemic activity. And the heart produces neurotransmitters that affect the brain. Additionally, heart rate variability (how heartbeats differ) can be used to diagnose anxiety and depression. Heart rate variability is also used to increase flow/zone in high-level athletes like NFL players. In short, the heart's electrical and chemical processes are complicated and amazing. They affect the brain more than most realize. This explains a lot, doesn't it?

Emotion is tied to the heart. If you're angry or afraid, where is the emotion *felt?* Generally emotions are "heart-felt". Emotion is sometimes undesired. Some want to eliminate it altogether, or at least the emotion sensing parts of the brain. But if this part of the brain is damaged, normal function is impossible. This part of the brain is essential. So emotion is important for function. But research also indicates that the heart is important in self-control and obtaining flow/zone (not in cardio ways but in heart-brain function). Did you ever think that the sayings "he did it with all his heart" or "his heart wasn't in it" might involve more than meets the eye? The effect of the heart on outcomes is physiological not just emotional or psychological.

Let's look more deeply. I'm going to get technical for a bit so hang tight, we're going to have some fun. The heart sends info through afferent vagus nerve fibers to the amygdala in the brain (which regulates emotion). The brain's limbic system, including the amygdala, and insular cortex, are preprogrammed to quickly respond to possible threats. This activity is then relayed to the medial prefrontal cortex. One of the jobs of the medial prefrontal cortex is to assess if there's real danger and tone things down if the amygdala and insular cortex are whacked out over nothing (like they think a stick is a poisonous snake, a test is the end of the world, or a sports event is life and death).

This system works great except for a little problem. Those with anxieties tend to have high emotional input from hyper amygdala and insular activation, and less prefrontal cortex override. So they tend to get worn down as they're yanked around by too many warnings coming in. Research shows that this is not so much due to *actual* threats, but whether a person thinks they can *control* a potentially threatening situation. Does that sound like "fear of coming out okay"? Research proposes that those with anxiety have an altered interoceptive prediction signal, which is just a fancy way of saying that potentially bad situations trigger extra worries.

So if a person is born with an overactive amygdala, an underactive medial prefrontal cortex, and a hyper-sensitive insula, is all lost? No! The brain *and* heart can be "trained." This can change emotions! This type of "heart training" is not cardio endurance—it's *waaay* different. It's more like savvy emotional override training. The heart has a kind of "neuroplasticity." Or is that "emotional cardioplasticity"? (This isn't the cardioplasticity that happens when the heart develops other pathways of functioning after a heart attack.) This is an improved heart function due to emotional savvy.

In my clinical psychology PhD program, I heard about combined heart and brain training that can increase ability. Specialists working with world-class athletes discovered a correlation between an individual's unique heartbeat patterns and peak performance. They studied heart records and found micro-sawtooth-heartbeat patterns that are as unique to an individual as fingerprints. They also found that these patterns can be altered by life experiences. Even seemingly insignificant experiences could permanently limit ability unless there was specific intervention. Intervention included emotional healing and biofeedback. The resulting heart micro-variability became permanently less jagged, which corresponded to an immediate increase in flow/zone performance. So, processing emotional experiences permanently increased ability. The word "processing" is just a fancy way of saying that a person comes to terms with past experiences and increases *awareness* of *thoughts* and *feelings*. So increased ability wasn't just tied to thoughts. It was tied to measurable changes in the heart.

A correlation between ability and past experiences was observed long before specialized heart monitors and high-level athletes documented it. Teachers observed a decline in the work of students who experienced trauma. Ability then improved as trauma healed. Additionally, educational researchers found that addressing anxiety immediately increased ability without any additional instruction or practice. They thought the students simply concentrated better, and neuroscience does show improved brain function when emotion decreases. But new evidence indicates that *body function* also changes. Other research indicates that life experiences may even change DNA and affect one's kids. If so, it's conceivable that some limitations (and aptitudes and talents) could come from ancestors. That puts a different spin on things, doesn't it?

It is well established that life experiences trigger heart reactions like heart attacks. But new research reveals that small, nearly imperceptible things can affect ability thereafter and change the heart. When this happens, it is said to be like driving with the gas and brake on at the same time. Experiences can cause lingering decreases in overall ability (not just heart function). This may account for some of the challenges athletes experience after injuries. Fortunately, processing experiences can remove the "brakes." When experiences are processed, ability increases. More can be done with less effort.

Yoga masters and researchers have also identified an interplay between meditation, ability, and the heart. When the heart chakra is "cleared" of emotional blocks, body function increases. It is said that one third of a person's life force is in the heart chakra because this chakra directly affects the heart and lungs. Emotional trauma has been known to decrease air capacity and physical endurance. This decrease can persist despite cardio training. But respiration and cardio capacity have been known to *immediately* increase when a blocked chakra is cleared. It usually takes weeks to months to build significantly increased air capacity, so significant or nearly doubled air capacity from a few minutes of specific yoga exercise is unique. Those who have experienced trauma—like betrayal, divorce, or death—and then "unblock" are more likely to report significant changes. Imagine how more lung capacity can relieve anxiety for those who rely on it, like musicians or athletes.

It was mentioned that the causes of anxiety and flow/zone issues are unique to the individual. Empirical evidence regarding the heart supports this. Furthermore, if anxiety is rare in children and common in adults, *something caused a change*. The change can be traced to life experiences. Not only are memories stored in tissue, but memories may permanently change heart and lung capacity (unless there is specific intervention). Processing negative experiences may restore one's core and improve heart function, lung capacity, emotional strength, mental clarity, physical skills, and confidence.

Whether changes take place directly in the heart or brain, or through a heart-brain connection is still being determined, but the fact that a change takes place is well documented. Emotional experiences affect heart (and lung) capacity. This puts a different twist on why a person might feel *unsure*, doesn't it?

Very small things can affect outcome anxiety and flow/zone. Things that would not even be considered "traumatic" can affect output. As you will see in the case study below, this cyclist didn't have anxiety, or even apprehension. He was just trying to improve race times. You can see how flow/zone and anxiety are related, and why ability is unlocked similarly for each. The research is new, but if preliminary studies are correct, eliminating anxiety and increasing flow/zone may involve literally lifting negative experiences out of body tissue—and apparently it's not that difficult. But even easy things are hard if unknown.

According to theories, physiological change happens as awareness of thought and feelings increases. If so, your mind isn't just changed by reading this book. Your body is changed. Anxiety improvement takes effort, but not an overhaul. Some performers become frustrated when flow/zone seems illusive, but this information opens new possibilities. Suzie had to look in the right direction to eliminate her fear; performers must look in the right direction to eliminate their fear. So while research is still new, preliminary studies indicate that *something* is going on and it may be quite significant.

This preliminary research puts a new twist on the importance of a balanced life and a healthy emotional core. It's common sense that these things allow a person to work harder and more effectively. So, is elaborate counseling, lengthy yoga, or bio-feedback needed in order to improve ability? No. Why? Their primary purpose is to increase an awareness of *thoughts* and *feelings*. Did you see that coming? And while there are many helpful resources that can be used to improve awareness, ultimately the individual does the work.

Life experiences affect performance. They may be more deeply embedded in tissue and the body than realized. Emotion-heart-output correlations are documented in a variety of academic research such as education, yoga, physiological responses, neurological data, and biofeedback. Ability improves with attention to the affect of emotion on the heart. This improvement has been seen in high-level athletes routinely monitoring outcomes in hundredths of a second. The brain can be trained; so can the heart—both for cardio stamina and *core stamina*. Strengthen your core by considering your heart.

Next up, heart training...

Summary

Thinking involves the brain and body. The heart and brain are more connected than realized. More information goes from the heart to the brain than the brain to the heart, and the heart can override the brain. Flow/zone is affected by emotional memories that are either directly embedded in the heart tissue or embedded somewhere else, indirectly affecting heart function. A heart-brain link was discovered by specialists working with high-level athletes increasing flow/zone. Similar improvements are supported in education and yoga research. When memories and anxieties are processed, there are documented positive changes to the heart and lungs. (This is different than cardio endurance; it's a sort of "emotional cardioplasticity".) Even things that would not be considered traumatic can affect ability. The heart can stimulate the amygdala. Those with anxiety have a hyper amygdala and a hypo-overriding medial prefrontal cortex. The heart-brain connection can be trained. The connection is likely affected right now as you learn. All memory is stored in tissue. Processing is recognizing and understanding thoughts and feelings. Deliberate processing seems to lift the negative impact of memories out of cells in a way that improves heart function, lung capacity, and overall ability. Sometimes great effort is made to improve ability without attention to emotional things. High-level athletes have trained the heart-brain connection to improve ability, could you?

Case Study

Dart's cycling race speeds had dropped. He was inexplicably slowing down in the turns. He had heard that biofeedback coupled with counseling could improve his times. In counseling, a couple of minor incidents were discovered that affected his race. When he was a boy, he was riding down the street when his mother suddenly screamed. From her vantage, she thought a car was going to hit him. Though he was safe, this brief moment was recorded in his memory. Later, he saw someone skid out while turning in a race. He'd seen racers skid out before, it was common. But for some reason these experiences mentally linked and his turns slowed. Though these two memories were relatively insignificant, they negatively impacted his output. Once they were identified and processed, Dart's race speeds shot up—not just on the turns, but through the entire race.

Case Study

Caryn was a woodwind player and was having difficulty with air in the short phrases, let alone the long ones. She had experienced extreme trauma. A therapist recommended yoga for emotional centering and exercise. Each day at the end of the DVD "chakra clearing" session, there was a meditation chant which she did not have enough air to complete in one breath. She was discouraged thinking it would take significant cardio training to get her air control back. The introduction to the heart chakra session said that heart and lung capacity could increase when "cleared." She doubted it. At the end of the exercise session, she did the chant as usual. But she was astounded to complete it in one breath! She replayed the chant and then kept going to see how long she could go. She almost did two full chants in one breath! She could hardly wait for her next music rehearsal! [She was told that if a chakra isn't blocked, differences are not noted; it's believed that issues can affect function in any chakra, but trauma is said to especially affect the heart chakra.]

Empower Yourself:

Repress your heart, or...restore your heart.

Fast-Track ReflACTION

1) When have you sensed emotions overriding your brain; what

might be causing this?

2) What type of brain and heart function did you apparently inherit; how does it influence your emotional responses?

3) Processing involves noticing fleeing insights or ideas. What fleeting thoughts have you had this week that may be beneficial to further consider?

16

A Change of Heart

Researchers report that changing the heart is relatively easy. Whew! There are various ways to affect this change, including controlled breathing, gratitude, genuine service, trigger awareness, yoga, and energy awareness. But before elaborating on these, it's helpful to know about body and mind baselines in order to understand the process of change.

The body naturally works toward dependable baselines through physical and emotional homeostasis—which is a fancy way of saying the body and mind like things to stay the same. Baselines and homeostasis are natural protections. When something is within a normal baseline, the body and brain relax. When something is off the normal baseline, the body and brain go on alert. Even positive changes are initially perceived as stressful. So a better job, an improved living arrangement, or a new friendship is a little stressful. Baselines are also why your house can make little creeks and groans that you're not aware of until there's a noise out of the norm. Then your ears prick up. Have you noticed this? Baselines affect responses to all types of situations.

How are baselines changed in positive ways? Changing a physical baseline is pretty obvious: make the change—like losing weight—and stick with it until the new baseline is accepted. However, homeostasis is stubborn. For example, it can take up to 3 months for weight hormones to stop trying to regulate back to the old baseline. That explains a lot, doesn't it? But despite strong pulls, the process of physical change is fairly straight forward. And there's a good flip-side. Once a physical baseline is changed, homeostasis tries just as hard to maintain the new one.

But how is an emotional baseline changed? Most people think that emotional baselines are changed simply by changing attitudes. But, this is only a small part of the process. Baselines also change through changing the brain (neuroplasticity) and changing the heart through changing heart function (literally). These things are influenced by triggers.

Remember triggers, the layers of emotion waiting to be heard? Triggers act like a "bruise." They indicate an "emotional ouch" that needs care and healing. That's why sudden waves of emotion are stronger than the situation appears to merit. And that's why they're difficult to control. Triggers increase reactions due to influences from past experiences. For example, a person who has been repeatedly lied to will react more strongly to lies than a person who has not been repeatedly lied to. It was previously thought that triggers develop exclusively from personal experiences. But new research hints otherwise. Triggers may also be intergenerationally passed down through DNA (similar to the way that instinct is intergenerationally passed down in animals).

Outcome anxiety, like performance anxiety, is a stronger reaction than a situation merits. So triggers are involved. Smaller "triggers" affect flow/zone. They're embedded in current baselines. They affect emotional homeostasis. So it's important to become aware of these influences and address them. This has been shown to literally and immediately change the heart. It improves long-term function and *emotional* and *physical* ability. Removing negative things, like triggers, is important. They diminish physical energy *even when the person is calm*. It's minuscule, but it's real.

So let's say that right now you want to change your heart baseline, go ahead. Do it. I'll wait. Done? How did it go? The heart can't generally be changed on command (unless maybe you're a meditation Zen master). But respiration can be controlled on command. Why is this relevant? A change in respiration can change heart function. Not only that, afferent vagus (body to brain) nerve impulses change the brain's emotion centers. So controlled, deep breathing is one way to change the emotional baseline in the heart (and brain). This strengthens your core. It takes fear away, both in the moment and permanently, as triggers are released.

This has been intuitively known for centuries. But now EEGs and ECGs empirically verify it. But controlled deep breathing is not the only way to change the heart. The heart and emotional baseline can be changed through gratitude. Gratitude and breathing are each powerful. But they are even more effective

88

when combined. This is called "gratitude breathing." It can strengthen the core. It changes baselines. How is this done?

Think of something you are truly grateful for. Take the feeling into the heart area while inhaling. As air enters, expand the gratitude throughout the chest. Hold the breath as long as is comfortable. Exhale and repeat. The hand can be placed on the heart to increase focus. This can change the micro variations in the heartbeat signature. Changes directly and immediately correlate to improved performance. And micro changes add up.

A gratitude breath is similar to deep breathing, but there are significant differences. The goal of deep breathing is to calm and relax. The goal of genuinely expressed gratitude through deep breathing is *to permanently change the heartbeat micro pattern* (which also happens to calm and relax). Do you see the distinct difference? The motive is *much* deeper. Gratitude breaths can literally change the heart and permanently improve functional micro pattern signatures.

So, gratitude can have a positive effect on eliminating triggers, changing heart patterns, and increasing ability, as shown in high-level athletes. This puts an additional twist on the impact of an "attitude of gratitude," "a grateful heart," or to "be grateful in all things," doesn't it? Is it a coincidence that the major religions of Hinduism, Christianity, Islam, Buddhism, and Judaism all advocate gratitude?

There are different levels of gratitude. A superficial level yields minimal change. For example, a person could say "I'm thankful for the sun." But it's more effective to sense the sun rays, soak in the warmth, appreciate the light, recognize the energy given to plants which become food, etc. In our society, enormous blessings are taken for granted. *This literally makes us sick.* There is constant clamor for more and disregard for bounty. Gratitude shifts these baselines. Profound gratitude increases optimal function. It reduces stress. It minimizes wear and tear on the mind and body. It rejuvenates and changes both the physical heartbeat and the emotional baseline.

Gratitude can be extended to almost any situation. For example, "I'm thankful for my family" or "I'm thankful for my job" can be genuinely expressed even if your family or job is crappy. Sincere gratitude attunes a person to benefits that are otherwise overlooked. Gratitude provides a deeper perspective and new sense of support. There's a reason for this. The amygdala is preprogrammed to notice negative things. *Gratitude balances this out.* It enables a broader, more accurate view. Theories also propose that gratitude isn't just a choice to change one's attitude; it's a choice to change one's cell function. Could this strengthen the core? We know that choices physiologically change brain function, and there is evidence to support that they physiologically change heart function, too.

But what if an *extremely* difficult, traumatic, or even criminal situation makes gratitude difficult? Place the right hand on the heart, skin to skin. Recall the situation and say to yourself, "*Of course you* would hurt; anyone would feel that way in this situation." Self-validation and self-nurturing help heal and change the heart. (This is different than self-justification, which is a quick-fix method to sidestep taking responsibility.) Victims sometimes self-condemn for not having prevented things. They take on responsibility that is not theirs. This damages the heart. One way to overcome difficult situations is to reclaim your core power. Baselines can be reset in a positive direction after trauma, as documented in counseling and biofeedback. Self-nurturing is appropriate. It's part of being aware of thoughts and feelings, and it opens the door to other types of positive change. It strengthens the heart and core.

Another strengthening tool is service if it's *genuinely* given "from the heart." This is different from grudging, obligated service. A mother of a young child looked at nighttime interruptions as an imposition on sleep. But energy surged when she determined to view interruptions as an opportunity for extra, special bonding. This type of decision not only strengthens the individual, it strengthens those in proximity. Genuine service is shown to change respiration, heartbeat, blood pressure, and rejuvenate the mind and body. And since it usually involves others, it also supplies beneficial doses of oxytocin, the brain's "love" neurotransmitter. Regular service improves physiological baselines, not just psychological. All these things improve performance.

As stated previously, yoga has also been found to change the heart and lungs. Certain types of yoga, involving 20-30 minutes of specific moderate exercises are said to "clear the heart chakra," along with other chakras. Whether or not chakras are real or actually "cleared", research shows positive physiological correlations. Yoga calms and balances. The exact mechanisms are still being examined, but empirical studies support various benefits of yoga. Certainly it involves mindful awareness. From both psychological and physiological angles, it appears to help reset the body toward more positive physical and emotional baselines.

The heart can also be changed by visualizing emotion as energy states. For example, a calm, peaceful emotion would be rated as a low energy level. An extremely angry, frustrated emotion would be rated as a high energy level. (In some theories, the names are reversed: calm, peaceful emotion is rated as high, meaning a higher quality; angry, frustrated emotion is rated as low, meaning lower quality.) Athletes are taught to identify negative experiences. These are processed. Residual negative energy is replaced with positive energy through visualization. This increases ability. Do you see how awareness is involved? Initially, improvements were simply attributed to beneficial visualization. But physiological research and quantum theories point to the possibility of literal energy changes. The question arises: Do thoughts change *matter*? It is not yet known. But it is known that thoughts matter.

Athletes use biofeedback to learn to control emotional energy as desired. But it does not take fancy equipment or a trained therapist to piggy-back on these techniques and experience benefits. Anyone can become more aware, choose gratitude, breathe deeply, genuinely serve, clear chakras, or adjust emotional "energy vibrations" to a more peaceful state. These techniques work for others, why not for you? They range from commonly accepted concepts to uncommon innovations. But they are all backed by research.

Now, before concluding, here's a couple of fascinating tangents related to the heart. Some coaches encourage heartbeat awareness (as opposed to heart rate awareness) for their entire teams. It appears that this emotional and physiological awareness not only increases an individual's ability to hit the "zone," it increases a *team's* ability to "zone" together. Additionally, it's known that the electromagnetic field generated by an individual's heartbeat can affect the heartbeat of others up to several feet away. So it's hypothesized that when individuals sincerely work together, they may affect each other on physiological or even quantum levels rather than just cooperational levels. Initial research seems to confirm the possibility.

There is further evidence of a physiological impact. A study done in Sweden hooked each member of a choir up to heart monitors. When the group began singing, the heartbeats of the entire choir synchronized within a few seconds. The researcher, Björn Vickhoff, hypothesized that there is collectiveness in performing. He believes that this extends beyond those participating to those watching. Individuals may influence each other in a way that is not yet understood. This new discovery may explain why a good crowd can rouse a sports team or theater cast. It is known that advertising and media affect behavior. Maybe influences extend beyond behavioral changes to include physiological changes.

Perhaps there is an intuitive understanding of the heart. Consider the many common sayings regarding the heart: *My heart is broken. He gave her his heart. Listen to your heart. He has a big heart. She learned it by heart. He had a change of heart. She stole my heart. My heart is bursting (with joy or sorrow.) They were pure in heart. Follow your heart. She played with her whole heart. Be of one heart....*

It is not yet known the extent that the heart plays on individual and collective performance, but mounting research indicates there are stronger correlations between the heart and brain than formerly realized. Further research will no doubt be insightful. In the meantime, current research supports the benefits of a change of heart! Baselines can positively change and change positively. Strengthen your core by changing your heart.

Next up, what causes "heart conditions"?

Summary

There are physical and emotional baselines that affect how the body and mind react. The body maintains baselines through physical and emotional homeostasis. Anything out of a normal baseline puts the body and brain on alert, even positive changes. Triggers cause stronger reactions (like anxiety) and indicate an "emotional ouch" that needs attention. Triggers can affect physical energy even when a person is calm. Addressing negative triggers permanently improves the heartbeat pattern. The heart can't generally be controlled, but breath can be controlled, and it affects the heart. Deep gratitude, genuine service, yoga, and visualized energy states also improve ability and heart function. The electromagnetic field caused by one heart is known to affect the heartbeats of others nearby. A study showed that choir heartbeats synchronized when singing. Heart research introduces a new dimension to team work, the influence of an audience, and the concept of being of "one heart." While further research will clarify the scope of these theories, current research supports the benefits of changing one's heart.

Case Study

Valerie felt her emotion rising, but she wasn't too worried. Though it was the championship match, she had been working on skills that she knew would reduce her nervousness. She sat in a quiet place, deeply breathed and thought of one thing after another that she was truly thankful for. She had made it this far! She was healthy! It was a beautiful day! Her grandpa traveled to see her! She liked this court! She had eyes and could see! She had hands and could use them! She made a game of finding more and more things to be grateful for, and feeling the gratitude more and more deeply. As she did, she realized how many things she took for granted and how insignificant this championship was in comparison with the rest of life. When she stepped on the court, she felt grounded and empowered. She was completely ready to enjoy the moment!

Empower Yourself
Deadbeat, or...elite heartbeat.

Fast-Track ReflACTION
1) What emotional and physical baselines would you like to change; how could you do it?
2) Take several sincere gratitude breaths and reflect on the benefits; what might routine gratitude breaths or other heart-changing activities yield?
3) In a typical week, when would you most benefit from deliberately changing emotional energy states to be more of "one heart" with someone; what might be the benefits?

17
Culture Shock!

Technology has had an amazing impact on culture. This has resulted in *huge* advantages and *huge* disadvantages. For thousands of years, the world has been essentially the same. Then the industrial revolution barged in, followed by the technological revolution, and suddenly the world is in your palm—and it's a full-time job to keep up. Have you considered the impact of technology, the internet, and social media on outcome anxiety and flow/zone? There is increased stress that's considered a "new normal." It actually has negative physiological, psychological, and interpersonal effects, but these can be managed.

It's easy to take technology for granted. For example, a TV movie set in the Wild West showed two young men walking down a street, when one suddenly freezes in front of an open window, "I've never heard piano music before!" Think about it. Can you imagine never hearing music before? It's almost unfathomable. Music is everywhere—even on ringtones and alarms.

Yet, in the entire history of the earth, only the last three generations have had easy access to recorded performances. Before that, live performances were the *only* performances. It is hard to imagine no recorded music—no phonographs, records, reel-to-reels, 8-tracks, cassettes, CDs, I-pods, smartphones, or other technology (that is outdated as soon as it hits the news). At a click you may "attend" the most astounding performances in the world in sports, music, business, dance, and education.

Have you considered how technology impacts individuals *culturally*? It used to be that great participation was expected; now only the great are expected to participate. In the past, all joined while the talented led; now only the leading talent joins. In the past you were only compared to the best in your local circle; now you are compared with the best in the world. In the past there was low pressure and high appreciation; now there is high pressure and low appreciation. In the past all performers were valued; now only the best are valued. In short, technology has *completely* changed cultural expectations.

In the past, tests were local evaluations given to a few at a time. Now there are standardized measures that pit a person against everyone across the nation and spit results out in impersonal computerized evaluations. Colleges and universities used to apply several measurements to evaluate and admit applicants. Now there is high pressure attached to very few measurements, such as ACT/SAT tests.

Even live performances have changed. They have become mega productions. They are enhanced by special effects, lighting, and camera shots projected on huge screens. And they are augmented by recorded material that has been edited, punched or reshot to perfection (whether it's a sports, performing arts, or business event).

It is bad enough to be compared to the best in the world, but in many cases there are comparisons to things that don't even exist because they are *impossible* in real time. A few years ago when recording and mixing a CD, one song had a track that required extra edits to align. Time was tight and I apologized to my sound engineer. He laughed and said that he just read in a professional sound engineering magazine that the current, top-chart song had *over 1000 edits in 10 seconds of music*! Do you see how easy it would be to unconsciously compare our recording to things that didn't exist in real time? Additionally, others may have compared themselves to our recording. Comparisons happen almost automatically. Is it any wonder that discouragement is common? And this type of unrealistic comparison isn't just found in music.

A famed TV hostess was contacted for a feature story on her new baby. She was not excited to have her postpartum figure plastered on newsstands. The editor laughed, "We Photoshop *everything* in our magazine." I attended a webinar where a motivational speaker described two years of edits, rewrites, and practice so that his 15 minute TED talk would look natural and effortless. Similarly, sports figures are coached on giving interviews, and spokespersons receive extensive media training....

These days everything is reduced to sound bites, edited, punched, reshot, Photoshopped, and computer generated to perfection. Whether you're in business, sports, or the performing arts, this is the culture. Talk about pressure! Comparisons are made to fictional things thought to be real. But that's not all; the sheer volume of information is also a problem.

Terms such as "infobesity," "digital downpour," "information overload," "fear of missing out [FOMO]," and "information fatigue syndrome" have become common. Too much information availability causes individuals to feel overwhelmed, out of control, and extremely stressed. (Yes, it causes anxiety.) Research also shows that too much information reduces memory, cognitive function, self-esteem, and brain grey matter. And it is addictive. It affects the brain similar to drug addiction. So information can strengthen or weaken the core. Have you considered that outcome anxiety and loss of flow/zone can be partially due to the web and social media?

This generation experiences unique pressure. But don't despair; there's a positive flip side. One of the biggest benefits is *inspiration*! Inspiration strengthens the core. It's easy to underestimate how powerful this is. There was a time when no one thought a four-minute mile was possible. It was believed that heart and lung collapse would occur if the human body was pushed that hard. But then in 1954, Roger Bannister ran a 3:59:4 minute mile. Within months, others broke the four-minute mile, and now the record has been lowered by several seconds. In fact, competitive male runners are currently *expected* to run a mile in less than four minutes.

This is just one example of what inspiration can do. It's happening all the time. An internet video is released, and within a few weeks things previously inconceivable are practiced and perfected (just ask my daughters who love hip hop). Technology assists and standards rise. Gold medal Olympians of one or two decades ago would not even qualify now, except maybe Michael Phelps—talk about inspiration!

Inspiration is not the only advantage in this generation. Daily resources provide support. They free up time and energy. It's easy to take cars, washing machines, and electric lights for granted, let alone video cameras, surgical repair of injuries, and neurological data. A large part of the population lives better than kings lived a century or two ago. Specialized servants were required to do tasks that are now done by simple appliances. Could ancient kings have conceived of an automatic furnace or water heater, let alone a microwave or smartphone? How about lightning-speed automated food packaging and distribution across the world?

But forget looking centuries back. Consider just the past three decades. Thirty years ago, music students scraped to buy expensive cassette players to record voice lessons. The concept of audio recording was novel and deemed a huge advantage. Now lessons can be taken remotely, instantly videoed, immediately emailed, and used for practice. Even slow-motion recordings of actual vocal chords and other research affects vocal technique. Similar advancements can be seen in every field. Yet, current leaders in many fields went to school without a personal computer or the internet. These things didn't exist.

So let's put technology into perspective. There are unlimited benefits and one primary detriment: pressure. *But pressure is a choice.* It was believed that stress was always damaging, but new research shows that the damage isn't caused by stress, per se. Damage is caused by the *perceptions and reactions* toward it. Some people thrive in stress—really. Awareness and attitude determine if pressure is damaging or invigorating. Negative perceptions, too much information, and unrealistic perfectionism increase pressure. But these can be countered.

So step back and look at the whole picture. Be mindful. Be aware. Perceptions can be positive. Technology can be managed. Expectations can be realistic. It can be done. And when it happens, every cultural advantage is there for the taking. Strengthen your core by making choices that put you ahead of kings.

Next up, decrease pressure while increasing output...

Summary

Technology's impact on culture has resulted in huge advantages and disadvantages. Higher stress is the new normal. Technology's impact has changed cultural expectations. Performers are now compared to world standards; previously they were only compared to local standards. Comparisons are made to things that are not even possible in real time due to extensive editing and enhancing. Personal comparisons are frequently made to fictional things. The negative result of technology is pressure. The positive result is inspiration. Inspiration strengthens the core. Information overload weakens the core. Technology addiction affects the brain like drug addiction. Technology also provides resources that save time and energy, so there is time to pursue inspiration. There are unlimited benefits from technology and one primary detriment: pressure. Pressure is a choice. Attention to thoughts and feelings results in the ability to make good choices and maximize the benefits of technology.

Case Study

Laura wanted some fresh dance lifts to put in her choreography. She searched online and within seconds was thumbing through YouTube videos. She posted links so her dancers could analyze and envision before rehearsal. Even though rehearsal was in just a few hours, she knew they'd all see the group post on their phones. Rehearsal was going to be fun; these were great lifts! Now to *immediately* get off YouTube and Facebook before getting sucked in! Otherwise she wouldn't get her choreography or paperwork done.

Empower Yourself

Deny saturation, or...devour inspiration.

Fast-Track ReflACTION

1) Name something, only available this generation, that positively impacted you this week and how you can maximize the benefits.
2) Name something, only available this generation, that negatively impacted you this week and how you can minimize the detriments.
3) How does awareness of the impact of your choices give you an edge in a technological culture?

18
Stop Trying to Get it Right

Performers often get sucked into trying to do things right. This cranks up the stress. They can even lose a sense of self. Traditional ways of doing things shouldn't be ignored, but they shouldn't stifle either. Technique, interpretation, style, artistry, timing, rules, and strategy are all subjective. They are a means to an end, not the end-all. Too much focus on doing things right can impede creativity and awareness. The bottom line is: what works?

Technique is subjective. What's the "right" way to dance, study for a test, manage a department, or handle a ball? Ballet's upward control looks ridiculous in hip hop's downward looseness, and vice versa. There is no "right" way to do things. A teacher mentioned that mix, belt, pop legit, rap, and even some whistle-tone singing were all considered "wrong" not long ago. Shifts have happened in other fields, too. When one statistician applied his skills to baseball, *every* sport changed. Teachers, business managers, and coaches approach skills and training differently. The reason for technique is to discover ability. Tailor technique.

Interpretation is subjective. At a large music conference, a prominent music professor said, "No lie, in a major national competition with highly competent adjudicators, my student had these comments from judges: 'You played this too Romantically;' 'You played this just right;' 'You should play this more Romantically.'" Does this happen in sports or business? You bet. Ask any gymnast, or advertiser! Individual interpretations contribute to success. Inspire interpretation.

Style is subjective. Beethoven raised eyebrows when bridging the light, classical style and expressive, Romantic style, yet he stirred generations. Bing Crosby turned classical musicians in their graves, yet audiences loved his pitch-sliding croons. Martha Graham dazed ballet with her earthy, modern choreography, and paved the way for other styles. Where would movies be if theatrical acting were not replaced with screen acting? And don't even get me started on sports changes—a few film clips tell all! Innovation expands expression. Sculpt style.

Artistry is subjective. One voice teacher said, "There is no such thing as singing 'right' except to protect the vocal chords." Every sound has potential for artistry. It's better to collect sounds and styles than self-condemn. Coloring words like "lonely" or "death" with a harsher sound is more moving—meaning is lost if sung "beautifully." How many amazing athletic moves were discovered from "mistakes"? Don't hate unexpected results. It's impossible to improve without change. Explore artistry.

Timing is subjective. Often there's an assumption that if training doesn't start just past infancy, there's no hope. My favorite ballet teacher defied this. She took her first lesson at age 17, danced with the Joffrey Ballet, and taught for decades. What if she paid attention to traditional timing? Similarly, there are older college students who have successfully made career changes. There are NFL players who had never been on a field or worn pads two years earlier. There are speakers whose passion quickly propelled them to TV. There are novice comedians whose sketches went viral in weeks. Don't worry about timing. Worry about passion. Experience is an advantage, but it isn't the only advantage. Desire, drive, and innate talent are all factors. Jump on the timing that's available to you. Tackle timing.

Rules are subjective. Okay, don't break competition rules. But certainly break rules in *how* you compete! A director demonstrated a weak, wobbly, bleating note and asked an elite choir if they would ever deliberately perform the weird sound. The emphatic, "No!" melted as they "sheepishly" recognized Doctor Dillamond from the Broadway hit *Wicked*. In a national music journal, a top Broadway vocal coach detailed how to judiciously but deliberately sing sharp or flat to enhance a character. That throws out the rule of "always sing in tune," doesn't it? Use rules to find something wonderful. Rehash rules.

Strategy is subjective. Documentaries occasionally reveal innovative strategies. In sports alone, changes can be seen in ball handling, player selection, equipment, training techniques, teamwork, and rules. One college coach devised a new offensive strategy. Eventually it was adopted across the nation and into the pros. Similarly the Ford Motor Company restructured production. McDonalds restructured the restaurant industry. Make your contribution. Spark strategy.

Now don't get lazy or misunderstand. I am not saying to abandon traditional "correctness" or careful training. These are important. I'm just saying that trying too hard to *comply* can slow development, increase stress, and waste energy. Part of progression is to understand the causes of stress and strategize to maximize ability. Doing things "right" can hint at perfectionism, which can limit expansive growth. One professor drilled, "Learn the rules in order to break them intelligently." Second-guessing strategies or a judge, coach, teacher, boss, or audience can drive a person crazy. It is impossible to please everyone. Doing things "right" may leave you disappointed and disappointing. There really is no "right" way to do things. Right is what works. Ultimately, training is not to teach conformity but creativity. Let your uniqueness blossom. Find what works. Who knows, someday your way may be the "right" way. Strengthen your core by looking beyond "right."

Next up, appearance factors...

Summary

Those with outcome anxiety often try to do things "right." The "right" mentality increases pressure, stifles learning, hints at perfectionism, and crushes creativity. Ultimately, there is no "right" way. Even top experts can disagree. And opinions change as improvements are made. Careful training and practice is a means to an end, not the end-all. Traditional ways of doing things are tools to build on. Interpretation, technique, style, artistry, timing, rules, and strategy are subjective and change. Rules are learned in order to break them intelligently (except competition rules). Training is not to teach conformity but creativity. Those who chase doing things "right" may stifle their own contributions. Someday your way may be the "right way."

Case Study

Anne moved across the country to train and was surprised to find that what they considered to be "right" was completely different from what she had learned. There were even different names for moves. In time she found that exposure to both types of training enhanced her ability. It gave her an edge. She had more tools to work with.

Case Study

Ryan hadn't had private coaching for a while. When he returned, everything had changed. The new way was better, but a decade of muscle memory was already trained into his muscles. It was frustrating. He got to work. After a few months, he was proficient in the new technique. He confessed that retraining was tough, but worth it.

Case Study

In a national teachers' workshop, one professional concert pianist encouraged scales that crawled sideways up the piano using two fingers. Another professor introduced an innovative "flattened" technique to reduce injuries common to pianists. Another suggested that non-career students abandon technique altogether and just enjoy making music. Teachers determined what was "right" for their students.

Empower Yourself

Obediently conform, or...intelligently explore.

Fast-Track ReflACTION

1) In what ways would you benefit from trying harder to do things "right"?
2) In what ways would you benefit from not being as concerned about doing things "right"?
3) What specific change could improve technique, inspire creativity, and release pressure for you?

19
Appearance Anxiety

Have you ever felt frustrated about your hair? Maybe you've tried on multiple outfits, unsure of what to wear. Perhaps insecurities surface at times regarding your car, house, education, job, or status? This is appearance anxiety. But the problem isn't appearance; it's feeling *unsure* of coming out okay. Ironically, performance anxiety is a form of appearance anxiety, and appearance anxiety is a form of performance anxiety. And ultimately, they're both outcome anxiety.

Some people think they can compartmentalize anxieties. But it's impossible to obsess about hair and expect it won't affect performance. Appearance anxiety clouds judgment. The part of you that second guesses hair is also the part that second guesses test questions, game plays, or business decisions.

In the end, there is no "right" appearance. For example, what's the proper attire for a job interview that requires an advanced college degree, supervises a large staff, and oversees millions of dollars of assets? A smart suit might come to mind. But what if the position is a commercial farm manager? A fancy suit and posh car would be laughed at. But the same would be true of a truck, work jeans and sturdy boots on Wall Street. Yet, both jobs are important.

In some high schools, the popular kids are the athletes and the academic kids are considered backward and inept. In other high schools, the popular kids are the academic kids and the athletes are considered backward and inept. It's all subjective. Those from areas that admire athletics may be surprised that other areas admire academics, and vice versa. The world can turn upside down in an instant. Admiration from appearance is unreliable, even when staying in a single location.

If worth is tied to others' perceptions, adaption is difficult. For example, some find it difficult to dress up (like Mia's friend, Lily, in the movie *Princess Diaries*). Others find it difficult to dress down (like the cheerleaders and their boyfriends in that same movie). These are both forms of perfectionism. One group is perfect at being imperfect. The other is perfect at being perfect. Both hide insecurity. Whether the look is grungy or pristine (or somewhere in between), perfectionism is involved whenever there's anxiety regarding appearance.

Appearance anxiety can manifest in many ways. People or situations may be avoided to prevent status or power from being lowered. (And this isn't limited to cliques in high school.) Appearance anxiety is also behind teachers or coaches playing favorites, or business personnel manipulating stats. There are different ways that behavior aims at controlling a good appearance.

Appearance anxiety regarding social media manifests through screening content and editing pictures. A speaker at a conference illustrated this: a close-up picture of a plate of beautiful home-baked muffins was shown. A second picture revealed the muffins next to piles of dirty baking dishes, a chaotic room, and a crying child. Individuals are certainly more likely to present the first, edited picture to control appearance.

Appearance anxiety may also keep people from trying new things. Honestly, isn't there such thing as leotard anxiety, paint brush anxiety, ice skates anxiety, etc.? Similarly some students do not take certain electives because of appearance anxiety. How many guys might enjoy ballroom dance or girls enjoy woodworking? Additionally, how many avoid that big hamburger on a date for fear of looking like they eat too much? I'm not advocating letting go of all restraint, but how much joy is missed due to appearance anxiety? There is encouragement to "be yourself" but also a fear to do so.

It is impossible to be truly authentic without addressing core concerns. Understanding self is the source of true confidence. Inner confidence allows a person to adapt. Great people adapt. They're okay if their hair gets wet in a water fight. They're okay dressing up or down. They're even okay appearing weak, like when getting ideas from subordinates or owing up to a mistake. True power comes from abandoning the need to be right or look right.

It's okay to stop trying to have the right hair, clothes, car, house, education, or status. This doesn't mean that these things are abandoned. It means that self-worth is not tied to them. One mother said to her daughters, "If you have a bad hair day, smile as if you planned it. Someone will complement or even copy!" What was really said? Hair shouldn't determine self-worth.

When efforts are exerted to "measure up," core power is given to others. Not only do others have power over personal worth, the underlying primary fears are not addressed. So there's permanent insecurity. The "high" from "shopping therapy" is usually short-lived because primary needs aren't met.

Primary fears are behind all outcome anxieties, including appearance anxiety. Primary fears are conscious or subconscious concerns about filling primary needs such as feeling loved, valued, secure, important, and capable. No matter how imperfect the appearance, a person will be okay if feeling loved, valued, secure, important, and capable. Conversely, no matter how perfect the appearance, a person will not be okay if feeling unloved, unvalued, insecure, unimportant, or incapable.

Businesses exploit these vulnerabilities. Appearance anxiety can numb discernment regarding value or quality. One person jokingly noted that some styles (and performances) are "well-done garbage." A documentary on the clothing industry revealed that in the past, styles changed seasonally. Now they're changed about every six weeks. Clothing was made to appear to fill primary needs and consumption increased. And since primary needs aren't filled, the market perpetuates indefinitely as worth is attached to looks. This strategy is not limited to clothing. Even cars and houses go out of style.

Appearance anxiety *drives* behavior. What clothing, transportation, or shelter is *actually* needed to function well? I'm not advocating reverting to rags, walking, or shacks. I'm talking about seeing a bigger picture so that decisions are *truly* made in one's best interest.

Appearance anxiety can ruin enjoyment and interpersonal enrichment. Have you ever felt deficient compared to someone's exotic vacation, amazing accomplishment, or restaurant excursion? The discontent from underlying anxieties results in feeling like an isolated hamster on a wheel. Great effort goes nowhere. In reality, pleasure costs nothing, just breathe deeply and feel genuine gratitude.

Anxiety depletes resources. Attempts to satisfy anxiety can drain time, energy, and money. The drain on time and money becomes apparent. But often the drain on energy isn't recognized, such as the cost of insecurity or indecision. Additionally, how many years are spent paying off debt due to appearance anxiety? Some think that appearance anxiety is worst among those at the "top," but it's equally robust across the spectrum, including those at the "bottom."

The problem isn't stuff; it's dysfunctional attempts to meet primary needs. Two people might have exactly the same hair, clothes, car, house, and status; and one might have anxiety while the other doesn't. Internal anxiety can drive a person to make unwise expenditures of time, money and energy. If appearance comes at the expense of stability, relationships, sleep, or genuine self-kindness, it may be time to rethink things.

When time, energy, and money are expended, there ought to be a solid return on the investment (not a drain). New things can be fun when well-considered. However, a drain indicates a problem. Could an old convertible sports car or home renovation save tens of thousands and yield more overall pleasure than new things? You bet! There's a movement to rethink belongings, but without an understanding of anxiety even extreme swings like tiny houses and modular wardrobes may still leave an individual feeling empty. Deepest pleasure comes from understanding, not just changing.

It's possible to go from exhausted and depleted to replenished and abundant. Financial makeovers are real like reducing debt and high-yield, long-term-satisfaction expenditures. Recognizing anxiety allows the crazy over- or under-drive to settle. Focused choices increase beneficial change. There's an art to deep satisfaction. Finding it may involve trial and error. In that process it's very helpful to understand the underlying influences of appearance anxiety. Even seemingly little, focused choices can yield big benefits when maximizing enjoyment and minimizing depletion.

In reality, clothes, cars, education and other things are tools. No more, no less. Most of the world values appearance. I do. I imagine you do. It's important. So make decisions *truly* in your favor. Let go of perfectionism and be proactive. Understanding appearance anxiety reduces unnecessary expenditures of time, energy, and money. It's the art of reasonable decisions (see the case study below).

Are you influenced by appearance anxiety? There's a difference between dressing up for fun or uniqueness and dressing up to hopefully fit in okay or defiantly make a statement. There's a difference between scurrying to clean house out of genuine enjoyment of tidiness and scurrying so as not to look bad. The difference between security and insecurity can be felt. One gives to self and others, the other takes from self and others. A person without appearance anxiety can enjoy a friend's unexpected visit even if caught in a real-world mess wearing pajamas.

Convention should not be thrown out the window. But it is more effective to focus on reasonable solutions than to anticipate others' reactions. A lot of resources can be wasted without meeting basic emotional needs. Appearance anxiety is eliminated the same way as other outcome anxieties. Become aware of thoughts and feelings. But honestly, change is hard unless primary needs are met; otherwise anxiety naturally drives behavior. So upcoming chapters will address this.

When confidence is dependent on others' reactions, core power is given away (even if the reaction is positive). You need your core power. Appearance isn't for compliance but for confidence. Confidence comes from being okay with reasonable decisions. Genuine confidence is attractive and powerful. Knowledge focuses core power. Abandoning appearance anxiety isn't a compromise. It's a crowning jewel. Strengthen your core through reasonable decisions.

Next up, how to be mega safe...

Summary

Insecurity regarding hair, clothes, car, house, education, job or status indicates appearance anxiety. It's a form of outcome anxiety because it is due to being unsure of coming out okay. Obsession about appearance usually affects other areas of performance. Appearance anxiety clouds judgment. The "right" appearance varies according to the situation and where you're from. If worth is tied to perceptions, it's difficult to adapt. All appearance anxiety is tied to perfectionism—some may be perfectly imperfect (grungy), others may be perfectly perfect (pristine), still others may be perfectly in between. Perfectionism is more about getting worth from others. Discomfort regarding the "perfect" look drives behavior. There is insecurity (anxiety). Appearance anxiety may manifest in avoiding people or situations, meticulous social media editing, and passing up opportunities. Appearance doesn't solve self-worth anxieties; meeting primary needs does. Businesses exploit appearance anxiety and pseudo primary needs. Time, energy, and money are drained chasing primary needs. Greatness doesn't have to be right. Clothes, cars, education, status, etc. are tools. It's important to know how to use them. An understanding of appearance anxiety allows a person to be authentic, adapt, and make decisions truly in their favor. Appearance anxiety is eliminated by becoming aware and authentically meeting primary needs. It's most effective to focus on reasonable solutions rather than to anticipate others' reactions. Anticipating what others think (even if their reaction is positive) gives away core power and derails genuine confidence. Genuine confidence is attractive and powerful. It comes from being okay with reasonable decisions.

Case Study

Karalyn was in the boutique on a mission. She was determined to get a great outfit for the regional meeting. It was the first big meeting since she was promoted, and she wanted to make a good impression. She pulled a couple of suits off the rack and proceeded to the dressing room. But as she looked more carefully, they were similar to some other things she owned. Why spend the time and energy to try them on? What she really needed was a crisp blouse and a new purse since hers was getting worn. On her way to the cash register she spotted some great accessories. They'd be out of style soon, so she chose only one. She didn't labor over the decision since she wanted to get home and enjoy a hot bath with a great book. The next day she had her suit dry cleaned so it would be immaculate. She was ready.

Empower Yourself

Appearance depletion, or...reasonable completion.

Fast-Track ReflACTION

1) In what ways should you spend more time, energy, and money on improving appearance?
2) In what ways should you spend less time, energy, and money on appearance?
3) How does an awareness of anxiety and reasonable decisions increase your effectiveness and overall enjoyment of life? What changes would be beneficial?

20
Emo Safety

The ability to maintain emotional safety is called "emotional IQ." This is the greatest predictor of success. It is more important than talent, grades, position, or education. Maintaining emotional safety for yourself and others is powerful. Emotional IQ might seem unrelated to outcome anxiety, but it's actually at the very core.

Those with outcome anxiety worry whether they will do (or have done) well enough to merit respect. It's a *huge* emotional safety issue. This is why outcome anxiety is common. The fear isn't just about a performance or other outcome. A person's entire sense of self can be at stake. No wonder anxiety can be strong!

Whether an individual is a mammoth football player or a petite ballerina, there's a vulnerable place inside that *MUST* be safe. All outcome anxiety—like apprehension, frustration, and flow/zone issues—happens when a person is unsure of emotional safety. Emotional safety includes feeling loved, accepted, appreciated, secure, valued, and capable. Humanity is *driven* to get emotional safety one way or another. Emotional safety is not optional.

A person becomes vulnerable when performing (or just being alive!) Performance vulnerabilities happen whether the performance is observed by just one person grading a test or by millions watching a televised event. Performers simply have no control over the challenges that might be encountered or the response of others, even if the performance is fantastic. This is why unsure feelings surface.

Individuals get a little wacky when they don't feel emotionally safe. Quick-fix reactions like anger, exerting authority, withdrawing inside, blaming, subtle bullying, shouting, crying, denying, excuses, belittling, running away, exaggerating, or cowering are all reactions to a lack of emotional safety. Can you see that fight, flight, freeze behaviors are as common when emotional safety is at risk as when physical safety is at risk? There's a good reason; when emotional safety is injured, it *hurts*! It's a type of emotional wound.

Emotional wounds are real—ask any person who has endured the death of a loved one, suffered through a break up, received devastating news, endured a betrayal, or been stripped of emotional safety in other ways. There are always reasons for emotional pain, just as there are always reasons for physical pain. Things like fear, anxiety, depression, sorrow, anguish, dread, confusion, or anger are warning alerts that *something internally or externally needs attention*. Whenever emotional safety is at risk, it can be felt, whether the emotional pain is as small as an unsettled feeling or as large as an overwhelming slam.

There are two ways to get emotional safety: manipulation and respect. Individuals generally gravitate to one or the other. Manipulation focuses on extrinsic worth and being the best because worth is *earned*. Respect emphasizes intrinsic worth and achieving personal bests since worth is *inherent* (more in upcoming chapters). "Kissing up" and prejudice are both types of manipulation that are used to gain position and secure emotional safety. Manipulation operates from a mindset that says, "To be safe I must get others to treat me right" and subconsciously asks "What do I need to do to get them to do this?" Respect operates from a mindset that says, "Others may or may not treat me right. It's my responsibility to appropriately safeguard my core" and asks "Where do I need to communicate clearly, learn better skills, take responsibility, and/or set boundaries?"

It's common for people to seek emotional safety by producing something that is "good enough" that others will think well of them. If that doesn't work, manipulation can surface in things like excuses or putting others down (such as referees, editors, adjudicators, exam writers, or business managers). Manipulation can happen before, during, or after performance. There are many forms of manipulation. In all its forms, manipulation seeks to persuade others to think well of self or one's close associations (or sanction those who don't). Manipulation tries to get something from someone else.

Manipulation trips up otherwise competent people. It's common and largely unrecognized. For example, there are salesmen who are educated, skilled, and prepared, yet persuasively manipulate. They push with information that doesn't quite feel reliable. The client squirms and leaves as quickly as possible. There are salesmen who are educated, skilled, and prepared, that respectfully influence. They support the critical evaluation of options based on accurate information; they are appreciated and referred to friends. Can you see the difference? (Sales isn't the problem; manipulation is.)

Manipulation causes a lot of problems, so why isn't it addressed? *Emotional safety!* The whole reason for manipulation is to gain emotional safety. Admitting to manipulation doesn't exactly provide bragging rights! It takes courage to address this issue. A lack of understanding about emotional safety is the root of most interpersonal and performance problems.

Sometimes manipulation and artistry are confused. Artistry is the skill to take an audience where you want them—like an actor making an audience laugh or cry, or an amazing athlete taking crowds to their feet. Artistry is *giving a gift to others.* Manipulation is *getting something from others* like esteem, praise, or agreement. This distinction is extremely important.

Eliminating anxiety hinges on understanding this concept. Manipulation is determined by how a person gets their *own* emotional safety. Actors often play manipulative characters, but it's *the actor's* reason for being on stage that determines manipulation. This is also true of other occupations. Why is the song sung, the game played, the business started, or the test taken? If it's to get something from others, manipulation is likely involved. Anxiety surfaces. Manipulative outcomes are uncertain.

There are three different kinds of manipulation that range from malicious to seemingly benign. Manipulation that's malicious is easy to spot. It's deliberate maltreatment, intimidation or criminal behavior. Manipulation that's insincere warmth is fairly easy to spot. It's found in calculated "kissing up" and "crafty positioning." Manipulation that consists of sincere kindness with an expectation of returned kindness is a type of manipulation that is hard to spot. If expectations weren't attached, it wouldn't be manipulation at all.

"Kind" manipulation is especially difficult because it's hard to identify. Though it's common, those doing it are often unaware. The person is kind and wants something in return, like smiling in order to receive a favorable response back. One way to tell if manipulation is involved is to consider what happens if the other person doesn't return a kindness. Is there judgment, self-consciousness, confusion, frustration, hurt, defensiveness? These reactions indicate underlying manipulation. If others can affect your feelings this way, you have given them your power.

It might seem that "kind" manipulation isn't a problem. After all, a lot of the world runs on this. But it's problematic because even a molecule of manipulation changes the relationship. For example, genuine gratitude feels different than gratitude that is expressed to get something in return. Kind manipulation is a symptom of insecurities, outcome anxiety, and a need for emotional safety. Kind manipulation often results in hurt feelings. At the very least it results in attention diverted to others' perceptions.

Genuine people are kind because that's just who they are. Genuine interaction increases the joy of returned kindness and eliminates the frustration of unfilled expectations. But more importantly, it gives power back to you. Your worth is not dependent on what others think. You're independent. There are times when expectations are appropriate. However, expectations should be clearly delineated and agreed on. This involves taking more personal responsibility to clearly communicate, but it works better. It not only clarifies expectations between people, it clarifies internal reasoning.

Kind manipulation can be reversed by dropping expectations, being genuine, and communicating clearly when there are needs. Genuineness doesn't mean becoming a doormat. It just means that kindness is real. Unspoken, unmet expectations are not safe for either side. There is greater safety.

Emotional safety can increase through the support of genuine friends. Often friends are trusted and disclosed to. Disclosing is about building a support system of trust, safety, and compassion. If someone isn't trustworthy, safe, and compassionate, it's not a good idea to share. Manipulative people aren't safe. Carefully selecting safe support before disclosing is wise and different than ignoring, denying, or suppressing problems. A deliberate choice to not disclose to an unsafe person is not running away from the problem; it's choosing to actively address it in healthy ways. It's choosing to retain core strength.

Emotional safety is not optional. Genuine friends strengthen. They can pop up in unexpected places. It's more important to have two or three genuine friends than two or three thousand manipulative ones. Genuine, supportive, non-manipulative friends are out there. Strengthen your core through being genuine and seeking genuine friends.

Next up, how is emotional safety increased...

Summary

The ability to maintain emotional safety is called emotional IQ, and it's the greatest overall predictor of success. Emotional safety is not optional. It includes feeling secure, respected, appreciated, loved, confident, and capable. People get wacky without emotional safety. Losing it hurts. Emotional wounds are real. Worry cannot change being vulnerable when performing. Performance fear usually involves emotional safety. There are two ways to get emotional safety: manipulation and respect. Performance manipulation is trying to persuade audience approval through a good enough performance. Artistry and manipulation are different. Artistry is skillfully giving a gift to others; manipulation is seeking something from others (like esteem, praise, etc.) Manipulation can surface in underhanded maltreatment, crafty maneuvering, or kindness with strings attached. Kind manipulation is damaging to giver and receiver. It can get messy due to unexpressed expectations. Genuine kindness is being kind because that's who you are, no reciprocal strings expected. Genuine people can pop up in unexpected places and they make great friends. Being a genuine person increases emotional safety and produces a strong core.

Case Study

Alison left the building, shut the door, and leaned on it. Her heart pounded as tears tugged at the corners of her eyes. She felt eaten alive and wondered if she had what it took. The elderly janitor was outside sweeping. She'd seen him before but hadn't paid attention. He glanced at her and spoke as he continued sweeping, "It can be tough, can't it? Take a break and then go back in. I've seen a lot come and go, and you've got what it takes. Don't let the competition get to you." Alison looked over at him through different eyes as she gathered herself and considered his words. He had nothing to gain by being kind to her, but his kindness meant a lot. After that day they occasionally chatted during breaks and became friends. She even brought his favorite doughnut now and then.

Case Study

Anger was rising, accusations were flying, and the production meeting was getting out of hand. Jem stepped back, took a deep breath, and calmly asked everyone to sit down. She waited until she had everyone's attention and then took charge, "I know that we're under a tight deadline and there are some problems, but if you want to speak, it will be done one at a time and with respect. We are still a team, and we need to work together to find a way to meet everyone's needs and make the deadlines."

Case Study

As the branch director, Shelly bent over backwards so the company could move solidly into the next phase. But then the bosses dismantled her work with decisions that contradicted their earlier instructions. This confused clients, doubled her workload, and tightened deadlines. The problem had happened before, and she had hinted at how damaging it was. These people were great to work with other than this problem. If she took the slack another round, would they fix this and be more responsive? Oh wait. Stop. She realized she was manipulating them with kindness and ambiguous expectations. They were also manipulating her by being kind on the outside but not taking responsibility as the unaddressed issues grew and requests fell on deaf ears. Irritation was beginning to surface both ways. It was time to stop manipulating and address the problem directly. Things could not continue as they were without significant damage.

Empower Yourself

Emotionally wacky, or...emotionally savvy.

Fast-Track ReflACTION
1) In what ways do you seek emotional safety? How can you increase emotional IQ?
2) How does wanting something from someone change the relationship; when have you manipulated and not realized it?
3) Who are your genuine friends; are you a genuine friend?

21
Intrinsic vs. Extrinsic Worth

Outcome anxiety is related to how a person obtains self-worth. There are two types of self-worth: intrinsic and extrinsic. Intrinsic worth eliminates anxiety. Extrinsic worth causes anxiety. Personal worth is so intricately intertwined with anxiety that it's essential to understand both intrinsic and extrinsic worth.

Intrinsic worth is the belief that each person is priceless just because they exist. It doesn't matter if that person is young or old, intelligent or mentally challenged, physically adept or handicapped, male or female, famous or unknown...each person has automatic, unlimited value. Worth comes from being a part of the human race. *So worth never has to be proven.* When put in context of performing, a person's worth cannot be changed by a performance. Whether a person performs well, poorly, or cannot perform at all, he or she is priceless.

Intrinsic worth is not dependent on ability. All are valued, regardless of ability. In a fair court of law, they don't say, "Well, he isn't the best performer, so it's okay to commit a crime against him." They say, "As a human being, he's automatically of infinite value and automatically protected under the law." Since each person is priceless, energy need not be diverted to prove worth. As a result, there are more resources available for creativity and growth.

Extrinsic worth is the belief that value increases according to what people can do, how they look, what they own, or what they have achieved. *So worth must be constantly proven.* Those who operate from an extrinsic worth viewpoint endlessly compare themselves to others to see how they measure up. Extrinsic worth is dependent on perceptions of what others think.

Some believe that only those who excel have extrinsic worth. But extrinsic worth is not due to achievement. It's due to *comparisons*. Rank is irrelevant. Extrinsic worth is measured by comparisons whether the person is first place, last place, or not competing. Conversely, intrinsic worth comes from within and is not affected by comparisons. Intrinsic worth can be found in people with amazing honors and those with no honors.

Research solidly shows that a focus on extrinsic worth hampers ability while embracing intrinsic worth maximizes ability. If asked, most agree that intrinsic worth is better. But in reality, there's a cultural fear of it. There's a fear that motivation will drop. There's also a fear of not looking good which affects individuals, coaches, teachers, and executives. As a result, most people operate from extrinsic worth.

One way to determine reliance on intrinsic vs. extrinsic worth is to ask: Do I feel better if others admire me? Do I feel worse if I don't measure up? Do I feel the same at the *core* whether a performance goes well or not? Do I feel the same about others whether they perform well or not? Am I genuinely compassionate? Do I compare myself with others? Do I enjoy my growth, independent of comparisons?

Extrinsic worth is a major cause of outcome anxiety. Extrinsic worth also leaves those who don't have anxiety susceptible to developing it. Why? Self-worth is a primary need. As challenges unfold if worth is not obtained one way, it will be obtained another. The pursuit of extrinsic worth is insatiable. Those at the top are on a slippery slope as others claw up to supplant them. Even if others smile on the outside (which they often do), there is constant comparison on the inside. It's a dog-eat-dog way of getting worth, even if done politely. The result is a perpetual, subconscious, gnawing insecurity regardless of whether the person is on top or not.

This erodes relationships. Extrinsic worth is a way to seek worth, but it is not the best way. Those motivated by extrinsic worth are caught up in being better, so it's not in their best interest to be supportive (unless doing so provides leverage or prevents them from looking bad). However, often individuals don't understand where the resulting insecurities come from or why relationships are hollow. Genuine efforts may be made. It is particularly heartbreaking when authentic relationships are desired and not understood. Fortunately there are better methods than outmaneuvering, comparing, or pseudo interactions with others.

It's possible to instantly climb off the extrinsic merry-go-round and immediately embrace intrinsic worth. It's simply a conscious decision to not worry about what others think. No more comparisons! But ingrained fears and fallacies may strongly tug back. These might include concern that those who embrace intrinsic worth aren't motivated or can't *really* achieve.

In reality, research shows that those with intrinsic worth have deeper focus, stronger motivation, higher-functioning brain patterns, more enjoyment, and better outcomes. This can all happen by genuinely shifting focus from interpersonal positioning to personal improvement. Not only does ability improve, interpersonal support is increased. Intrinsic worth is contagious! This is because intrinsically motivated people are safe. The difference can be felt. So an intrinsically motivated person naturally influences others toward healthier interpersonal interaction. Let me illustrate:

A new university music professor stepped up to perform a cello solo at the community benefit. There was a lot at stake. It was the first time many community members and many of his new students and orchestra would hear him perform. Additionally, the program was composed of top musicians from all around the area, to whom he would naturally be compared. He took the stage and carefully placed the music. Soon virtuoso cello music filled the hall and mesmerized the audience. All went well until he reached to gently pull down some pages and all the music tumbled. Uncertainty gripped the room as the audience held its breath.

What did he do? Loud and strong, he sang his part with a wide grin as he scooped up the music. Then he resumed bowing, and continued beautifully to the end. The audience applauded wildly. In fact, he received more applause than any other performer, yet he had the most obvious error. In the moment of uncertainty, intrinsic worth pulled him through and the audience response was delight and admiration! When asked to use this story he said, "Oh, I recall that! Yes, you can't predict what will happen in a live performance. You just go on and do your best." What is notable is that he is consistently genuine. So under pressure this reaction was second-nature. Essentially, he "practices" intrinsic worth daily in how he genuinely and warmly interacts.

There are things that cannot be anticipated during performance, *but a person's stance can be anticipated.* It is not a perfect performance or an awesome test score that determines if a person comes out okay; it is the internal attitude about self. Intrinsic worth cannot be faked. Intrinsic worth is embraced by letting go of comparisons and genuinely valuing self and others. This automatically radiates out. Strengthen your core through the power of intrinsic worth.

Next up, an intrinsic power boost...

Summary
There are two types of self-worth: intrinsic and extrinsic. Intrinsic worth is based on internal worth as a human being. This invites personal bests and mutual support. Extrinsic worth is based on rank and comparisons. This results in continual competitiveness. The difference between intrinsic and extrinsic worth is not honors but *comparisons*. Society is built on pursuing extrinsic worth. Most agree that intrinsic worth is best, but in reality, fears and fallacies preclude it. Extrinsic worth is unstable as others climb to the top to supplant. Research strongly supports the value of intrinsic worth. A person can have intrinsic worth and receive honors. Intrinsic worth is obtained by abandoning comparisons and focusing on self-improvement. Genuine value of self and others can be felt. Intrinsic worth is a choice.

Case Study
Lori was being taped in front of a live audience for an internationally broadcast TV special comprised of celebrities. In the middle of her solo her microphone caught feedback. In a single smooth movement, she instinctively changed body direction, extended the mic away, and lowered her volume. But these split-second, professional responses didn't correct the problem. So, without skipping a second beat, she delightfully chimed, "Sing mic! Sing!" and continued. The potentially embarrassing moment immediately turned to laughter and warmth. It was just enough time for the sound engineer to correct the problem, and the performance continued without a hitch. It didn't matter that future audiences would see the replays; their reaction would be the same as the live one.

Empower Yourself
Constantly climb, or...automatically shine.

Fast-Track ReflACTION
1) Do you operate from a perspective of intrinsic or extrinsic worth? (Consider comparisons.)
2) What might hamper your sense of intrinsic worth? (Consider social and personal influences.)
3) What advantages might be experienced from a consistent focus on intrinsic worth?

22
THE Best vs. MY Best

Have you ever dreamt of being the best at what you do? There can be reasons to go for it and reasons to slam on the brakes and add the emergency brake! Let me explain why and present an option that may be better.

The problem with aspiring to be the best is that only *one* person on planet earth can be the best at any given time in any given thing. Can you see the pressure? And where does that leave the millions of other people? If only the best person in a field shared their talents, the world would be a very sad place! Imagine if only the best violist bowed, the best actress recited, the best composer created, the best dancer expressed, the best skateboarder shredded, the best drummer rocked, the best quarterback threw, the best salesperson pitched, the best speaker presented, the best teacher mentored, the best executive led, the best student excelled, the best skater glided, or the best coach trained...

This world needs *every* person, not just the best. Additionally, every person starts at the bottom. Without all levels, the top performances would never happen. And it's almost impossible for a person to get to the top alone. It takes teams of people on many levels. Instead of simply abandoning a focus on the best, society has gone in the opposite direction.

Categories have been divided into subcategories. If a person can't achieve being the best in the world, he or she can aspire to be the best in the nation, region, state, area, school, class, or group. And if that's not enough, there are sub-subcategories, such as the best musical theater singer, rock singer, country singer, opera singer, or yodeler; the best Latin dancer, hip hop dancer, lyrical jazz dancer, or ballet dancer; or the best salesperson in the northwest region, the toy division, the insurance division...and the list goes on and on.

And if that's not enough, then there are sub- sub- sub- sub-categories by group size, gender, age, type of performance, and time period. For example, the best ACT score achieved by a Native American female high school junior this year. There are awards for just about everything—clear down to the biggest pig at the county fair. It is hoped that there are enough awards to satisfy self-worth. But, if not, participation awards fill in the gaps.

"The best" mentality is detrimental—both for those who lose and those who win. It's not that competitions or awards are a problem, or that winning or losing is inherently detrimental. It's that a *"the best" mentality shifts focus from patience, process and progress, to pride, pursuit, and put downs*. That's the problem.

For example, there are people who fear looking stupid, so they don't try things they really want to learn, and never enjoy potential gifts. There are others who could excel much further, but stop if they think they can best others. Some experience regression due to injury or circumstance and drop out rather than enjoying progression where they are.

Sometimes the problem goes even further. Individuals engage in damaging actions toward themselves and others—from harmful things like abusive use of legal* or illegal drugs or eating disorders to criminal sabotage of a competitor. Detrimental thinking can engulf people: "I'm better because I can hurt myself" or "I'm better because I can hurt you." It's sad and it happens. These attitudes indicate a need for deeper core power through intrinsic worth. Damaging physical and emotional behaviors can be replaced in healthy, happy ways.

There are other times self worth is sought in dysfunctional ways. *Any time* individuals seek worth extrinsically in *any way,* there is a degree of damage to self and relationships even though some methods are less damaging and may go unnoticed. This problem is not widely understood. Much effort is expended in ways that leave individuals empty and relationships uncomfortable. It's sad and sometimes even tragic.

A "the best" mentality is damaging regardless of whether an individual is winning or losing. It increases pressure, causes performance problems, injures the sense of self, damages relationships, and implies that individual worth must be earned. But, is the person on top the only one that matters? Are the rest of the masses worthless? No. Every person is priceless.

So, whether you compete or not, I suggest throwing "the best" out the window and switching to "my best" instead. What's a "my best" mentality? It's consistent, diligent focus on self-improvement regardless of rank.

How many people can simultaneously accomplish "my best"? Everyone. "The best" is exclusive; "my best" is inclusive. "The best" is cutthroat and damages relationships; "my best" is cooperative and supports relationships. "The best" is demeaning and demanding; "my best" is delightful and deliberate. The difference is not whether a person receives recognition or honors. It's the attitude and mental focus. It's *how* honors are approached and *why* they are sought. Honors aren't a problem, *but achieving them to prove self-worth is.*

Some think that switching perspective from "the best" to "my best" is unrealistic. Can it be done? Yes, in an instant. It just takes a shift in focus. For example, a talented student once said to me, "I've had more fun this week. I stopped comparing myself with others and just worked. I decided to be my best in private." That's when she took off. Prior to this she won most competitions; afterwards, she was unstoppable. Ironically, she said that when her attitude changed, winning competitions didn't mean as much to her. Instead she loved seeing how far she could push herself. *That's* the difference between "the best" and "my best."

One of the major benefits of changing is increased ability. But "my best" can't be faked. If a person tries "my best" to be "the best" it doesn't work. Why? There are still comparisons. The focus must *absolutely and completely* be on self-improvement. Rank and comparisons must be completely abandoned. Since it's easy to regress, constant awareness is wise. Even a molecule of comparison shifts the person back. I'm not talking about abandoning self-evaluation, feedback, or observation. Nor am I talking about abandoning careful, analytical, assessment of competitors. I'm talking about *worth* being tied to besting someone else. The highest core strength and ability is always found in "my best."

Is this tactic only used by people who can't really make it to the top? No, it's used by top athletes *to get to the top.* Here are some stories of Olympians: In the 2014 Olympics, Kate Hansen garnered profound respect because of her remarkable attitude. She was featured multiple times and captivated the world. In an internationally broadcast interview, she said, "I worked half my life for this. I wasn't going to waste it being stressed out." Was she lax about those 80 MPH luge runs? No. Video clips of her unbelievable conditioning routines and her comeback from a shattered leg would quell any argument. She deliberately ignored "the best" and focused on "my best." It helped her heal, gave her a competitive edge, and resulted in admiration as she defended her World Title at the Olympics.

But, she is not the only athlete with this powerful focus. Following a winning game, an Olympian was asked how he felt when his team was behind several points before rallying to win. His eyebrows furrowed thoughtfully and then he candidly replied, "Honestly, I don't know what the score is when I'm playing. I just concentrate on executing each play *my best*. I didn't know we were behind."

An Olympic gymnast was asked how she felt when she and her teammate were clearly going to take gold and silver medals. The winner was still in question with one event to go. She said, "If I do *my best* I'm happy either way, and I think she will be, too. We're friends."

Imagine the pressure these athletes took off themselves by a "my best" focus instead of a "the best" focus. Imagine also, the improved relationships. It is an accomplishment to be an Olympic athlete. But it's an even greater accomplishment to be able to say that your fiercest Olympic competitor is your friend. This competition is *designed* to determine the best. It includes the potential for record-book fame and million-dollar contracts. How did these athletes unlock their highest ability? They chose a "my best" focus. You can, too. Strengthen your core through choosing "my best."

Next up, ability and relationships...

Summary

There are two mindsets: "the best" and "my best." "The best" focuses on recognition. Instead of society minimizing a focus on recognition, this has been expanded through subcategories and participation awards. This emphasis can be damaging. Competitions aren't the problem. Winning or losing isn't the problem. Extrinsic focus is the problem. *Attention goes from patience, process, and progress to pride, pursuit, and put downs.* Fear of looking stupid keeps people from trying; others stop trying when a title is wrapped up; still others drop out rather than enjoying progression. All are shortchanged. Sometimes competition drives people to damage themselves or others through harmful substances, dangerous eating disorders, criminal sabotage, or other things that harm self or others. Mentalities emerge of "I'm better because I can hurt myself" or "I'm better because I can hurt you." A "the best" mentality implies that worth must be earned, sometimes at detrimental costs. *Any time* a person engages in extrinsic worth, self and others are damaged to some degree. Extrinsic worth indicates a need for greater core power. "My best" is a better mentality. "My best" is consistent, diligent focus on self-improvement regardless of rank. "The best" is exclusive, cutthroat, damaging to relationships, detrimental and demanding. "My best" is inclusive, cooperative, supportive of relationships, delightful, and deliberate. The distinction is not whether a person has honors or not. It's *how* and *why* honors are sought. Honors aren't bad, but achieving them to prove self-worth is damaging. "My best" can't be faked. It's achieved instantly by shifting focus. It's easy to regress, so constant awareness is wise Top athletes are usually grounded in "my best", which gives them an edge. A major benefit of "my best" is to unlock highest potential.

Case Study

Mae always wanted to take ballet, but her family couldn't afford it. Now she longingly watched her daughter's lessons. One day she asked herself why she didn't just start! Sure it would take years to become proficient, but she could wait inside the class as easily as outside. The next week she squeezed into a leotard, told her daughter to suck up any embarrassment (it couldn't be worse than her own), gathered courage, and joined. She ignored the stares from the kids and other moms and just did her best. After the initial adjustment, it wasn't so bad. In fact, it was fun. In time Mae's waistline shrank, muscles took shape, and confidence soared. She said, "Kids don't get to have all the fun. Adults can grow."

Case Study

The director of a children's theater company returned from a vacation to New York. She commented to a staff member that doing a show on Broadway was a piece of cake. The friend asked why. She pointed to several names in the Broadway program and said, "I do the jobs of all these people. I direct, do most of the tech, and manage all the publicity! We're not Broadway, but we don't have to be the best to make a difference and change kids' lives!"

Empower Yourself

The best, or...my best.

Fast-Track ReflACTION

1) What are the advantages and disadvantages of "the best"? What are the advantages and disadvantages of "my best"?

How can abandoning comparisons and rank increase success?

2) Have you seen or experienced these things: "I'm better because I can hurt myself" or "I'm better because I can hurt you?" What are the long-term effects? Should you get help to overcome one of these?

3) In what ways do pride, pursuit, and put downs hurt you? In what ways can increasing (or encouraging) patience, process, and progress help you?

*Note: Though a strong core can sometimes reduce or eliminate the need for pharmaceuticals, the appropriate, supervised use of them is different than dependency, addiction, or abuse. Dependency, addiction, or abuse indicates core problems and a need for assistance building core strength. It's wise to get help with these problems, especially if past efforts have failed.

23
Subtle Bullying

"Subtle bullying" is responsible for a lot of anxiety, so it's important to know what it is and how to handle it. Subtle bullying affects emotional safety, brain function, and ability. It's common and damaging. Yet it receives little attention. There are significant advantages in recognizing it. So, let's take a look.

Subtle bullying happens constantly. It's found in nearly *every* social situation. It happens when people compare, one-up, put down, throw weight around, revel in mistakes, judge, and display badges of superiority. Subtle bullying can turn to subtle group emotional abuse. This is when unconscious (or conscious) solicitation is directed at thinking less of someone. It happens through insinuations, side glances, tight lips, sighs of frustration, squirming, weight shifts, widened eyes, turning away, tensed muscles, smirks, rolled eyes, or other body language.

Usually there's no verbal exchange when abusers "band together." In fact, most don't know they're doing it, but exchanges take place nonetheless. Solicitation comes through non-verbal communication. Exchanges can happen between spouses, co-workers, friends, or even strangers. Insinuations are seen and joined. Usually the bullying is nonverbal, but other times it includes small snide remarks, snubbing, bits of gossip, etc. (Open degradation is not subtle bullying or subtle group emotional abuse. It's overt, especially if repeated defamation and degradation occurs.) Group emotional abuse can take place in front of a person or behind their back.

There are two reasons for subtle bullying and subtle group emotional abuse. One is to subtly build superiority and support by tearing another person down. The other is to subtly manipulate a person toward a desired behavior or outcome. Anyone can be targeted, but subtle bullying is often directed at those who are physically, mentally, or socially different. Sensitivity has risen, but some situations are still overlooked like highly capable individuals who may feel a full brunt of bullying yet receive little compassion. But bullying is devastating to any individual. Subtle group emotional abuse is common, tolerated, and, unfortunately, sometimes even expected.

If confronted, ill behavior is demurely denied. "I didn't put you down. You're too sensitive." But in reality, the nonverbal messages are clear and proficient. The common reaction is, "Quit being so sensitive; toughen up." What is really being said is, "Your sensitivity is another indication of your deficiency. Ignore my actions so I can continue to feel better about myself by putting you down."

Is ignoring inappropriate behavior the best course of action? Does it prevent the bullied person from becoming vulnerable, hurt, or *unsure*? No. The solution is to become *more* sensitive, not by running around with hurt feelings, but by becoming an expert at spotting and appropriately handling it.

Let's start by looking at an example. This case study includes subtle bullying and group emotional abuse: Sheela was eager to start her first day in this prestigious dance company. It would take a little while to "learn the ropes," but she figured others would understand and help. She jumped in, but it didn't take long to make a minor mistake. As she quickly fixed it, she noticed disapproving looks from the person next to her and covered whispers from two people across the room. Sheela felt a little unsettled and her movements became tenuous. She cleared her thoughts, brushed away the fleeting desire to hide in embarrassment, and resumed her tasks.

Sheela experienced subtle bullying which caused physical, mental, emotional and behavioral symptoms. These included tense muscles, confused thinking, an unsettled feeling, and the desire to get away. Did you spot all that? Subtle bullying caused her to become *unsure* which resulted in anxiety symptoms. This interaction was small, but cumulative patterns are problematic.

Perpetual emotional wounds can be very damaging, even if small. An insignificant, stubbed toe isn't a big deal unless it happens again and again and again. And the injury is compounded if there is insufficient recovery time. The same is true of "insignificant," emotional wounds. The damage from compounded emotional wounds depends on the amount of bullying, an individual's resilience, the amount of recovery time, and the ability to address problems.

Stories like Sheela's happen daily. It is a rare class, team, school, stage cast, or business that does not have subtle bullying. The interplay can be boiled down to abusers, enablers, and users. Abusers essentially say, "I'll walk on you, you will let me, and this will prove I'm good." Enablers essentially say, "I'll let you walk on me, in time you will see I'm good and change, and this will prove I'm good." (In other words, "I'll stop abuse by allowing it.") These stances are unhealthy and based on extrinsic worth. Users essentially say, "I'll try not to walk on you, but if it's inconvenient, I'll indirectly assist or remain silent as you're walked on, and this will keep me looking good." This still supports bullying and is an indirect form of "I'll walk on you, you will let me, and this will prove I'm good."

Subtle bullying effects everyone, not just the person bullied. No one can relax in this environment because everyone has to watch their backs. Subtle bullying is even damaging if the person bullied is not present (as with gossip) since all become *unsure* if they're next. If Sheela's worth is tied up in how others feel about her, she'll try to prove herself (enable). And if those engaged in subtle group emotional abuse get their worth by putting others down, they will find reasons to disapprove (abuse). There's constant clawing for elusive security. It's a no-win situation. Yet, this is a common, extrinsic way that individuals attempt to get self-worth.

Subtle bullying *causes* anxiety and a lack of emotional safety in the person bullied. Subtle bulling *is a sign of* anxiety and a lack of emotional safety in the person bullying (and those allowing or joining). Bullying can negatively change personalities in both the person bullied and the person/s bullying (especially if confronted). Why? Emotional safety.

Sometimes the intent of subtle bullying is clearly detrimental and delight is taken in others' suffering. But usually subtle bullying is unrecognized and simply a dysfunctional, subconscious effort to maintain personal safety. If confronted, the subtle bullying is strongly denied since the person bullying honestly does not know. *Intent* is defended. But when *intent* is defended, understanding is blocked. Problems can't be solved. (Often both sides bully at times; however, there are usually predominant roles.) Even if a person's intent is so innocent that bullying would stop if it were understood, subtle bullying is damaging.

The person bullied may struggle with self-doubt and loneliness. The person bullying may be at a loss to solve problems or improve relationships. It can be painful for either to recognize.

This is especially true when bullying happens in families or between close friends. When bullying goes unrecognized, minor problems can become serious. The person bullied usually recognizes problems before the person bullying. (Sometimes the person bullying never recognizes.) When recognized, the person bullied may feel betrayed. The person bullying may feel shame or remorse. Trust erodes or guilt engulfs. Neither is helpful. The answer is to address things and move on. The short-term solution to bullying is boundaries (see next chapter). The long-term solution is to build core emotional safety (previous chapters).

If the leader in an organization ignores or joins subtle bullying, restraint is removed and bullying increases. Leaders matter. Perpetual exposure to emotional wounds can result in emotional issues and serious stress-induced health problems. Both sides can experience them, but they're usually worse for those bullied. Bullying can lead to depression, addictions, cutting and suicide. The overall effect on performance can range from slight flow/zone inconsistency to outright incapacitating anxiety.

Many think that overt bullying between groups (like rivals, races, or gangs) is because of differences. But this is not true. It does not account for the bullying going on *within* their groups. Clashes happen because individuals are the *same*—they lack emotional safety. Emotional safety is the real problem and the only solution. Brains can't even function without emotional safety. Better solutions can't be comprehended without it. Most attempts to solve bullying involve manipulation. This does not work (see next chapter). The core of the problem is emotional safety. Change starts with seeing the actual problem. The earliest stages of bigger problems are found in subtle bullying.

There are many advantages to spotting subtle bullying. It's another angle of awareness of thoughts and feelings. Strengthen your core by becoming an expert at spotting subtle bullying.

Next up, a subtle bullying shield...

Summary

Subtle bullying is a form of manipulation. It affects emotional safety and performance outcomes. Subtle bulling is putting someone down to build self up, and it happens in a variety of ways. When individuals unconsciously (or consciously) band together to put someone down or pressure them toward compliance, subtle bullying turns to subtle group emotional abuse. A common response is "You're too sensitive." In reality, more sensitivity is needed by becoming an expert at spotting and handling subtle bullying. Subtle bullying causes physical, mental, emotional and behavioral symptoms. Abusers say, "I'll walk on you, you will let me, and this will prove I'm good." Enablers say, "I'll let you walk on me, in time you will see I'm good and change, and this will prove I'm good." Users essentially say, "I'll try not to walk on you, but if it's inconvenient, I'll indirectly assist or remain silent as you're walked on, and this will keep me looking good." Users are indirect abusers. All three pursue extrinsic worth. Just as small physical wounds can be disruptive, small emotional wounds can be disruptive. Repeated wounds can result in significant problems, especially if there is no recovery time. It can be painful to recognize that one has been bullied or has bullied. Rather than blame or shame, grow and move on. Overt and subtle bullying have the same cause and solution. Gangs and races don't clash because of differences. They clash because they are the same—they lack emotional safety. Bullying happens *within* these groups, not just *between* them. Subtle bullying must be spotted to be fixed. There are many advantages to understanding subtle bullying. Knowing how to handle it reduces anxiety.

Case Study

A teacher's eyes widened after learning the effects of subtle bullying at a conference. She exclaimed, "No wonder I had difficulty reading! A girl in my kindergarten and first grade class wouldn't leave me alone. She moved and reading became easy."

Case Study

Karl walked into the locker room. Wow! He couldn't believe he'd made the varsity team! Ard, the varsity captain, openly welcomed him. Then Jim strolled in. Karl and Jim usually walked home together. Ard looked at Jim, rolled his eyes toward other varsity players and they quietly smirked. Karl ignored and warmly responded, "See you guys around!" He waved as he left with Jim. Karl figured he'd first try genuine respect and friendship since Ard seemed decent. If that didn't work, he'd go from there. Other people did not determine his friends. [Karl is using emotional safety and boundaries (see next chapter). Boundaries can be increased, if needed. In extreme cases adult intervention may be necessary.]

Case Study

For four years Mara was bullied in elementary school. It started with snubs and snide remarks and escalated to daily spitting and hitting. Visits to the teachers, principal, and even higher administration fell on deaf ears. Mara's grades went from the top of the class to the bottom and her extrovert personality became withdrawn. Then she was beat badly enough it was not certain whether she would lose permanent teeth. She begged not to return the last three weeks of the year. Her parents agreed and then moved in the summer. At the new school Mara's grades were back up within weeks. [This story includes both subtle and overt bullying. It is used to illustrate how bullying affects ability and personality. When leaders failed to intervene the problem slowly escalated from subtle bulling, snubbing, and snide remarks to overt bullying and serious injuries.]

Empower Yourself

Bully ignore, or...address and soar.

Fast-Track ReflACTION

1) When have you seen/experienced subtle bullying; name the physical, mental, emotional, and/or behavioral symptoms?
2) Have you subtly abused, enabled, or used? If so, when, why? (Consider emotional safety.) What positive things could result from healthier interaction?
3) How can spotting subtle bullying (especially in the moment) help prevent or reduce anxiety?

Please note: In rare cases, addressing subtle bullying may instigate overt bullying and require addressing safety issues. Err on the side of caution and do not hesitate to seek assistance. See Appendix B for more information.

Much of the content of this chapter is adapted from my relationship book *Just Respect* and is used by permission. For more in depth information see that publication.

24
Choose Respect

Coaches encourage their traveling players to ignore the home crowd. Teachers say not to be deterred by other students. Business CEOs tell managers to focus on tasks and not worry about competitors. Directors tell performing artists to block out the audience. What's really being said? Set respectful boundaries! Boundaries place a protective, emotional fence around individuals so that tasks can be attended to. Respectful boundaries are a big deal in eliminating anxiety.

In fact, boundaries are possibly the most important skill to improve performance. Yes, you read that right, the *most* important skill. Boundaries are right up there with a musician learning to read music, a dancer learning control, a businessman learning the trade, and a student learning test material. *Whenever there's outcome anxiety, there's a boundary problem.* Basic boundaries can be intuitive, such as those mentioned above. But boundaries are not used skillfully or deliberately enough.

Wise sayings such as "what others think of me is not my business" are difficult to implement without boundaries. Boundaries free individuals to interact in more positive ways. Boundaries are healthy and helpful. It is good to develop them, but this is almost impossible without understanding respect and manipulation. They were introduced earlier; now we'll go in depth. They are the foundation of a solid, powerful core.

As stated earlier, there are two ways to get emotional safety: manipulation and respect. Manipulation and extrinsic worth go hand in hand. Manipulation is perpetuated by a fallacy that a person deserves less respect if they haven't "measured up." This viewpoint opens the door to "walking on others" if they're not measuring up, or "being walked on" if you're not measuring up. So, individuals scurry to make sure they measure up. But there's a problem. Only pseudo safety can be obtained because standards constantly change and performances are not always predictable. So even if a person measures up, there is constant underlying anxiety. This is a big reason why anxiety is so persistent.

There's an alternative. A *chooser* says, "I won't walk on you and you won't walk on me. If you treat me respectfully, I'd love to interact with you; if you treat me disrespectfully, our relationship will be limited to the degree that you are disrespectful."

In other words, a chooser expects respect 100% of the time, even if they mess up; and gives respect 100% of the time, even if others mess up.* A chooser is grounded in intrinsic worth. Choosers are okay with or without others' approval. Respect for self and others is a *big* deal. It's basically impossible to achieve emotional safety, embrace intrinsic worth, implement "my best," reach full potential, or eliminate anxiety without consistent respect.

There are counterfeits to respect. Pride is fake self-respect. Flattery or "kissing up" are fake respect for others. So what is true respect for self and others? True respect is humble confidence, a sense of worth, and profound dignity toward self and others in equal amounts, regardless of whether you or someone else messes up or measures up.

Giving and expecting respect 100% of the time* is the safety valve that prevents hurting others (because "I won't walk on you"), and it prevents getting hurt (because "I won't let you walk on me"). This means that even if someone messes up enough to require correction or dismissal, it should be done respectfully. But what if someone's an absolute jerk? Good question! There's a difference between respect and trust. Respect is absolute civility that is given to everyone *all the time*. Trust is openness that is *only given when it has been earned*. Consistent respect, reserved trust and selective boundaries protect more effectively than manipulation.

If trust is given freely, it undermines emotional safety. If respect is *not* given freely, it undermines emotional safety. *This is the single most important concept in eliminating outcome anxieties.* Respect, trust, and boundaries affect brain and body function. The brain and body work differently when there's anxiety; anxiety can't be eliminated without emotional safety; emotional safety depends on boundaries; boundaries are tied to understanding appropriate respect and trust. This provides the foundation for a strong performance core. Respect is essential.

But honestly, is respect shown 100% of the time? No. When conflict arises, respect is thrown out the window and quick-fix manipulations surface instead. But this is when respect is needed the most! During conflict, enablers abandon self-respect, abusers abandon respect for others, and then messy interactions happen that zap time and energy. Maintaining respect during conflict is important. But how! It requires knowing what to do when there is disrespect.

At some point someone is going to disrespect you. Disrespect happens all the time—the rude comment on social media, the screaming fan at the game, the condescending teacher passing out grades, the grouchy boss on a bad day. Disrespect can be as small as rolled eyes and side glances, or as large as devastating betrayal and criminal action. How can safety be maintained without quick-fix manipulation? Boundaries!

Boundaries are common in society; that's why there are security officers at events and police officers on highways. Laws and jails handle severe disrespect. These boundaries maintain safety in society. Boundaries are just as important in private life. Very few people grow up in environments where healthy boundaries are second nature, so most learn to implement personal boundaries as adults. Every person benefits from understanding boundaries. Boundaries are built on the understanding that you don't have a right to determine what others will do, but you do have a right to determine what you will do.

You are the VIP security for yourself. It's your responsibility to determine the boundaries and consequences that provide your personal safety. It would be nice to be able to delegate this task, but it's not possible. Even if it were, it would not provide the same level of core strength or self-respect. So knowing how to use boundaries is important. Those with outcome anxiety usually don't understand boundaries. That's why there's fear. *There's a lack of safety!* It's not the performance that's frightening; it's a lack of boundaries!

Most people think that boundaries are punitive. But in reality *all healthy relationships have boundaries 100% of the time* (just like society has boundaries 100% of the time but, they're usually only noticed during punitive enforcement). Boundaries aren't noticed in healthy relationships because boundaries are intuitively sensed and honored. So the only time boundaries are noticed is when an unhealthy relationship brings attention to actively "setting" and/or "enforcing" a boundary.

When there is disrespect, a boundary is needed to some degree. A boundary is a substitute for respect. A boundary may feel like manipulation to a disrespectful person; after all, if respect were understood, there would be no need for a boundary. Most people attempt to get emotional safety through manipulation instead of boundaries. Usually manipulation is not consciously recognized by the person manipulating or the person manipulated. Boundaries provide emotional safety without manipulation.

Boundaries and manipulation are sometimes confused, but they are *distinctly* different. A boundary protects by *shielding* a person from disrespect—there is no attempt to change or control. Manipulation protects through things like persuading forcing, coercing, or pacifying others—all involve some sort of influence or control on someone else. Do you see the difference? The chart below from my relationship book *Just Respect* further clarifies:

Boundary	*Manipulation*
Respectful/firm	Disrespectful/calculating
Protect/shield	Persuade/intimidate
If/then consequence	Varied contingencies
Accept others	Change others
No agenda	Agenda—do what I want
Self determines worth Control self	Others determine worth Control others
Minimum intervention	Maximum intervention
MY Best	THE Best
Intrinsic Worth	Extrinsic Worth
Peace	Pressure
I teach others how to treat me kindly, responsibility, communication	Others should respond and treat me kindly implication, coercion
Limited use	Always use
Boundary does the work	Manipulation does the work
Suspends judgment	Extends judgment
Disagreement ok	Disagreement disturbing
Share	Compare

Source: *Just Respect*. By M. R. Adams. Reprinted with permission.

Boundaries are *respectful* and *firm*. A boundary can be big to small or short term to long term (seconds to years). Setting a boundary is not saying that the other person is bad or that the relationship won't change. It just says something damaging needs addressing now. A boundary says to others, "Think and do what you would like, and if it happens to be hurtful, I'll protect myself and those I'm responsible for." Boundaries have two parts: the clarification and the consequence (similar to society's laws). They follow the pattern, "If you ____, then I will ____ to protect myself." A boundary can be as small as "if you are rude, then I refuse to look at you," to as big as "if you threaten me despite the restraining order, then I will call the police and you will go to jail."

There are many types of boundaries. For example, "If you are respectful of me then I will perform for you; if you are not respectful, then I will perform for the others in the room." "If you don't like my performance, then you can leave." "If you don't appreciate what I'm doing, then you can take my place." "If you rant at me, then I refuse to listen or value your opinion." "If you do not believe my honest disclosures, then I will seek understanding and friendship elsewhere." "If you betray me, then I will not interact with you." Many boundaries are unspoken.

Mental, unspoken boundaries might look the same from the outside, but they are decisively different on the inside. Mental boundaries are like putting on armor! Boundaries definitively say, "I deserve and expect respect." During a performance the performer has relationships with either 1) specific audience individuals or 2) the collective audience as a whole. Even when walking into a room of strangers, there is a "relationship" with everyone. Mental boundaries clarify relationships and are *huge* in eliminating anxiety and unleashing flow/zone.

Boundaries toward an audience are important, however, they are not enough. Boundaries must be comprehensive. If you're only safe when performing, you're still not safe. Non-performance relationships affect performance reactions, so boundaries are important in all aspects of life.

Boundaries make it possible to implement "what others think of me is not my business." Worry happens when unsafe; boundaries provide safety regardless of reactions. Some say boundaries are so important that they should be set any way possible—screaming and shouting if necessary. I disagree. Why? *It's disrespectful.* Disrespect is manipulation even if used to set a boundary.* That said, boundaries are *important* and setting them appropriately usually takes trial and error practice like any other skill.

One last point, disagreement does not equal disrespect; individuals can passionately disagree and still be absolutely respectful. In fact, passionate disagreement combined with equally determined respect can be an amazing catalyst for great problem solving and deep insights! This can strengthen the core and deepen performance.

Respect is the foundation of non-manipulation. A person who *gives* respect can more easily *expect* it; a person who *expects* respect can more easily *give* it. *Choosers* give and expect respect 100% of the time* and they use boundaries. Boundaries are huge in eliminating anxiety and increasing peak flow/zone. Strengthen your core through using boundaries and choosing respect.

Next up, a squeaky clean core...

Summary

Boundaries are like a protective, emotional fence so that tasks can be attended to. They are probably the most important performance skill. Whenever there is outcome anxiety there is a boundary problem. A chooser says, "I won't walk on you and you won't walk on me." Choosers expect respect even if they mess up, and give respect even if others mess up. Respect is given freely; trust is conditional. Abusers disrespect others; enablers disrespect self. Boundaries are common in society and appropriate in personal life. Boundaries provide emotional safety. Boundaries are a substitute for respect and eliminate the need for manipulation. The quality of a person's boundaries is reflected in their relationships and personal safety. There are defining characteristics between boundaries and manipulation. Boundaries are if/then statements. New boundaries may feel uncomfortable. Mental boundaries dramatically strengthen the inner core; they are like putting on armor. Worry happens when unsafe; boundaries provide safety. Respect is given freely; trust is given conditionally. Earned trust and selective boundaries protect better than manipulation. Boundaries are respectful and firm. Disagreement does not equal disrespect. A person who gives respect can more easily expect it; a person who expects respect can more easily give it. Choosers give and expect respect 100% of the time* and use boundaries.

Case Study

Sheela (from the last chapter) limited interactions with those who were unkind. She finished her year contract with the internationally acclaimed dance company and then chose to leave. She said, "I didn't like the daily cat fights. I traded the prestige of being in the chorus of that company with the prestige of being a principle dancer in my regional company. I'm happier." [Boundary: *if* you are unkind, *then* my relationship with you will be strictly professional; and, *if* I am not treated with respect, *then* I will not dance for you.]

Case Study

Jed was surprised when his manager burst in. She ranted on about him not fulfilling his responsibilities. He calmly waited and then responded, "No one told me of this policy change. If you don't inform me then I can't make the change. If you will email me a copy of the new policies I will read it and make the necessary changes." [When he calmly waited, he did two things. He avoided quick-fix responses and shut down brains that would have made the situation messy, and he implemented the mental boundary, "I refuse to take responsibility for your mistakes." He then implemented a verbal boundary which essentially said, "If you let me know, then I will do it; if you don't, then I can't and won't." By remaining calm, he showed her respect; by setting mental and verbal boundaries, he expected respect.]

Empower Yourself

Endlessly maneuver, or...always respect.

Fast-Track ReflACTION

1) Why should respect be unconditional, while trust and boundaries are conditional? How does each protect?
2) If a person deserves less respect when they mess up, how does this negatively impact you and others even if no mistakes are made?
3) Think of a situation that you could improve by expecting or giving more respect; what if/then boundary could help?

*Please Note: The 100% respect rule does not apply in cases of extreme physical danger or abuse. See Appendix B for more information.

Much of the content of this chapter is adapted from my relationship book *Just Respect* and is used by permission. For more in depth information see that publication.

25

Strong and Squeaky Clean

Anxiety and flow/zone problems come from attempting to function without a solid core. It's like crossing a deep ravine on an unstable bridge, as mentioned earlier. *Emotional safety is not optional.* When the core is not safe, fear sets off internal alarms. Most try to get rid of the fear instead of reinforcing the core. It's backwards.

Core strength improves ability and reduces fear. Yet, have you heard a coach say, "Okay team, we're upping our game, so today figure out who you're walking on and stop!" Have you heard a teacher say, "We're going to improve our test scores, so set a boundary and report how it increased self-respect and respect for others!" Have you heard a boss say, "We'd like to improve company productivity this month, so go talk to your spouse, agree on boundaries with the kids and fix any problems!" Most wouldn't even know what was being asked!

The result of internal "unsure alarms" is self-consciousness. Self-consciousness is "checking the bridge." Sports, education, performing arts, and business research amply document the detriments of self-consciousness. Self-consciousness is thought diverted to self, others, or the environment to *come out okay*. It causes second-guessing and stress. It doesn't work.

Some think that self-consciousness is a "loss of focus." But there's no such thing as losing focus. Focus happens *continually*. The problem is focusing on the *wrong* thing. But focus can't be forced. If you try to not think of a white bear, guess what happens? When an unintended focus creeps in, there's always a strong internal reason. It's almost always tied to emotional safety. Focus problems are not fixed by a stronger focus; they're fixed by boundaries. An unsafe "rickety bridge" will *always* get your attention no matter how much you try to focus elsewhere. When focus fluctuates, there's an inadequate boundary somewhere. Boundaries come before laser focus.

There are two types of focus: *self-awareness* and *self-consciousness*. Self-awareness is beneficial and associated with peak flow/zone, higher-level brain function, expanded attentiveness, emotional safety, better body function, and *giving* to others. It improves performance. Self-consciousness is detrimental and associated with anxiety, flow/zone problems, lower-level brain function, constricted attentiveness, a need for emotional safety, lower body function, and *getting* from others. Self-consciousness is no big deal. It's a hassle and can lower performance, but it's simply an effort to secure emotional safety. It can be fixed when addressing the right thing.

No one is completely self-conscious. In fact, even a self-conscious person spends most focus on performance awareness. (Otherwise, performing would be impossible.) Self-consciousness just causes a fluctuation of focus between the performance (self-awareness) and coming out okay (self-consciousness). So the goal is to become more consistently self-aware. This isn't done by attempting to focus on self-awareness; it's done through boundaries that build core safety. Then self-consciousness is not needed. It's basically impossible to abandon self-consciousness in performance without boundaries.

There's another form of self-consciousness that requires boundaries. Have you heard of impostor syndrome? It's feeling that if others could peer inside they'd see a fraud, that success was luck, and that others must have been tricked as parts of self were hidden (like anxiety). It's fear of "being found out." But why would that be a problem? There are unsure feelings of not coming out okay if "unlovable stuff" were known. (Ironically imposter syndrome is most common in the most capable people.) Imposter syndrome is a form of outcome anxiety that results in constant self-consciousness. Why? Emotional safety. What's the answer? Boundaries. There's a need to feel respect despite "unlovable" imperfections. Boundaries maintain self-respect and allow for imperfections without discrediting accomplishments.

Boundaries are developed through increased awareness of *thoughts* and *feelings*. But, there's a problem. When a person already feels *unsure*, efforts to be more aware can increase self-consciousness. *Awareness must first be channeled into constructing boundaries to be beneficial.* Without this, unhealthy self-consciousness squeezes out the healthy self-awareness needed for peak flow in the zone. Figuring this out is a process but it works (see first case study below).

Proactive self-improvement requires proactive safety. A safe environment allows a person to clean their side of the street, which means to fix mistakes. Admitting a mistake is like venturing out on a rickety bridge. It feels vulnerable and scary. If that bridge isn't stabilized by boundaries, manipulation and quick fixes take over to attempt to increase safety. That's why defensiveness is common. Boundaries strengthen the bridge, reduce defensiveness, and keep a person safe while growing. Even very capable people will struggle without boundaries.

Boundaries protect interpersonally, but failed attempts to improve can lead to self-bullying. Self-bullying is a dysfunctional attempt to sure up a bridge. One person said to her friend, "If you talked to your children the way you talk to yourself, you'd lose custody for emotional abuse."

Is your self-talk respectful? Don't walk on yourself! Negative self-talk immediately changes the chemicals in the body, which can cause discouragement and depression. Within a few weeks, negative self-talk can even negatively change the shape and function of the brain (which can be reversed with positive self-talk). Negative self-talk does not motivate or strengthen. It is detrimental. It's okay to be kind to yourself.

Negative self-talk can lead to "negative self-care". Addictions, avoidance, and distraction can cause life to become crazy. They're usually due to discouragement, or internal or interpersonal disconnection. These actions are usually conscious or subconscious attempts to manage deeper concerns. But problems aren't addressed, they're compound. This weakens the core. It's better to clean things up in healthy ways that support yourself.

Just as it can be necessary to set boundaries with others, it can be necessary to set boundaries with yourself. Some try to fix things through internal manipulation. Interpersonal manipulation runs over someone else; internal manipulation runs over a part of you. It disconnects internally and exerts unhealthy control.

Have you ever felt two parts of yourself warring (like the inner couch potato with a doughnut and the fitness guru with a hearty salad)? Forcing self is based on control and manipulation. Who likes that? No wonder there are internal fights! Part of core power is to respect self, *all* of self. So instead of force (a form of manipulation), consider *why the resistance*? This engages high-level thinking and opens the door to discovering dysfunctional "shoulds" and "oughts". Self-examination makes space for greater self-awareness. This encourages healthy motivation, internal integration, self-connection, and self-compassion. Respectful internal boundaries and respectful interpersonal boundaries are both important.

Boundaries work, but using them is a learned skill. This skill includes carrying out consequences respectfully. If a boundary says you won't look at someone, don't look (instead of giving nasty looks). If the boundary says you'll leave, leave (but don't slam the door on the way). If the boundary says you will call the police, call (instead of yelling threats).

Boundaries require treating others respectfully 100% of the time,* even when out of earshot. Core strength builds as respect is considered, even when processing or venting. It might not seem like this matters, the other person can't hear when out of earshot. But respect changes *your* core. Respect increases *your* internal power. Giving and expecting respect builds core power. If you want to perform well, you'll need all the power you can get. It's an art to stand up for self without stomping on others. It yields solid core strength.

Walking on others (or stomping on them) is a common boundary mistake. There are other common boundary mistakes like taking responsibility for someone else's stuff (a form of enabling) and not taking responsibility for your stuff (a form of subtle abuse). Both manipulate a situation to one's favor. Neither is healthy.

Another common mistake is trying to get another person to understand when it just isn't happening. This may be motivated by a genuine concern that misjudgment is causing the other person undo pain. But if explanations are resisted, additional efforts usually backfire and fall into manipulation.

You are not responsible for cleaning their side of the street. Misjudgment happens. Misjudgment is a reflection on them, not you. You're not bad and usually they aren't bad. There's just a lack of better coping skills. Feeling inadequate when another person isn't cleaning their side is taking responsibility for their stuff. It's a form of enabling. It increases pain, usually for both sides. Boundaries stabilize things and give space for growth. Boundaries can be removed in an instant when growth has occurred. However, when assuming another person needs to do the cleaning, watch out for self-deception. Handling things appropriately requires absolute self-honesty. *No self-deception.* High emotional IQ is required to step up, step down, or step away, as appropriate.

Many people don't admit to their own mistakes because they didn't mean to make a mess. So, they defend their *intent* instead of cleaning up their unintended *mess*. But even if someone else is 95% at fault and you're only 5% at fault, there's still a responsibility to clean up your part (and not take responsibility for the rest). But don't fudge on your stuff. It's never appropriate to dodge responsibility, whether the intent was good or the amount of damage minuscule. Messes should be directly and openly fixed except when doing so increases pain for others.

Do you see that regardless of what others do, you can keep your side of the street clean? Cleaning your side of the street is a one-sided, no-defensiveness, total-responsibility, pure-integrity deal. Initially it's scary. (Imagine an alcoholic standing the first time in an AA meeting.) Admitting to faults can be hard, especially if the intent was good and the mess-up unintentional. That's why so many people won't address problems until rock bottom situations force it like divorce, addiction, job crisis, or health loss. Why wait for big heartache and loss? There are better ways to meet emotional needs: clean your side of the street and use boundaries to ensure giving and expecting respect.

The same action can be an appropriate boundary or an inappropriate manipulation depending on *motivation* and *intent*. If an "if/then" action is done to change someone, it's still manipulation. Boundaries are for protection (but manipulation is also protective). A boundary doesn't try to change others (though sometimes it results in change). It also does not try to punish others (though sometimes it is interpreted this way). If things aren't working, check whether there are adequate boundaries and/or if manipulative intent snuck in to subtly change someone. Manipulation is so common that usually both sides do it.

Respect tends to lower others' defenses so problems resolve easier. But, if respect is given *to change someone,* it's manipulation and doesn't work. Cleaning up your stuff so others get the hint and clean up their stuff isn't cleaning up; it's throwing more manipulative trash around. Most emotional pain, relationship problems, and performance problems are due to some sort of minuscule or major manipulation. (For example, what's self-consciousness? It's thought directed toward manipulating a situation to come out okay.)

So, part of cleaning up is to stop manipulating your audience, your boss, your friends, your family, strangers, and even yourself! There's a difference between wisely using principles in a way that may result in positive outcomes for everyone and manipulating. Abandoning manipulation does not mean to abandon influence. The line between respectful, knowledgeable, positive influence and manipulation is force. It's the line between respectfully resolving concerns versus resolutely overcoming resistance with increased pressure. A respectful person is willing to work things out but walks away if others are not willing. A boundary is only used if needed. A manipulative person breaks ties using punitive silence, overt degradation, or undermining jabs.

Even a molecule of manipulation causes problems. Cleaning your side of the street means to: do good things just because that's who you are, not because you want something; set and enforce if/then boundaries instead of manipulating; learn to maintain emotional safety while addressing problems; give and expect respect; distinguish earned or unearned trust; clean up your messes, even if others don't clean theirs; and take responsibility. To eliminate anxiety and flow/zone problems, focus on these things with complete integrity. They form the foundation of emotional IQ.

Research repeatedly supports that emotional IQ skills are indispensable and more closely tied to success than any others. However, just as an athlete does not learn his skills in a day, these skills are not learned in a day. Everyone starts where they are. It's an art to be accountable and respectfully hold others accountable. Proactive persistence and patience pays off. Perfection is not needed to benefit; even small gains in reducing manipulation and street cleaning make a difference.

Whether during a performance or not, there are continual opportunities to practice emotional IQ. This is how core strength is developed. You'll be interacting anyway; those efforts might as well propel you forward. It's particularly beneficial to consider your reactions to your mistakes or others' mistakes. Personal improvement is enhanced by specific goals. Sometimes performance improves fastest by improving non-performance skills. That's why the *CPPro-LP* supports all types of goals and tracks their effects on performance.

One person said, "When I focused on only one thing—not manipulating (and taking responsibility if I slipped)—not only did my performance shoot up, everything in my life improved." This is common. Things change in a positive direction for those who understand emotional IQ skills. Self-consciousness turns to self-awareness, self-judgment to self-acceptance, self-righteousness to self-observation, and self-criticism to self-compassion.

These result in self-support, self-confidence, and self-delight. But that's not all. They open up non-judgmental acceptance, compassion, and increased delight toward others. There are more benefits than just emotional safety and improved performance.

Take responsibility to keep your side of the street clean. It strengthens the core. When core power is strong many things improve. Strengthen your core by reinforcing bridges and cleaning streets.

Next up, how to fail and other smart things...

Summary

Most try to improve backwards. Most fear is from a lack of core power. Core power requires boundaries and cleaning your side of the street. Manipulation of self, others or environment is a common quick fix attempt to grasp emotional safety. There's no such thing as losing focus. There are two types of focus self-consciousness and self-awareness. Self-consciousness causes a fluctuation of focus between the performance (self-awareness) and coming out okay (self-consciousness). Self-consciousness is addressed by boundaries. Imposter syndrome is a form of outcome anxiety. Negative self-talk is a form of emotional abuse. It reduces the function of the body and brain. Manipulation is not limited to interpersonal interaction. Self-manipulation can be addressed by considering *why the resistance?* It's common to defend intent instead of cleaning messes. Intent and amount of wrongdoing in relation to others is irrelevant; there's never a time when it's appropriate to dodge responsibility. Cleaning messes can be vulnerable without boundaries. Emotional pain, relationship problems, and performance problems are almost always due to manipulation. Subtle enabling and subtle abusing are forms of manipulation. Manipulation includes attempts to be understood when there's resistance, even if the motive is to reduce others' pain. True respect and street-cleaning is one-sided, and done because that's how the person wants to be. Respect, boundaries, non-manipulation, responsibility, and integrity provide the ultimate emotional safety, and opportunity for maximum ability. These skills melt fear.

Case Study

Dylan prepped for the final play of the game as someone yelled from the stands, "If you miss we lose the championship!

This season's on you!" Tension gripped him. He stepped back, took a breath and shot up a mental boundary. *Everyone on the team is responsible for where we are. I am only responsible to do my best.* Core strength surged. He set the ball and let it fly. [Boundary: *If* you are unreasonable or disrespectful, *then* I won't listen. However, I will take responsibility to fulfill my commitments as best I can.]

Case Study

Annette extended kindness. But, "friends" took advantage of her time and money. At first she gave the benefit of the doubt. Maybe they didn't understand. But inconsideration grew and then she heard jokes behind her back. She channeled the initial anger into firmness. She would not interact with those who were disrespectful; and, despite her kind heart, she would not provide opportunities for the less advantaged if they were not respectful. [Boundary: "*If* I'm respected, *then* I'd love to be friends and help; *if* I'm not respected, *then* I won't." If she tried to *change* them, especially if for recognition, appreciation or emotional safety, then this action would be manipulation despite that it's in the form of an if/then boundary. Also, if her actions were meant to *punish* (whether successful or not), it would be manipulation. Only she would know her true intent (and intent can change). Other people's judgments—accurate or inaccurate—would be conjecture. If she attempted to correct inaccurate conjecture, they resisted, and she persisted, it would be manipulation even if her motive was to reduce pain and re-establish assistance in a healthy way.]

Empower Yourself

Messy manipulation, or...boundaries and responsibility.

Fast-Track ReflACTION

1) Name a recent internal self-manipulation; answer *why the resistance*? (Consider deeply.)
2) Name a recent time in which you were manipulated; what boundary would provide a good response? (Remember that a boundary that isn't strong enough doesn't provide protection; a boundary that's punitively strong is manipulation.)
3) Name a recent time in which you manipulated someone; what boundary would be better?

*Please Note: The 100% respect rule does not apply in cases of extreme physical danger or abuse. See Appendix B for more information.

Much of the content of this chapter is adapted from my relationship book *Just Respect* and is used by permission. For more in-depth information, see that publication.

26

Fail... and Other Smart Things

This chapter is filled with smart tips to maximize progress....

Please Fail. Will Smith says to fail early, fail often and fail forward, that growth is in failure, and practice is controlled failure. An Olympian said that she failed 90% of the time, and it resulted in a World Title and the Olympics. Edison said that his 10,000 failures to make a light-bulb put him that much closer to finding what worked! Physical trainers deliberately encourage muscle failure because that's when the micro muscle tears produce hormones to increase strength. So it is not failure that's discouraging but *perceptions* regarding self and the task. Perceptions can be changed to your advantage. It's critical to know how to make mistakes. Failure is actually constructive feedback. Successful people *deliberately* fail! They push limits until weaknesses surface and then turn them into strengths. Changing perspective regarding failure is smart and enhances progress. Be smart: deliberately fail.

Never Perform. A good way to get rid of outcome anxiety is to never perform! This doesn't mean to never play sports, get in front of an audience, take a test, or present a business proposal. It means to treat performances as a learning experience. Performance is practice...in front of an audience. But watch out, some treat practice as a performance, thinking about how a future audience will react or how to cover a mistake. This "trains in" the possibility of undesirable things and reduces your power in practice and performance. Renee Elise Goldsberry teaches that performance goals give your power back to you. She encourages performers to always have a specific goal. This approach encourages authenticity and greater quality. After auditions or tryouts she encourages leaving immediately, evaluating whether the goal was achieved, choosing a new goal, and leaving it at that. Judges and audiences are just the means of testing whether private goals are achieved. The advice to focus on goals fits any situation including sports, business, tests, relationships, and the performing arts. Treating performance as simply practice with an audience increases the chances of a good outcome and solid progress. Be smart: never perform, always practice.

Tell Stories. Research shows that thoughts create emotions and emotions affect outcomes. So monitor the stories in your head. Rather than accept any narrative that comes to mind, consider the story most beneficial and accurate. One person was in a minor accident and unable to do anything for her husband's birthday. On top of that, he was out of town and on a diet. The initial story in her head was that it was awful that her injury prevented doing something special before he left, that it was sad he was alone on his birthday, and that they couldn't even do something fun when he returned because of the diet. But then she changed the story. Without the accident they wouldn't have shared all the sweet moments as he tenderly helped her. He now had well-earned quality time for himself, and a trim waistline was a hundred times better than a piece of cake! Do you see how stories can be changed? Be smart: tell great stories to yourself!

Recovered Perfectionist. Perfectionism is not about *what* is done; it's about *how* and *why* things are done. For example, extreme organization to achieve better function and more joy is different than harried organization to impress. Meticulous attention to performance quality for the joy of improvement is different than meticulous attention to performance quality in the pressured hope of being more highly esteemed, such as not letting your team or parents down. Problems surface when quality isn't about product, but about proving worth (even if just a molecule is directed toward proving worth). Wacky overdrive is a sign of perfectionist triggers and an underlying concern of "not being good enough." A "recovered perfectionist" examines *how* and *why* things are done in order to ensure that healthy things are backed by healthy reasons. Be smart: consider how and why.

Take It Down a Notch. As stated earlier, high emotion slows and/or shuts down the thinking parts of the brain. Some believe that emotions rule and nothing can be done. But in controlled therapy sessions, individuals are sometimes asked to deliberately increase emotion. Why? This shows that emotion can be regulated. Lowering emotion *just one notch* facilitates creative problem solving. Higher level thinking kicks in. So why not lower emotion more than just a notch? This tends to backfire. So taking emotion down just one notch avoids both suppression of emotion and over-expression of emotion. It gets the brain working again. Be smart: take emotion down a notch.

Challenge, Counter, Credit! At some point negative self-talk invades the brain, and it's all too easy to believe it. But most negative self-talk is either completely untrue or ridiculously imbalanced. Sometimes it can be downright brutal. You have as much right to kick out the hecklers in your head as a security officer does to kick out hecklers in a quiet concert or testing center. Most negative thoughts deserve an outright boot. But in cases where there might be some truth, 1) *challenge* negative thoughts, 2) *counter* them, and 3) give yourself *credit.* For example: Challenge: am I really incapable or is this harder? Counter: I'm actually doing great in a very difficult situation! Credit: in any event I deserve to be treated respectfully as I grow. Many times what looks like regression is actually progression. Often steep learning curves are not initially recognized. Be smart: challenge, counter, and give yourself credit.

Balance. A university coach with an amazing record was asked his secret. He said, "I don't over-train my athletes." Later, comparisons revealed that his program had more recovery and personal time than most. The coach expected *deep* commitment during practice, but he also expected his athletes to have balanced lives. Life balance is important and no one can do it for you. If you're pressured by those who do not understand the importance of balance, it's even more important to take responsibility to balance your own life. Balance is fluid, requiring daily adaptation. Balance is not an excuse to avoid preparation, but rather a means to more effectively enhance preparation. Be smart: be balanced.

Everything. One way of determining if life is balanced is the "everything" test: a time for everything and everything in its time; a place for everything and everything in its place; a budget for everything and everything in its budget. Management of time, belongings, and finances is a pretty good test as to whether life is balanced. When life is unbalanced these things will start to slip. Sometimes there's a belief that accomplishing amazing things in one area of life compensates for neglect in other areas. This is not true. Of course, there are differences in circumstances and personalities, and there's no need for perfectionism. Nevertheless, if these three things are significantly out of whack, there are probably issues to consider. It may be wise to carve some time to systematically ground yourself. Improvement is beneficial, even if it takes time to reorder. Balance increases core strength. It increases overall ability and resiliency through stable grounding. Be smart: consider "everything."

No Benefits Please. When tempted to cut things from the schedule it can be helpful to ask a simple question, "Do I want the benefits of doing this?" If the answer is yes, act accordingly. The brain is hard-wired to pull back. This trick can help engage the prefrontal cortex to move forward.

Don't Be So Responsible. Being responsible is a positive thing; being overly responsible is not. There are many ways to be overly responsible. For example, a performer has three responsibilities to an audience: prepare, give best effort, and graciously appreciate. Did you ever consider that the audience has these same responsibilities toward performers: prepare, give best effort and graciously appreciate? The same is true toward other situations like employers/employees and friendships. Recognizing others' responsibilities isn't to change them; it's to change you. There are many situations where taking too much responsibility for others' reactions can tip the scales in unhealthy ways causing anxiety. Boundaries may be needed. Be smart: don't be so responsible.

Abandon Embarrassment. Is it possible to choose to never be embarrassed? Sure! Some people fall in the trap of thinking that embarrassment proves they are sorry or that something unexpected went wrong. But often others don't even know there's a mistake unless broadcast through embarrassment. When a situation can't be hidden, a sheepish reaction tends to enhance sympathy, but this is different than shame. Sidestep shame. If preparation was inadequate, set a goal to fix the problem; if preparation was adequate and something weird happened, let it go. It's okay to expect respect, even if mistakes are made. Embarrassment and shame are negative emotions that can shut down the brain. Not being ashamed (even if someone is shaming you) increases core strength. If someone is shaming you, it's a reflection on them not you. Set a mental boundary, and while you're at it, consider if you're taking responsibility. If not, step up to responsibility rather than cower to the shame. It's more productive. Be smart: abandon embarrassment.

Lower Expectations. Does that sound funny when trying to improve outcomes? But expectations increase pressure. Some even say that expectations are premeditated disappointment. There's no ability to control an audience, judge, scout, adjudicator, or client. Focusing on things that cannot be controlled causes *unsure* feelings. Focus on things that can be influenced like achieving an improvement goal. *Changing* expectations can feel like *lowering* expectations. Why? There's less pressure, and that's good! Be smart: lower (change) expectations.

Never Lose. One coach related that her son lost a major sporting event and was ready to quit. Her response was that you either win or learn; the only time you can lose is when you quit. I would add that winning isn't about the score or outcome. Winning is about accomplishing private goals and learning (so it's possible to win even if you "lose"). If learning has taken place, it's always a win! And those wins add up. There's an easy way to never lose, always learn. Be smart: focus on learning.

Blast Past Procrastination. As you know, outcome anxiety can start *long before* a performance and affect preparation. (If you experience this, you know it's hard.) Pushing forward without considering feelings is likely to compound problems and affect quality. So take a second to ask, "what about this seems too hard," "why do I feel unsure of successfully handling this situation," or "why the resistance?" This takes only seconds, but it addresses anxiety and can magically get things rolling. Then get to work. (Repeat as needed.) Procrastination is often related to perfectionism, so also check out *how* and *why* things are done. Be smart: understand procrastination.

Reverse Procrastination. This is a tool to combat perfectionism and procrastination. Start preparations immediately, but *deliberately* do only 80% of your best and 80% of the task. Why? It takes the pressure off. No preparation is an "F", but 80% is a "B." Any way you look at it, you're ahead. If there's time later, the last 20% can be finished. When I first learned this strategy, I had a speaking engagement covering new material. I tried the strategy and prepped "80%" immediately. As things turned out, I didn't have any more time later. But the initial prep ended up about 95%. I didn't realize it because there was so much less pressure! Be smart: procrastinate—in reverse.

Time to Time. If overwhelmed, try breaking big things up into smaller tasks and pitting yourself against time. Stop watches aren't just for athletes. One day, long before I read research supporting this tactic, I was *not* excited at the prospect of housework. The to-do list created dread in my head. On a whim, I timed how long it took to make my bed: ten seconds. What! Seriously? I couldn't believe that a ten-second job dragged me down. Research shows that a lot of us do that. In fact, freaking out about tasks often takes more time than completing them! How smart is that? "Today I think I'll double my workload with some excellent freaking!" This problem can be easily taken care of by timing tasks. There are several ways. Time the task, and next time try to beat the time. Set a timer, see how many tasks can be accomplished in the allotted time, and stop when the timer goes off. Time two people doing the same task and have a friendly competition. Timing can make personal and professional tasks more enjoyable. Be smart: time.

Work. Don't Worry! Save the worry for after most of the work has been done. The worst part of any task is right before starting. Worry shuts down the brain, so reverse worry. *Worry after, not before.* Jump right in. Keep your brain functioning. You can always worry later if there's still a "need." Be smart: work; don't worry.

MY Best Rewards Club. Set small goals and reward them, and don't skip the word "small." The whole point is to rack up as many successes as possible and reward *each.* There are many types of rewards like voraciously checking off a list, soaking in some sunshine, reading a book, or giving yourself a victory fist high in the air. Maximize enjoyment and recognize achievements. Be smart: honor yourself.

Five Seconds to Success. Research shows there's about a 5 second lapse between success and failure. Those who notice a beneficial idea and act within five seconds, have a huge edge over those who don't. Another version of this is "act on first promptings." This concept overcomes emotional drag. (A reverse benefit of understanding this concept is to deliberately delay action five sections when an idea is *not* beneficial. Strategize, like move a candy dish off your desk and into another room to create effort and delay.) Consider your goals and the underlying resistance or lure that might occur. Be smart: win the first five seconds.

"Enslave" Yourself. Remember, the right hemisphere of the brain is happy to take over routine tasks. It can be used to create an internal "personal assistant" to keep you on track. The word "habit" has gotten a bad rap because habits can be hard to break, but that's the point! A good habit is as hard to break as a bad one! Good habits can propel a person forward. The more that tasks are done in a routine way like the same day, same time, or same place, the more habits can take over. And parents, or those with other jobs that have frequent interruptions, adapt by doing things in the same *order.* This also builds habits but is flexible regarding the time interruptions. And don't forget things like the habits of thinking positively or expressing gratitude. Be smart: "enslave" yourself to good habits.

Go Play. Part of productivity is taking time to play. It rejuvenates the body, enhances creativity, resets the mind, increases productivity, and assists problem solving. Downtime is an important part of self-care. But play is subjective. What is work to one person may be play to another. A medical professional who enjoys fixing cars would have a different perspective on this task than a mechanic. You are the only one who knows what play is for you. When you find it, you know because it's *fun.* (When possible, select an occupation that's fun.) Be smart: go play!

Be Selfish. It's nice when others support you, but support from others can never make up for a lack of inner support. Many times support from others is chased when a lack of inner support is the real problem and could be immediately obtained. Inner support is tied to intrinsic worth, self-respect, boundaries, and personal bests. Sometimes there is concern that self-support is selfish. But respect keeps selfishness in check (because part of respect is "I won't walk on you"). So go ahead, be selfish. Be kind and support yourself. There are lots of people you can treat with kindness, but the most important one is you! Choose the power of showing up for yourself. Be smart: be "selfish."

This chapter was filled with tips to improve outcome and enjoyment. Don't just endure, enjoy! Find tricks that work. Strengthen your core by failing and other smart things.

Next up, the ultimate in ability...

Summary

There are several skills that are smart and increase productivity. Little changes shift force to fun. The most important person to treat with kindness is you. Don't just endure, enjoy! Find tricks that work.

Case Study

RaNae looked at the work list and felt overwhelmed. But she knew better than to let apprehension sink in. Out came her stopwatch app and the race was on! She triumphantly checked off items. Going at lightning speed not only moved her forward faster, her mind was more clear—she was pretty sure it had to do with the train-your-brain stuff she'd heard about. The last item on the list wasn't due until next week. It was almost time to go but she knew that sticking it out could make a big difference. She broke the task into sections, tackled the first small section, checked it off, and left work on time. She was the champion of the work list. Wahoooo, cheers, applause! She took a victory lap down the hall and out the building! Now to go home and play...

Empower yourself

Work harder, or...work smarter.

Fast-Track ReflACTION:

1) How could you increase your success by routinely planning to fail; how can changing your stories help?

2) Which of the anti-procrastination skills could be most fun and beneficial to; why?

3) Which of your three "everything" areas need the most attention, what other skill/s listed may help you improve it; what might be the benefits?

27
Core Integrity

Some think that peak "flow in the zone" is the Mount Everest of performance outcomes. But there is something even better: core integrity. It unlocks peak flow and more. Core integrity isn't optimal performing; it's optimal *being*. Everyone talks about how to get optimal performance, and no one talks about how to get optimal being. But optimal *being* is where optimal *performance* comes from. This book's concepts unlock inner power. The skills help, but they only go so far.

If there's a gap between your current self and your better self, it can be felt. Narrowing the gap changes the core. Growth isn't stressful perfectionism or extrinsic worth. It's not impossible goals or discouragement. It's core awareness and mindfulness. Tuning in improves everything.

Being genuine, responsible, non-controlling, intrinsic, reasonable, respectful, and letting boundaries do their job produces a tough, reliable, emotionally-safe performance core. Internal power flows toward the person without effort. It's not that the world suddenly changes. Integrity changes you. This is real power; the rest is an illusion.

Most performance psychology deals with control. But control over skills, control over what others think, or control over self all have a common element—control. Power emerges when control is banished. Is this an abandonment of performance skills, social awareness, or self-restraint? No! It means it's more powerful to "trust your practice and practice your trust" than to exert control over skills; it's more powerful to "share rather than compare"; it's more powerful to "understand and integrate" the inner self than to force and control the inner self. These higher approaches toward performance preparation, social interaction, and self-control yield higher ability. The *need to control* limits ability. The idea is not to ignore, coerce, or force; it's to *understand*.

Hopefully there have been clear paradigm shifts, *but a molecule of control or self-deception* can still muddy and weaken. Control is ingrained in our culture, at least control of self if not subtle control of others. (Performance anxiety is about control of outcome.) Some literature advocates shifting from things that can't be controlled to things that can. But ultimately *all* control should be eliminated. It *IS* more powerful to "trust your practice and practice your trust" than to exert control over skills; more powerful to "share rather than compare"; and more powerful to "understand and integrate the inner self" than to force and control the inner self.

Control assumes that something needs to be coerced into compliance or agreement. This is manipulation. Even minuscule amounts are damaging. Control offers an illusion of strength and inner safety. Integrity unlocks true strength and inner safety. *That's* when there's full core power. This level of emotional safety *literally* increases neurological and physiological function.

It takes courage to let go of control. It's like jumping off a cliff. Why is it hard to admit when wrong, take responsibility, say "I'm sorry," confront respectfully, initiate needed change, express genuine gratitude, give full support, or focus only on growth rather than awards? Vulnerability. It can feel emotionally unsafe. But ironically it's the place of maximum safety. This isn't reckless vulnerability without boundaries. It's strong, responsible, respectful vulnerability within a core framework. It's a gift given to self. It takes emotional IQ and skills. Relinquishing control can't be faked.

So how do you know when manipulation dissipates, boundaries are adequate, control is relinquished, and integrity genuine? *You KNOW.* It's distinctly different. Others' judgment becomes irrelevant. Self-criticism melts. Effort increases without force. This inner change is similar to science-fiction movies with an energized barrier between worlds. There's a distinct difference between feeling the strength of an energized wall and slipping through the energized barrier into a new amazing world.

Most anxiety information goes to the wall. Why stop? Why not step into the other world? Valuing intrinsic worth, eliminating brain shorting, shifting from manipulation, sensing deeper gratitude, deliberate neuroplasticity, etc. touch the wall and draw energy. There's noticeable improvement. But a person may still be in the old self-conscious world attempting to control outcomes and others' perceptions. When core skills combine with core integrity, another world opens. It's there for the taking, but inaccessible without relinquishing control and focusing on integrity.

Stepping through isn't difficult but it does require depth. For example, one student questioned: why am I afraid to take this ACT test? *I might not do well enough.* Why does that matter? *I might not go to a good college.* Why does that matter? *It may affect my success.* Why does that matter? *It may affect whether I'm worth loving.* Jackpot! When the core concern is known, superfluous things can be bypassed: *I choose to love myself. And I'll put in my best effort regardless of the test outcome.* Do you see the shift to intrinsic worth, integrity and personal responsibility? This core strength gives power back to you. Fear diffuses power and scatters thinking. Core integrity collects power and focuses thinking.

An employee got news of a boss dismantling his work in publicly humiliating ways. The employee was devastated. He questioned: Why is this situation so difficult? *I feel tremendous rejection.* Why does that matter? *I have nothing to show for my work.* Why does that matter? *I feel looked down on.* Why does that matter? *I don't feel respected.* Jackpot! He hit the core concern. *He determined that he was important, if only to himself.* This gave him perspective, courage to address problems, ability to use respectful boundaries, and ultimately, confidence to look for a better job when efforts to resolve problems were disregarded. Taking care of the core steadies many things.

Most core concerns are ignored instead of explored. Why? There's a fear of being overwhelmed, especially with guilt and shame. But guess what? You deserve respect 100% of the time. *A person with the courage to examine and fix problems deserves the most respect of all.* Ultimately, whether others applaud or curse, self-applause is the only reaction that matters. Core integrity sustains with or without recognition from others. Genuine core strength is inherently stable.

Some try to fake core integrity. Integrity means "sound, unimpaired, perfect condition." A bridge with integrity can withstand the elements swirling around it as it reliably performs its function. What if a bridge only *looked* like it had integrity? Integrity is as important for a performer as for a bridge. Another definition of integrity is "the state of being whole, entire, adherence to moral and ethical principles, and undiminished." Doesn't this also describe an ideal core self?

Fake integrity does not yield core power. It's impossible to control and not control at the same time. It's impossible to manipulate and not manipulate at the same time. It's impossible to practice carefully and practice sloppily at the same time. It's impossible to have extrinsic worth and intrinsic worth at the same time. It's impossible to subtly bully and genuinely support at the same time. It's impossible to compare and not compare at the same time. It's impossible to engage in an addiction and not engage at the same time. It's impossible to disrespect and respect at the same time. It's impossible to be unaware and aware at the same time.

Real core power comes from real core integrity. At any given moment a person has core integrity or doesn't. If it's lost, it's regained by taking responsibility to make the necessary adjustments. So awareness *in the moment* is important.

Core integrity melts the dysfunctional crutches of comparison, pride, flattery, "kissing up", prejudice, subtle bullying, positioning, manipulation, enabling, quick fixes, group emotional abuse, control, and all the other quick-fix maneuvers. They are no longer needed. Emotional safety is stable (or if shaken, the restoration tools are known). This is stepping through the energy barrier. A rock-solid core radiates from the inside out. Paradoxically, self-love and self-value become abundant without seeking them from others.

Core knowledge is the power that unlocks ability. It is also the power that supplies *sustainability* and *stability*. No matter what heights are achieved, you will decline if you live long enough. Moments in the limelight, whether short or long, will eventually fade. "Olympic depression" can last for years, talents change, new competitors surface, markets evolve, injuries occur, life happens...and old age comes to all. A rock-solid core is beneficial not only in improving performance but in managing when spotlights shift and performance takes an irreversible decline.

So we come full circle. Suzie was afraid of monsters under her bed. Her fear automatically melted when she understood. There are different performance monsters described throughout this book. The information provided dissipates "monsters" and leads to core integrity. The acquisition and maintenance of core integrity is not a one-time deal. It's a lifetime pursuit. It's also a rock-solid gift you give yourself that provides emotional safety, awesome brain function, increased performance ability, improved relationships, and deep respect. The times that you have it, you *know*. Strengthen yourself through core integrity.

Next up, core power and leadership...

Summary

Peak flow in the zone is not the Mount Everest of performance; core integrity is. Core integrity isn't optimal performing; it's optimal *being*. Core integrity requires going deep enough to truly understand. Everyone talks about how to get optimal performance, but no one talks about optimal being—but optimal being is where optimal performance comes from. Integrity changes you. Control (of self or others) muddies understanding and ultimately limits ability. A clear focus on the core self unlocks an internal power that flows to you without compulsion. Core integrity can't be faked. The distinct change is like stepping into a new, amazing world. In this world, self-love and self-value become abundant without effort. Core integrity radiates from the inside out. Every person has access to the power of core integrity; it's there for the taking. Core integrity powerfully focuses thinking. Knowledge is the power that unlocks ability and supplies sustainability and stability. Everyone declines; a solid core provides internal strength in all stages of life. Core integrity is a lifetime pursuit. Suzie was afraid of monsters; her fear automatically melted when she understood. Core integrity is a rock-solid gift you give yourself. It yields emotional safety, awesome brain function, increased performance ability, improved relationships, deep respect, and intrinsic worth. When you have it...you *know*.

Case Study

A guest pianist, Marvin Goldstein, traveled across the nation to play for an enthusiastic, packed crowd in a huge university theater in California. The crowd cheered and clamored for encore after encore. The next night, he donated a free concert in another community. Though extensively advertised, the hall was empty except two people and one family who had driven a distance to see both concerts. The nearly empty building seemed cavernous and the attendees wondered if the concert would be cancelled or cut short. At the appointed time, Mr. Goldstein stood in his tuxedo and eagerly said, "Oh good! This means we can get to know each other! Come on stage where it's easier to see!" His virtuoso concert rivaled the night before, but also included personal touches. He addressed each person by name. He used their phone numbers as melodies in complicated improvisations and effortlessly combined their favorite songs into hilarious musical arrangements.

163

Afterward, the children got an autographed picture. It provided inspiration as they became skilled musicians. Why were both concerts powerful? Core integrity.

Empower Yourself
Reactive control, or...proactive integrity.

Fast-Track ReflACTION
1) Why is ultimate *being* more important than ultimate performance?
2) Why does abandoning control provide more "control"?
3) What obstacles stand in the way of core integrity; what benefits might be experienced from addressing obstacles?

28

Effective Leadership

The previous chapters were for performers. This chapter is for current or future leaders. It's one thing to perform well; it's another to inspire others. Leading is the crowning achievement and culmination of skill. Quality leadership is a powerful force. This chapter prepares future leaders and assists current leaders to harness that force while being realistic about the demands on leaders.

The most common factor in underachievement is anxiety. It's the most significant, fastest growing problem in education and other organizations. It's the underlying cause of discipline problems, illnesses, self-inflicted and accidental injury, substance abuse, emotional problems, eating disorders, insecurity, loss of pleasure, inability to think well, absenteeism, and dependence. Knowledge helps leaders avoid these problems and unlock potential in themselves and those they lead.

Leaders don't just supervise skill execution. They establish emotional environments. Environments accelerate or diminish peak ability. The principles introduced in this chapter apply to any leadership relationship. For simplicity teacher/student is used, but these principles also apply to coach/team, employer/employees, parent/child, etc. Consider your current or future roles.

When students ask for help with anxiety, a common response is, "Just get over it!" Ultimately this is true. But it's like giving third-graders an algebra problem and saying, "Just do it!" Even the brightest will likely fail. But with the right support most could succeed. The same is true regarding outcome anxiety and flow/zone development. Support doesn't mean pandering, wasting precious time, or reducing expectations. In fact, time is saved, ability increased, and higher expectations met. Research shows that ability *immediately* improves when anxiety is addressed. So why doesn't this happen more often?

Anxiety weeds people out of a field. For example, a person with science anxiety probably won't end up a scientist. Career choices are significantly influenced by anxiety. A teacher with little anxiety might naturally think that student anxiety is no big deal and not address it. There can even be inaccurate judging regarding a student's intent and feelings. A teacher may assume that a student is faking, pandering, or not working hard enough. This increases the problem. However, even when teachers sincerely address anxiety there can be unexpected issues.

A "teaching gap" phenomenon can happen. If a teacher's minimum anxiety is 0 and maximum is 4, but a student's minimum is 6 and maximum is 9, when the student seeks advice for "bad" anxiety, the teacher understandably gives advice appropriate for level-4. But this doesn't even address the student's *minimum* anxiety, let alone the maximum, and neither the teacher nor the student realizes it! Also, there are types of problematic anxiety that are not recognized without training. So teachers and students may not comprehend the *scope*, let alone the cure! This can be hard on both, especially on leaders who care.

Those who don't have anxiety must work as hard to understand it as those who do have anxiety must work to overcome it. Education and empathy are needed. Empathy may be easier than realized. For example, leaders often experience *unsure feelings* when asked how to eliminate anxiety! Additionally, empathy crosses over fields; a teacher who has no problem performing but is insecure doing something else like technology might consider those feelings when helping a student challenged by performance anxiety.

Feelings of incompetency can shut down the brain. (Imposter syndrome is common even in highly competent, admired leaders.) Anxiety and stress *literally* burn out energy. Have you felt depleted when grades are due, business reports are compiled, hiring or firing, or conducting auditions or tryouts? Leaders feel the effects of anxiety. Usually when a person says they're "burnt out" they *literally* are. There is a physiological depletion. This can happen in teachers and students. Understanding this is important in preventing long-term problems.

Support of self is as important as support of others. Leaders also need to feel loved, accepted, appreciated, secure, valued and capable. It's difficult to help others if feeling inadequate or burnt out. Avoid the epidemic of stress-related burnout.

Imperfection is okay and so are needs. Awareness and acceptance of self indirectly enhances the ability to respond to others. Genuine attention to both personal and interpersonal needs can head off burnout and even rejuvenate.

Dissatisfaction is also a form of anxiety. Usually someone becomes overwhelmed and blames others. There can be such certainty that problems are due to another person that the real causes and solutions are never considered. A leader may do this to others, but often it's the other way around. Anyone overwhelmed is experiencing outcome anxiety. They're unsure of coming out okay. Brains shut down and quick fixes are thrown around. Solvable problems feel unsolvable. (It's hard to do things without the brain.)

Others' dissatisfaction can nullify the effectiveness of even qualified, dedicated leaders. Others' dissatisfaction can increase stress for all and result in potential triangulation. For example, children can be caught between loyalty to a parent and a teacher. Triangulation problems can also happen between co-workers and supervisors, or teammates and coaches. Wise leaders recognize that dissatisfaction is an anxiety and they look for the real problems.

Usually dissatisfaction can be resolved, and this is best. But when honest, diligent effort does not resolve lingering problems other action may be necessary such as a strong boundary, especially if there's scapegoating. When a damaging, dysfunctional situation is ignored, the result is "kind manipulation" at best and outright emotional abuse at worst. Even if a situation is only damaging to one side, core energy is drained. It's not okay. Working through difficult situations requires awareness, honesty, and knowledge.

Accurate information is essential. Most anxiety research is new. The best information is only five or ten years old. Dedicated leaders deserve a shout-out for moving information forward so well, especially since even positive change is initially stressful. Relevant information has expanded to multiple fields.

Initially it was not known that different performance-based anxieties were caused by the same thing (*unsure*-of-coming-out-okay). Now that this is known, the research from multiple fields suddenly provides a more powerful response. This combined response has evolved. Some developments even required new medical inventions! Only recently has endocrinology, neuroscience, biofeedback, and other fields jumped in to support anxiety intervention. Valuable information has grown exponentially. But it's hard to keep up in one field, let alone multiple fields. Those that take time to learn deserve praise.

There are many things that teachers, coaches, directors, and executives can do to reduce anxiety. Small things can have a big impact like supportive comments, reflective questions, or even jotting down team-related anxiety observations. Some strategies will be mentioned in this chapter, others can be found in Appendix C. Attempting everything would certainly cause anxiety! So be selective, a few things may speak to you or the information may spark even better ideas.

In general, anxiety management includes breaking big tasks into smaller, manageable ones; providing a structured, predictable, positive environment; providing challenges without crushing workloads; and guiding toward effective practice/preparation. It also includes instilling hope. Sharing anxiety information is *very* empowering. Students change as they understand things like neuroplasticity, the ability to affect body reaction, the power of gratitude in enhancing body function, the power of positive interpretation of events, the power of boundaries, the ability to choose a focus, the freedom of intrinsic worth, the empowerment of non-perfectionist goals, the ability to overcome mental and physical drag, the power of respect and taking responsibility, etc.

In short, effective leadership empowers. This is particularly important when others' vision and experience is lacking. Empowerment is not time consuming. It's *how* a leader does what they're *already* doing. In the case study below, anxiety management took *no* extra time but completely changed the outcome. In fact, it saved time.

You're probably already doing some anxiety management. Deeper understanding maximizes the benefits. When anxiety surfaces an easy response is to ask simple questions: "How can I help you? What about this seems too hard? Are you okay? How do you feel about this? What do you think is possible? What do you suggest?" (If they say "I don't know" say, "If you did know, what do you think?") Research shows that simple, genuine questions can *immediately* improve ability without additional instruction or practice. Sounds good, doesn't it? Quick. Easy. Powerful. You're busy. It's nice when easy things work.

There's another beneficial strategy. Focus on the mental or physical *energy* while producing movement or thought. This bypasses anxiety and taps into flow/zone. This works whether the task is mental or physical. A test taker can sense thinking sensations. A musician or athlete can sense the energy sensations required in quality movement. I have tried this with students, musicians, and athletes. It is powerful. Research strongly supports it.

Another way to avoid problems is to realize that fear is contagious. It can spread in a team, class, or workplace. Heading it off pays off. Reframe perceptions in positive ways like, "Fear means your body is prepping to support you! This is good!" Counter negative talk with positive intervention. Challenge "I don't know if we can do this" with "What a great challenge! We've got this." Or counter their "I can't" with "Not yet!" Teach others to counter their negative talk. "I'll never get it" to "I've done tough things, I'll get this." I've actually assigned written countering as homework and graded it to increase core strength. It's powerful.

Some leadership methods reduce ability and increase anxiety. For example, rewards may seem beneficial, but they shift internal motivation to external (even in those previously motivated internally). Rewards reduce flow/zone and enjoyment. If discontinued, there's motivational fall-out. Extrinsic rewards reduce intrinsic pleasure. They undermine deep learning and effort. They only help when intrinsic motivation is already low and wouldn't be undermined anyway. Similarly, praise is beneficial when it's unexpected and sincere. All this research is very helpful in providing direction. Some is counterintuitive, such as the effect of rewards.

Intrinsic/My Best environments are more effective than Extrinsic/THE Best environments. The leader determines the environment. Sometimes honors are used to prove a leader's self-worth. This is detrimental to the leader and those they lead. Honors aren't a problem; honors *to prove worth* is a problem. Let's face it, honors are fun! But they're more fun when achieved through intrinsic means. It is impossible to face two directions at the same time—at any given moment a program is either intrinsic or extrinsic.

Extrinsic programs often have these problems: expectations and consequences are unclear, individuals are coerced, expectations and respect fluctuate, subtle bullying is evident, comparisons and gossip are common (between people in the program or about competitive programs.)

Intrinsic programs have these elements: Respect is valued. Subtle bullying, gossip, and comparisons are discouraged. There are clear expectations, and they can be high. Consequences are enforced equally, respectfully, and dependably. In an intrinsic environment, individuals can be pushed hard without damage. Similar expectations in an extrinsic environment can crush.

Intrinsic worth is not wimpy. It is rock solid and safe. A leader's job is to set up a challenging, clear structure and then enforce fair consequences all the way across, respecting everyone equally—the third-string to the first-string. All are valued. This not only strengthens the third-string, it strengthens the first-string. Why? Trust. Trust establishes emotional safety. Remember, *emotional safety is not optional*. When there's safety there's more emotional and physical energy to attack goals. This isn't just opinion. *It's science*. Emotional safety is important.

One year my high school daughter and I took advanced dance classes at one studio that specialized in one type of dance and then traveled across town to take class from a second studio which specialized in another type of dance. Both studios were nationally ranked and placed students in top professional situations. At the first studio the technique was superb. But the classes were ridged, mistakes were shunned, and coldness was common. Initially I thought the underlying discomfort was because I was an adult in a class of high school students. But I later learned that students in other classes also felt uncomfortable.

The second studio was a blast. Music blared, dance combinations were insanely difficult, mistakes were laughed at and second attempts encouraged. I loved the teacher and the class. Then one day it dawned on me that most of the class also drove over from the first studio. *The girls' personalities changed depending on the studio*. That's the day I realized the emotional power of leadership! The second teacher was an *expert* in teaching students how to make mistakes, unlock ability, and reduce stress. I'm sure that's why she consistently produced champions in record time. Too much emphasis on perfect execution stifles and sets the stage for subtle bullying. Of course, there must be discipline. But the second teacher did not shun mistakes *in order* to eliminate them more quickly. Good leaders positively encourage failing. They balance discipline and fun.

Leadership matters. The leader sets the tone. I would not have allowed my daughter to attend the first studio if I knew then what I know now about the brain. Children have more impressionable brainwaves and the effect on self-esteem can be long-lasting. The first studio lost many students. I found them in other studios when I decided to leave. The first studio was a good program. They just didn't understand anxiety and it cost them a lot of revenue. I don't condemn them. I made similar mistakes. It's easy for leadership styles to be hit and miss without solid information.

This chapter's case study comes from my experience with two high-level piano students. The stories happened a few years apart—before and after I knew about anxiety management. Both students were preparing for the *exact* same adjudication on the same material, with basically the same amount of preparation, levels of anxiety, and personalities. The first incident left both the student and I depleted, discouraged and frustrated; the second left us invigorated, excited and enthusiastic. To be honest, I was *astounded* at the difference in them and me. Anxiety information matters. The case study is not exaggerated.

Leading is more fun when anxiety management is understood. Anxiety information works. Other leaders have experienced similar success. What impact will you have? You may become astounded, too. Choose to decrease outcome anxiety and increase everyday flow in the zone. Understand anxiety and use anxiety reducing concepts. Strengthen core power in yourself and others.

Boost core power, and bust anxiety!

Summary

Outcome anxiety management and consistent peak flow/zone are skills. Skill can be developed in others. This doesn't mean pandering, wasting time, or reducing expectations. Anxiety management information is new. Dedicated leaders deserve praise for spreading information. It took time for seemingly unrelated fields to combine and inventions to help. The importance of anxiety management was not initially understood. Anxiety weeds people out of a field, causing a possible "teaching gap." Those without anxiety have to work to understand it; those with anxiety have to work to overcome it. Leaders can feel incapable of successfully handling situations. Stressful anxiety literally *burns out* energy. This depletion can be felt. Anxiety management reduces burnout. Often leaders are already doing some anxiety management. Knowledge maximizes potential benefits. Certain questions can immediately reduce anxiety. Fear is contagious. It can be countered. Some common leadership methods increase anxiety—like most reward systems. Leaders who set up clear structures and apply them equally within a framework of intrinsic goals increase emotional safety. Trust increases the ability to improve. Leaders set the learning environment. Reducing student burnout reduces teacher burnout. Boost core power and bust outcome anxiety!

Case Study

These two situations were about five years apart. One was before I studied anxiety, the other after. These students were advanced high school piano students with similar personalities and preparation. A nationally certified adjudicator was sent from the state teachers' association to judge them on the exact same material.

At lesson, I asked the first student if she wanted to do the adjudication. She said yes. I asked why she stopped practicing. She averted her eyes and said she didn't know. She was overwhelmed, embarrassed and ashamed. I was exasperated and out of ideas. (Notice *my* anxiety?) I strongly encouraged practice and proceeded to help her stumble through as best I could. It was painful for both of us. She did not pass the adjudication and soon dropped out. I thought the situation was primarily due to her lack of preparation...until the second student.

At lesson, I asked him if he wanted to do the adjudication. He said yes. I asked why he stopped practicing. He averted his eyes and said he didn't know. He was overwhelmed, embarrassed and ashamed. I said, "I think I know why." He turned his lowered head to peer at me, expecting the worst. I said, "It's just a little performance anxiety." (Of course it was a lot of anxiety, but I was using recommended anxiety management intervention.)

I asked, "Do you feel capable of successfully handling this situation?" He said, "*NO!*" surprising even himself at the strength of his emotion. I said, "That's what I thought. But it's really no big deal. Research shows that ability is usually higher than it seems and that things improve immediately when anxiety is addressed. You think you're miles from success but you're probably only inches." I asked him to play the first scale. It was a *mess*. (I honestly didn't think he could pass, but I put trust in the research.) I said, "What was wrong with the scale?" He said, "Everything!"

I said, "Really? Let's see." He played again. It was still a *mess,* but he noticed a thumb cross problem and commented on it. (My reactions reduced his anxiety enough for his brain to work.) I said, "Okay, everything else can be wrong but not that cross." He played with 100% accuracy. It was slower than required, but accurate. I was shocked.

I summoned all my acting ability and smiled as if I expected this, "See, you're closer than you think." I explained anxiety and that it's easier to play with the brain. We continued. I interjected anxiety information. I said his procrastination was just anxiety and provided tricks to jump past it. He left invigorated. He practiced harder than ever and passed. He was elated...and so was I.

The story doesn't stop there. I had contact with the first student. I shared anxiety information and apologized for not knowing what to do earlier. After long avoidance, she began dabbling and now teaches music. Anxiety information matters.

Case Study

Mark heard complaints about his service behind his back. He reached out in a sincere attempt to resolve the situation. But his emails and phone messages were not reciprocated, let alone mutual problem-solving engagement offered. He made another attempt and left the door open. When there was still no response it was now a reflection on them not him. It took both sides for a solution. They either did not have the desire or the skills to resolve the situation.

Empower Yourself

Reasonably instructive, or...amazingly effective.

Fast-Track ReflACTION

1) How can you reduce stress and burnout as a leader?
2) What clarifications regarding rules, expectations, consequences, and support could empower you and your students? Are you consistent and fair?
3) What challenging things give you anxiety empathy?

Appendix A

Core Power Pro-Launch Pad:
Propel Progress

Practice or performance (circle one)　　　　　**Date:**
TYPE of performance (circle) Tests/Sports/Business/Performing Arts/Other:
Observed problem/s:

Last goal completed? (circle) **Yes/No**
Type of Goal: (circle) Performance Ability/Emotional IQ/Life Balance/Respect self/Respect Others/No manipulation/Take Responsibility/Other:
Goal:

5-Qs about the problem	Observations
What happens	
When	
Where	
Why	
How Much	

OBSERVATIONS today	Circle	
Worst ever quality	1 2 3 4 5 6 7 8 9 10	Awesome over-all quality
Incapacitating anxiety, Totally unsure	1 2 3 4 5 6 7 8 9 10	Great flow/zone, Totally sure
Focus on THE Best/ compare/Extrinsic	1 2 3 4 5 6 7 8 9 10	Focus on MY Best/share/ Intrinsic
Totally degraded others	1 2 3 4 5 6 7 8 9 10	Totally respected others
Totally belittled self	1 2 3 4 5 6 7 8 9 10	Totally respected self
Nada zip zero preparation/progress	1 2 3 4 5 6 7 8 9 10	Amazing preparation/ progress
Total manipulation of others	1 2 3 4 5 6 7 8 9 10	No manipulation of others
Awful. Hated it. Grudges dragging	1 2 3 4 5 6 7 8 9 10	Great! Fun! No inner reservations. Flow/Zone

REFLECTIONS	Comments
Thoughts/feelings effecting output	
Possible cause of positive/negative changes	
Patterns or helpful observations	
Input from leader/mentor/friend	

Appendix B
Resources for Help

Abuse indicates a lack of emotional coping skills. This can result in safety issues. Use care when confronting abusive people or those who may become so. It is appropriate to address abuse. Abuse is not healthy for the person abusing or being abused. Abuse is usually aimed at one person or a very few. This is why abuse goes unchecked—few see it.

Some think that abuse is limited to open aggression. This is not true. Abuse can also be cold, punitive, and withdrawn. Abuse can be carried out directly by the abusive individual, or indirectly through others who have been consciously or subconsciously influenced by the abusive individual. Both direct and indirect abuse is harmful. Both cause high emotion which shuts down the problem-solving parts of the brain. When this happens fight, flight or freeze reactions take over with little prefrontal cortex override to intervene toward stopping aggression. Problems feel bigger and solutions are more difficult to see.

Abuse is an effort to control, often to dysfunctionally maintain a sense of emotional safety. Abuse can dangerously escalate out of control. Abuse intervention should be carried out with the assistance of others, particularly those who are specially trained. Interacting respectfully, keeping emotion low, and building emotional safety are all helpful, but these should be done in conjunction with additional safety precautions and outside support.

The 100% respect rule does not apply in situations where there is physical danger. Do not hesitate to call 911 if feeling threatened or in danger. A false alarm is better than a fatal one (for both the abused and the abuser). When confronting abuse, work with licensed professionals and/or law enforcement and always have a safety plan in place. Assistance is available. However, please note that computer/phone use can be monitored by abusers. Take necessary precautions. For more information see:
http://domesticviolence.org/personalized-safety-plan
http://www.thehotline.org
1–800–799–7233 or TTY 1–800–787–3224.

Appendix C
Ideas for Leaders

This list of interventions is gleaned directly from research in performance, sports, education, and business. Watch out! It will be like taking a drink from a fire hydrant. However, it should reinforce current efforts and spark new ideas. Adapt as needed to your type of leadership:

Scaffold learning; challenges that are too high or too low increase anxiety. Avoid high stakes situations; have several small tests with one dropped instead of one big test. Avoid negative labels. Work toward policies that support effort. Encourage boundaries. Rethink impressive, crushing workloads like multiple high school AP classes, or 70 hr work weeks. Encourage emotional awareness. Validate ability. Educate regarding anxiety management/flow. Use eye contact, smiles, and contact like handshakes and slaps on the back. Minimize institutional overlapping due dates.

Place emphasis on progress rather than outcomes. Emphasize physical and emotional self-care. Teach exceeding *own* ability rather than others'. Encourage attention to the moment rather than the outcome; even positive thoughts about outcome can distract. Do *CPPro-LP* logs, journals of thoughts, or other performance anxiety records. Have experienced people mentor the less experienced. Emphasize group support rather than group competition. Encourage emotional IQ. Teach brain function. Encourage self-nurture and repair. Model emotional maturity. Assist preparation by breaking big tasks into smaller ones; build anxiety management into performance preparation or assignments. Avoid favoritism. Minimize last minute changes in/before performance. Do not shame those with anxiety.

Examine the structure of a performance. Recognize that ability can immediately and dramatically increase after addressing anxiety. Encourage MY Best goals. Provide smaller performances leading to an important big performance. Teach visualization. Mention emotional safety and the positive use of negative emotions. Encourage performing exactly what was practiced. Bring attention to the impact of interpersonal interaction. Provide close replicas of the performance situation. Assist in the structure of realistic, but challenging goals. Enforce rules; be unbiased.

Discourage subtle bullying and group emotional abuse. Consider formal and informal biofeedback. Set high expectations. Believe in performers. Encourage a "never perform, always practice" mentality by structuring time for goals/evaluation. Use mental practice.

Have clear expectations. Calculate change carefully; even positive change adds short-term stress. Support autonomy. Assume underachievement is at least partly due to anxiety. React slowly. Point out growth. Recognize that if high achievers start to crash it is likely tied to anxiety. Give task-directed feedback. Increase group bonding in meaningful ways; built genuine trust. Understand that silliness or apathy is often due to feeling overwhelmed. Recognize that attention to anxiety can reduce injury rates. Discourage expectations of a perfect performance. Intervene if a situation is likely to result in damaging failure. Have clear rules. Bolster confidence. Use relaxation and deep breathing. Foster intrinsic worth. Foster gratitude. Use boundaries instead of manipulation. Build in fun. Consider vulnerability to be a strength. Understand triggers and boundary explosions.

Build perspective. Consider deeper awareness regarding the reasons for and use of cue relaxation, massage, progressive muscle-group tensing/relaxing, medication, stretching, and adaptations of yoga. Systematically reverse imprinting. Realize that what is done to one is internalized by all. Encourage failure. Use mistakes to move forward. Be aware of mini-group culture. Blame problems on anxiety and express faith in ability, like "Just a few jitters, you'll get it." Teach imagery and implement it into pre-performance routines. Recognize that procrastination is usually anxiety; address anxiety and teach tricks to reverse procrastination. Avoid extrinsic rewards. Use rewards more than punishers. Bring attention to little successes. Avoid rumination. Praise self-regulation. Recognize approach avoidance. Teach thoughts of desired outcomes, rather than avoiding undesired ones. Realize avoidance or drop-out is frequently due to anxiety. Express gratitude.

Use neuroplasticity aggressively. Notice incongruent goals. Realize that outside anxiety can affect performance; an athlete with a paper due may not play as well. Plan multiple strategies for solving a single problem. Plan dopamine hits (unexpected pleasure reward) and oxytocin dumps (enjoyable socialization.) Patiently listen. Teach and encourage taking emotion back one notch. Build specific anxiety management strategies into daily and performance routines. Teach cognitive restructuring and reframing. Recognize that drugs, alcohol, behavior problems are usually tied to anxiety. Realize that addressing anxiety reduces almost all undesired behavior. Educate and encourage healthy glucose breaks. Have pre-performance routines and keep them. Build experience. Show respect.

In short, genuinely enjoy and esteem those you work with. Supporting others ultimately supports self. Outcomes improve.

Glossary of Terms

Several terms are unique to this book or slightly different than commonly used. This glossary is provided to clarify concepts. Page numbers are provided for just the main references of each concept.

Abuser—someone who subtly or overtly damages others to build self up; "I'll walk on you, you'll let me; this proves I'm better;" a symptom of extrinsic worth. 127, 129- 131, 135, 138, 177.

Amygdala—the emotional processing part of the brain; involved in automatic safety systems and fear. 80, 83, 89.

Appearance anxiety—apprehension associated with how a person appears to others regarding physical looks, possessions, education, job, other status; based on comparisons and extrinsic worth. 2,105- 109.

Artistry—the skill and ability to take an audience where you want without manipulation (an actor moving others to cry or laugh; an athlete bringing a crowd to their feet; a teacher inspiring understanding; a salesman accurately informing.) 64, 101- 103, 113, 115.

Awareness—accurate internal or interpersonal assessment; mindfulness regarding thoughts, feelings and other factors affecting internal or interpersonal well-being, especially when done in the moment. Pages throughout book.

Baseline—the physical and emotional norm that homeostasis seeks to achieve. 87- 90, 92- 93.

Be selfish—self-care, self-awareness. Taking responsibility so that interpersonal action is healthy and others aren't eventually burdened caring for you. 157.

Blanking—a type of brain short that indicates a lack of processing; usually no discomfort. 1, 27, 51, 53, 55, 57- 60.

Boundary—an if/then statement that is not intended to alter another person's behavior but to protect self emotionally and/or physically. 133, 135- 139, 141- 148, 154, 180.

Brain short—a brain micro-shutdown when thought processes are impeded, includes crunching, fogging, and blanking. 50, 52- 53, 55, 58- 60, 64, 160.

Catastrophic thinking—thinking of major or minor things that could go wrong; mental symptom of anxiety. 5, 27, 49, 63.

Causes (of anxiety)—subconscious or conscious concerns, usually regarding emotional safety. Pages throughout book.

Chakra—one of seven energy centers yoga philosophy; "cleared" to increase ability. 81, 84, 90, 91.

Choking—drop in performance; often due to shifting mental processing from the right hemisphere to the prefrontal cortex. 9, 67- 69, 71.

Chooser—a non-manipulative person who expects and gives respect 100% of the time and uses boundaries; "I won't walk on you and you won't walk on me;" based on intrinsic worth. 134, 138.

Clean your side of the street—taking responsibility, especially to fix mistakes rather than defend intent. 143- 147.

Collecting data—noting factors, influences, and patterns affecting emotional well-being and ability. 23- 24, 37- 40.

Confidence—a strong core; greatest protector against anxiety. Pages throughout book, 17.

Consequence—the protective "then" part of a boundary. 135- 137, 144, 169.

Core—emotional base, resilience, stability, inner awareness and emotional safety. Pages throughout book.

Core integrity—optimal *being* including non-manipulation, release of control, taking responsibility, protection through respectful boundaries, and complete intrinsic worth [see also "strengthen the core" and "core power"]. 159, 161- 164.

Core Launch Pad—[see *Core Power Pro-Launch Pad*]

Core Power Pro-Launch Pad (*Core Launch Pad* or *CPPro-LP*)— this book's companion workbook; proactive tool to observe and eliminate anxiety causes. 7- 8, 37- 40, 146.

Core power—skills, understanding, integrity, boundaries, non-manipulation, responsibility, and respect of self and others. Pages throughout book.

Core stamina—improved, strong emotional and physical ability through emotional IQ. 83.

CPPro-LP—[see *Core Power Pro-Launch Pad*]

Crunching—a type of brain shorting that causes discomfort in the prefrontal cortex. 27, 50- 53, 55- 59.

Defending intent—not admitting an unintended a mistake. 129, 145, 147- 148, 166.

Direct cause—a factor limiting performance that is not affected by past influences, like a simple lack of performance skills or information. 22- 24, 34.

Disconnection—lack of internal or interpersonal awareness of thoughts and feelings; usually due to ignoring or hiding un-lovable things. 16, 18, 51, 143.

Disrespect—infringement on another's emotional core safety; ma-nipulation. 134- 138, 148, 162.

Don't be responsible—avoiding over-responsibility and enabling. 154.

Edgy fear—helpful, supportive, positive amounts of adrenalin that prep for success. 25, 28- 29.

Eliminating anxiety—having the core skills, knowledge and aware-ness that emotional safety alarms are not needed. Pages throughout book.

Emotional cardioplasticity—changing heart responses through specific exercises to increase ability. 80, 83.

Emotional IQ—ability to secure an emotionally safe environment and meet primary needs of self and others. 111, 115, 144, 146, 160.

Emotional safety—emotional awareness to sense and meet pri-mary needs, use boundaries, and maintain intrinsic worth. Pages throughout book, 111- 116.

Emotional warning—negative emotion, whether fleeting or over-whelming. 31, 55, 80, 112.

Emotional wound—an emotional trauma, whether miniscule or incapacitating. 112, 115, 128, 130- 131.

Enable/Enabler—a person that doesn't expect respect, helps an-other avoid responsibility (usually to feel better about self), a symptom of extrinsic worth. "I'll let you walk on me, and in time you'll see that I'm good." (I'll stop abuse by allowing it.) 129, 131, 135, 138.

Energy state—the intensity and quality of an emotion. 191- 192.

Heart attacking—deliberate effort to increase ability through emotional strategies shown to affect the heart such as awareness, mindfulness, gratitude, service, and processing trauma. 79- 86.

High-level, high-road, or transformational thinking—mental processing not inhibited by anxiety, involves more pre-frontal cortex, synapse connections and richer memory stores. 76.

Homeostasis—the built-in mental and physical attempts to stay the same; usually a protection. 87- 88, 92.

Imposter syndrome—feeling that others would see a fraud if looking inside; feeling success is from luck and hiding unlovable parts of self. 2, 142, 147.

Imprinting—the effect of positive or negative emotion experienced when first learning a skill or subject which affects future learning in that skill or subject. 10- 13, 180.

Indirect cause—a factor limiting performance that is related to a past experience with that specific type of performance or task. 22- 24, 34.

Inseparables—the two parts to every performance that can't be separated: the performance material and anxiety management. 21- 24.

Inspiration—the ability to benefit, from others abilities; especially from things available through technology, without becoming damaged, distracted or discouraged. 12, 97- 98.

Internal infrastructure—skills and emotional IQ that create inner core strength. 187.

Intrinsic worth—self-worth based on innate, infinite worth as a human being; self-worth devoid of comparisons. 117- 120.

Judging—assuming someone's thoughts, feelings, and intent; a form of disrespect, and a sign of extrinsic worth. 33, 35, 69, 166.

Kind manipulation—being kind with the expectation of kindness in return. 113 114- 115, 167.

Kissing up—[see also "flattery"]. 112, 113, 134, 162.

Low-level, low-road or anxious thinking—mental processing inhibited by anxiety; mental processing that's rerouted away from the pre-frontal cortex, memory stored in a "lump", fewer synapse interconnections. 76.

Manipulation—exerting influence toward a desired outcome that yields personal benefit and/or violates another's personal autonomy, especially if it puts another down; continued effort to be understood when resisted; a symptom of extrinsic worth, dysfunctional emotional safety. 133- 150.

Measure up—an attempt to be good enough to deserve emotional safety and having primary needs met. 107, 117, 118, 133.

Medial prefrontal cortex—reasoning part of the brain that overrides initial fear responses from the amygdala. 80, 83.

Mental hygiene—awareness of thought content, thought construction, and positive use of neuroplasticity. 55, 56, 62, 63.

MY Best—self-improvement devoid of comparisons or rank; effort based on intrinsic worth. 121- 126.

Negative self-care—addictions, avoidance, distraction done instead of meeting primary needs or other needs. 122, 124, 143, 165.

Neuroplasticity—the ability to shape the brain and neurologically adapt to needs. 61- 66.

Never lose—learning from every situation; progressing regardless of outcome or rank. 155.

Not think—(don't overthink) not switching material from the right hemisphere to the left frontal lobe. 67- 72.

Never perform, always practice—the mental state of performing with a pre-determined goal; using an audience to test specific goals and ability; performance devoid of self-worth concerns. 151, 152, 180.

Occupational hazard (performance)—the potential detrimental effect of anxiety and stress on a performer's physical and mental health. 3, 17, 18.

Outcome anxiety ("unsure-of-coming-out-okay-anxiety")—any anxiety with the underlying fear of not coming out okay (such as performance or test anxiety); also, most apprehension, insecurity, procrastination, indecision, frustration, and unsure feelings. Pages throughout book.

Over-edgy—too much adrenalin response, usually from outcome anxiety; part of fear cycle. 25, 28, 29.

Overthink—switching material from the right hemisphere to the left frontal lobe, or an inability to mobilize due to perfectionism and procrastination. 51, 67.

Perfectionism—dysfunctional attempts to meet a primary need done to an extreme, whether done extremely well or extremely badly; often associated with procrastination. 27, 98, 103, 106, 108, 109, 152, 153, 155, 159.

Pigeon-hole thinking—failure to recognize the effect of anxiety on ability; believing that ability is set and unchangeable; usually involves low-level thinking when engaged in a difficult activity. 11, 13.

Power through—mindless, ignore emotional, physical or other needs; disconnection. 50, 74.

Prejudice—lack of respect for others, maneuvering for position, and judging; a symptom of extrinsic worth. 112, 162.

Pride—fake self-respect, maneuvering for position; a symptom of extrinsic worth. 122, 124, 134, 162.

Primary fear—subconscious or conscious concern regarding having primary emotional needs met; lack of emotional safety regarding primary needs. 16, 18, 22, 26, 107- 109, 118.

Primary needs (emotional)—feeling loved, accepted, appreciated, secure, valued, and capable. 17, 18, 107.

Proactive safety—setting and maintaining boundaries. 143.

Processing—understanding the influence of past experiences and intergenerational influences. Pages throughout book, 81-83, 85.

Procrastination—avoidance of action usually due to outcome anxiety, lack of skills, and/or perfectionism. 2, 9, 27, 29, 70, 71, 155, 172, 180.

Questions strategy—quick way to increase awareness and address anxiety; using questions to increase internal or interpersonal connection, such as: what about this is too hard; why the resistance; or what can I do to help? 143, 167, 168.

Quick Fix—disrespectful reactions that create a false sense of safety through fight, flight, freeze manipulation or avoidance such as anger, blame, withdrawal, fleeing, or indecision; associated with extrinsic worth. 131- 136.

Record—proactive observation and notation of anxiety influences. 37- 48.

ReflACTION -a term that combines reflection and action; the last part is capitalized indicating momentum in creating positive change. Pages throughout book, 7.

Respect—humble confidence, sense of worth, and profound dignity toward self and others in equal amounts; consistent civility; regard without consideration to ability, rank, appearance, messing up or measuring up; an essential element of intrinsic worth and boundaries. 127- 150.

Reverse Procrastination—deliberately doing 80% of preparation immediately, and 20% later, tasks feel easier due to less stress. 155, 180.

Rickety bridge—unsafe core, inadequate boundaries, disconnection; insufficient self-understanding and confidence. 1- 4.

Self-awareness—full mental engagement without diverted concerns toward emotional safety; a sign of intrinsic worth, emotional IQ, and true giving. Pages throughout book, 12, 23, 142, 144, 146, 147.

Self-bullying—disrespect to self; control and coercion rather than deeper understanding. 143.

Self-consciousness—a portion of attention directed toward emotional safety; a sign of extrinsic worth, and taking and/or needing something from others. 23, 142, 144, 146, 147

Self-deception—inaccurate internal or interpersonal assessment; not taking responsibility for actions (abuse), or taking too much responsibility (enabling); incorrect assessment of a situation, particularly when avoiding responsibility. 144, 160.

Shifting—switching material from the brain's right hemisphere to the left frontal lobe; overthinking. 67- 69, 71, 119, 125.

Side-tracking—unduly blaming a situation or person; not recognizing when a problem is caused by a trigger, avoidance of responsibility, or an inadequate boundary. 32.

Sit with emotion—feeling and observing negative emotion without further arousal, judgment, or taking action; listening to feelings without quick fixes, especially when vulnerable. 33- 34.

Strengthen the core—increasing awareness, maintaining intrinsic worth, developing emotional IQ, and improving other internal infrastructures; decreasing self-deception and manipulation; expecting and giving respect. Pages throughout book.

Stress—pressure, usually anxiety producing. Pages throughout book, 95.

Subtle bullying—subtle unspoken or spoken ill behavior intended to "put down" another person in order to build oneself up; often not consciously recognized; a symptom of extrinsic worth; defending intent; not taking responsibility. 127-132.

Subtle group emotional abuse—two or more people exhibiting ill behavior toward another person/s to "put them down" in order to build themselves up; usually communicated through unspoken body language and often not consciously recognized. 127-130, 162, 180.

Support—being sustain by someone knowledgeable and kind who sees and meets primary needs. 16, 18.

Symptom (of anxiety)—physical, mental, emotional or behavioral manifestations of fear. Pages throughout book.

Take it down a notch—slightly lowering emotion to improve brain function. 152.

Take responsibility—acknowledging the effect of one's actions and fixing problems, including unintended results, regardless of whether others do so and regardless of whether others are more at fault. 145- 148, 153, 160.

Teaching gap—the difference between teacher/student experiences, such as levels of anxiety; usually not recognized by teacher or student. 166, 171.

THE Best—effort based on extrinsic worth, comparisons, and rank. 121, 126.

Thought construction—focus on thought sensations rather than thought content. 149, 152, 159.

Trigger—a wave of emotion stronger than the situation merits; indicates unresolved subconscious concern and possible genetic influences. 31- 36, 87- 89, 92.

Trust—openness that's given when earned. 134, 138.

Understand—the level of awareness that eliminates anxiety in self and assists anxiety elimination others. Pages throughout book.

Unlearn—to uncover the underlying conscious and subconscious factors affecting behavior and feelings, especially regarding negative emotions. 9- 14.

Unlovable stuff—things hidden due to shame or stigmas. 16, 18, 142.

Unrelated cause—a factor affecting performance that is related to a past experience not related to the performance, usually a childhood experience. 22- 24, 34.

Unsure anxiety (or "unsure-of-coming-out-okay anxiety)—see "outcome anxiety". Pages throughout book, 2.

Unsure shifting cycle—increased shifting from the right hemisphere to the prefrontal cortex due to self-consciousness and fixing during performance; associated with "choking"; common in inexperienced performers. 88- 89.

User—a person who joins or ignores overt or subtle abuse to maintain a more favorable position; indirect subtle abuse; a symptom of extrinsic worth. 129, 131.

VIP security—[see also boundaries] providing oneself with personal boundaries and emotional safety; not being reckless or negligent regarding core internal safety. 135.

Endnotes

These endnotes provide both documentation and a synopsis of book concepts. Concepts are documented according to the chapter they first appear in the book, and only once. When similar concepts are reiterated in later chapters, please refer to previous chapter documentation.

Preface:

Enjoyable, accessible information makes assimilation easier and reduces associated anxiety problems: Ashcraft & Krause, 2007; Boucher & Ryan, 2011; Ely 1991; Fredrickson, 1998; Goswami, 2008; Hinton et al., 2008; Isen & Daubman, 1984; Isen, Johnson, Mertz & Robinson, 1985; Isen & Reeve, 2005; Jalongo & Hirsh, 2010; Kenny & Osborne, 2006; Leffingwell, 2001; Lenhart, Arafeh & Smith, 2008; Nezlek & Derks, 2006; Putwain, 2009; Reeve, 2015; Tugade, et al., 2004; Wigfield & Eccles, 1989; Yondem, 2007; Young et al., 2012.

Chapter 1: Rickety Bridges

All ability is influenced by subconscious/conscious concerns: Ashcraft 2002; Assf, 2006; Ely, 1991; Meharg, 1988; Moors et al., 2013; Murphy, 2004; Reeve, 2015; Thayer & Lane, 2008; Thayer et al., 2012.

A performance can be known seconds to months in advance: (Emmons & Thomas, 2008; Studer et al., 2011; Van Kemenade et. al., 1995.

The underlying cause of outcome/performance problems is being unsure of successfully handling the situation, or being unsure of coming out okay: Ashcraft, 2002; Assaf, 2006; Bandura, 1983; Bandura, 1988; Bandura, Reese & Adams, 1982; Birenbaum & Nasser, 1994; Bloom, 2008; Cottny et al., 2006; Gregor, 2005; Jalongo & Hirsh, 2010; Lazaroff, 2001; Lazarus, 1991; McCraty et al., 2009; Moors et al., 2013; Murphy, 2004; Neimeyer, 2010; Ortony & Clore, 1989; Putwain, 2009; Reeve, 2015; Ryan & Deci, 2001; Tarrant et al., 2010; Thayer & Lane, 2008; Walker & Nordin-Bates, 2010; Weisinger & Pawliw-Fry, 2015.

A "performance" is any formally or informally demonstrated ability: Abril, 2007; Abu-Rabia, 2004; Ashcraft, 2002; Assaf, 2006; Birenbaum & Nasser, 1994; Bloom, 2008; Bradley et al., 2010; Cottyn et al., 2006; Day et al., 2006; Emmons & Thomas, 2008; Gregor, 2005; Jalongo & Hirsh, 2010; Lazaroff, 2001; Likar & Raeburn, 2009; Murphy, 2004; Neimeyer, 2010; Putwain, 2009; Small, 1998; Sternbach, 2008; Stolpa, 2004; Studer et al., 2011; Tarrant, Leathem & Flett, 2010; Young, 2016.

Every level of outcome anxiety, from inconsistent flow-zone to performance-based anxiety, stem from the same basic problem: Bandura, 1988; Gilman, 2012; Lazarus, 1991; Martin & Jackson, 2008; McCraty et al., 2009; Moors, Ellsworth, Scherer & Frijda, 2013; Neimeyer, 2010; Ortony & Clore, 1989; Reeve, 2015; Reisenzein, 1994; Thayer & Lane, 2008; Young, Wu & Menon, 2012.

Things that decrease anxiety improve peak flow in the zone: Bandura, 1983; Bandura, 1988; Gilman, 2012; Lazarus, 1991; Moors et al., 2013; Ortony & Clore, 1989; Putwain, 2009; Reeve, 2015; Reisenzein, 1994; Ryan & Deci, 2001; Thayer et al., 2012.

Emotional intelligence, relating to understanding outcome anxiety and how to proactively combat it, has enormous benefits: Bandura, 1988; Berenson, 2005; Bradberry & Greaves, 2005; Bradley et al., 2010; Chan, 2011; Cherniss & Goleman, 1998; Emmons & Thomas, 2008; Fernandez-Berrocal, Alcaide, & Extremera, 2006; Fredrickson & Barrett, 2004; Kirchner et al., 2008; Lazaroff, 2001; Likar & Raeburn, 2009; Loyd, 2005; Palmer, Donaldson & Stough, 2002; Ruiz-Aranda, Salguero & Cabello, 2012; Taylor, 1970 & Leffingwell, 1971 as cited in Leffingwell 2001; Wall, 2005; Weisinger & Pawliw-Fry, 2015.

Most anxiety information targets symptoms: Boucher & Ryan, 2011; Edwards, 2009; Ely, 1991; Khalsa et al., 2009; Likar & Raeburn, 2009; Murphy, 2004; Osborne & Kenny, 2008; Sweeney & Horan, 1982; Tarrant et al., 2010; Walker & Nordin-Bates, 2010; Wall, 2005.

Performance problems aren't caused by performing: Bandura, 1983; Bandura, 1988; Bandura, Reese, & Adams, 1982; Emmons & Thomas, 2008; Esch, 2014; Hedden & Gabrieli, 2004; Hong, 2010b; Ortony & Clore 1989; Reeve, 2015; Sorrentino, 2013; Weisinger & Pawliw-Fry, 2015; Winecoff et al., 2011.

Unique life experiences influence the nature and causes of outcome anxiety: Bandura, 1988; Boucher & Ryan, 2011; Buck, 1984 as cited in Reeve, 2015; Hong, 2010b; Izard, 2007; Kenny & Osborne, 2006; Ortony & Clore, 1989; Reeve, 2015; Wigfield & Eccles, 1989.

Frustration, limitations, health issues, injuries, and discouragement result from not performing well: Berlyne, 1975; Bragge, 2006; Cizek & Burt, 2005 as cited in Salend, 2010; Emmons & Thomas, 2008; Jangalo & Hirsh, 2010; Jensen, 2005 as cited in Jalongo, 2010; Keyes, 2007; McEwen, 1998; Meharg, 1988; Mogel, 2005; Murphy, 2004; Nolen-Hoeksema et al., 2008; Putwain, 2009; Reeve, 2015; Sena et al., 2012; Young, Wu & Menon, 2012.

Physical health, mental health/brain function; emotional health, ability limitations, and interpersonal factors relating to outcome anxiety (documented separately below):

Physical health: Belsky & Pluess, 2009; Berthoud & Neuhuber, 2000; Boucher & Ryan, 2011; Bragge, 2006; Cherniss & Goleman, 1998; Chrousos, 1995; Chrousos & Gold, 1992; Chrousos & Kino, 2005; Collishaw et al., 2010; Cottyn et al., 2006; Edmondson et al., 2012; Edwards, 2009; Ely, 1991; Emmons & Thomas, 1998, 2008; Forkey, 2015; Fredrickson, 1998; Fredrickson & Barrett, 2004; Gilman, 2012; Gross & John, 2003; Harvard Health Publishing, 2018; Hurrell & Murphy, 1996; Khalsa et al., 2009; McCraty et al., 2009; McEwen, 1998; McEwen, 1999; McGonigal, 2013; Murphy, 2004; NIOSH, n/a; Jiijima, 1992; Reeve, 2015; Studer et al., 2011; Tarrant et al., 2010; Thayer et al., 2012; Tiller et al., 1996; Trolinger, 2005; Tugade et al., 2004; Tugade & Fredrickson, 2006; Weisinger & Pawliw-Fry, 2015.

Mental health/Brain function: Adams, 2012; Ashcraft, 2002; Ashcraft & Krause, 2007; Assaf, 2006; Bawa, 1981; Boucher & Ryan, 2011; Boyle, 2015; Chrousos, 1995; Chrousos & Gold, 1992; Cloninger & Gillgan, 1987; Cramer et al., 2011; Davidson & McEwen, 2012; Draganski et al., 2004; Esch, 2014; Etkin & Wagner, 2007; Forkey, 2015; Giovanni & Csikszentmihalyi, 1996; Groves & Brown, 2005; Gardian, 2012; Harvard Health Publishing, 2018; Hinton et al., 2008; Izard, 1989; Jalongo & Hirsh, 2010; McEwen & Sapolsky, 1995; McEwen, 1998; McGonigal, 2013; Murphy, 2004; Neilsen et al., 2017; Neimeyer, 2010; Paton et al., 2006; Paulus & Stein, 2006; Reeve, 2015; Schreurs et al., 1986; Thayer et al., 2012; Thayer & Lane, 2008; Tiller et al., 1996; Weisinger & Pawliw-Fry, 2015; Winecoff et al., 2011; Young et al., 2012; Yuan, et al., 2011.

Emotional health: Andrus, Ashcraft, 2002; APA, 2013; Ashcraft & Krause, 2007; Assaf, 2006; Augustine & Hemnover, 2009; Bandura, 1983; Bandura, 1988; Bandura, Reese, & Adams 1982; Bloom, 2008; Boucher & Ryan, 2011; Boyle, 2015; Brach, 2015; Cherniss & Goleman, 1998; Chrousos & Gold, 1992; Collishaw et al., 2010; Cottyn et al., 2006; Davidson & McEwen, 2012; Deci & Ryan, 1985; Elliot & church, 1997; Ely, 1991; Emmons & Thomas, 1998, 2008; Esch, 2014; Etkin & Wagner, 2007; Fehm & Schmidt, 2006; Forkey, 2015; Fredrickson, 1998; Fredrickson & Barrett, 2004; Gilman, 2012; Gross & John, 2003; Haid, 1999; Hale III et al., 2009; Hamann, 1982, 1985; Hamann & Gordon, 2000; Harvard Health Publishing, 2018; Hinton et al., 2008; Hobson, 1996; Hong, 2010a, 2010b; Hunnicutt & Winter, 2011; Hurrell & Murphy, 1996; Isen & Daubman, 1984; Isen et al., 1985; Isen & Reeve, 2005; Iwata, 1987; Izard, 1989, 2007; Kenny, 2005; Kenny & Osborne, 2006; Khalsa et al., 2009; Kirchner et al., 2008; Kokotaski & Davidson, 2003; Lessingwell, 2001; Martin & March, 2006; McEwen & Sapolsky, 1995; McEwen, 1998; McGonigal, 2013; Miller et al., 2003; Moors et al., 2013; Murphy, 2004; Neilsen et al., 2017; Neimeyer, 2010; Nolen-Hoeksema et al., 2008; Osborne & Kenny, 2005; Putwain, 2009; Putwain & Best, 2011; Rae & McCambridge, 2004; Reeve, 2015; Reisenzein, 1994; Robertson & Eisensmith, 2010; Roughan & Hadwin, 2011; Ruiz-Aranda et al., 2012; Ryan & Andrews, 2009; Salend, 2012; Sena et al., 2012; Sorrentino, 2013; Sternbach, 2008; Studer et al., 2011; Sweeney & Horan, 1082; Taborsky, 2007; Tarrant et al., 2010; Trolinger, 2005; Tugade et al., 2004; Van Kemenade et al., 1995; Van Oort et al., 2009; Walker & Nordin-Bates, 2010; Wall, 2005; Weiner, 1985; Weiner et al., 1987; Weisinger & Pawliw-Fry, 2015; Wigfield & Eccles, 1989; Wortman & Brehm, 1975; Yodem, 2007; Zinn et al., 2000.

Anxiety limitations: Abril, 2007; Adams, 2012; Ashcraft, 2002; Ashcraft & Krause, 2007; Assf, 2006; Augustine & Hemnover, 2009; Birenbaum & Nasser, 1994;B Bloom, 2008; Boucher & Ryan, 2011; Bradley et al., 2010; Chrousos, 1995; Chrousos & Gold, 1992; Cloninger & Gillgan, 1987; Collishaw et al., 2010; Cottyn et al., 2006; Davidson & McEwen, 2012.

Injuries: Cherniss & Goleman, 1998; Chrousos, 1995; Chrousos & Gold, 1992; Collishaw et al., 2010; Deci et al., 1999; Edmondson et al., 2012; Edwards, 2009; Elliot & church, 1997; Ely, 1991; Emmons & Thomas, 1998, 2008; Etkin & Wagner, 2007; Fehm & Schmidt, 2006; Fredrickson, 1998; Fredrickson & Barrett, 2004; Gallwey, 1974; Gilman, 2012; Giovanni & Csikszentmihalyi, 1996; Gregor, 2005; Gross & John, 2003; Gross & John, 2003; Haid, 1999; Hale III et al., 2009; Hamann, 1982, 1985; Hamann & Gordon, 2000; Harvard Health Publishing, 2018; Hinton et al., 2008; Hobson, 1996; Hodgins & Knee, 2002; Hong, 2010a, 2010b; Hunnicutt & Winter, 2011; Hurrell & Murphy, 1996; Jalongo & Hirsh, 2010; Khalsa et al., 2009; Kirchner et al., 2008; Kokotaski & Davidson, 2003; Lazaroff, 2001; Leffingwell, 2001; Lenhart et al., 2008; Lehrer, 1985, 1987; Likar & Raeburn, 2009; Martin & Jackson, 2008; McEwen & Sapolsky, 1995; McEwen, 1998; McGonigal, 2013; Meharg, 1988; Mogel, 2005; Murphy, 2004; Neilsen et al., 2017; Neimeyer, 2010; Osborne & Kenny, 2005, 2008; Petrovich, 2003; Putwain, 2009; Putwain & Best, 2011; Rae & McCambridge, 2004; Reeve, 2015; Rideout, 2002; Robertson & Eisensmith, 2010; Roughan & Hadwin, 2011; Ruiz-Aranda et al., 2012; Ryan & Andrews, 2009; Salend, 2012; Sena et al., 2012; Small, 1998; Solar, 2011; Sternbach, 2008; Stolpa, 2004; Studer et al., 2011; Taborsky, 2007; Tarrant et al., 2010; Trolinger, 2005; Van Kemenade et al., 1995; Van Oort et al., 2009; Walker & Nordin-Bates, 2010; Wall, 2005; Weisinger & Pawliw-Fry, 2015; Wigfield & Eccles, 1989; Yondem, 2007; Young, et al., 2012; Yuan et al., 2011; Zinn et al., 2000.

Interpersonal Issues: Aylett, 2000; Cherniss & Goleman, 1998; Collishaw et al., 2010; Davidson & McEwen, 2012; Deci et al., 1999; Edmondson et al., 2012; Emmons & Thomas, 1998, 2008; Etking & Wagner, 2007; Fehm & Schmidt, 2006; Gilman, 2012; Gross & John, 2003; Hale III et al., 2009; Hamann & Gordon, 2000; Harvard Health Publishing, 2018; Hong, 2010b; Murphy, 2004; Patterson et al., 2002; Petrovich, 2003; Putwain, 2009; Putwain & Best, 2011; Reeve, 2015; Robertson & Eisensmith, 2010; Roughan & Hadwin, 2011; Ruiz-Aranda et al., 2012; Ryan & Deci, 2000, 2001; Small, 1998; Solar, 2011; Weisinger & Pawliw-Fry, 2015; Wiechman & Gurland, 2009; Yondem, 2007.

Inaccurate and insufficient information compounds problems: Ashcraft, 2002; Collishaw, et al., 2010; Goswami, 2008; Jalongo & Hirsh, 2010; Likar & Raeburn, 2009; Murphy, 2004; Reeve, 2015; Petrovich, 2003; Putwain, 2009; Putwain & Best, 2011; Sorrentino, 2013; Taborsky, 2007; Weisinger & Pawliw-Fry, 2015; Wiechman & Gurland, 2009; Woolfolk, 2010.

Stress is an occupational hazard for performers: Ashcraft, 2002; Collishaw, et al., 2010; Edmondson et al, 2012; Fehm & Schmidt, 2006 as cited in Studer et al., 2011; Goswami, 2008; Jolongo & Hirsh, 2010; McEwen, 1998; Mogel, 2005; NIOSH, n/a; Taborsky, 2007; Wall, 2005; Zinn, McCain, Zinn, 2000.

Anxiety information and training prevents problems: Ashcraft, 2002; Bradberry & Greaves, 2005; Collishaw, et al., 2010; Edmondson et al, 2012; Fehm & Schmidt, 2006 as cited in Studer et al., 2011; Goswami, 2008; Jolongo & Hirsh, 2010; McEwen, 1998; Mogel, 2005; Patterson et al., 2002; Taborsky, 2007; Wall, 2005; Zinn, McCain, Zinn, 2000.

Performance threats seen as only immaterial perception: Bandura, 1983; Bandura, 1988; Ely, 1991; Emmons & Thomas, 2008; Meharg, 1988; Thayer et al., 2012; Weisinger & Pawliw-Fry, 2015.

Performing carries real, sometimes high-risk stakes: Cizek & Burt, 2005 as cited in Salend, 2010; Edmondson et al., 2012; Emmons & Thomas, 2008; Gilman, 2012; Jangalo & Hirsh, 2010; Meharg, 1988; Mogel, 2005; Murphy, 2004; Nolen-Hoeksema et al., 2008; Putwain, 2009; Putwain & Best, 2011; Reeve, 2015; Sena et al., 2012.

Accurate knowledge increases individual and group success: Bandura, 1988; Cherniss, & Goleman, 1998; Gilman, 2012; Murphy, 2004; Osborne & Kenney, 2008; Palmer et al., 2002; Reeve, 2015; Weisinger & Pawliw-Fry, 2015.

Chapter 2: Measly Monsters

Addressing symptoms: Boucher & Ryan, 2011; Edwards, 2009; Ely, 1991; Emmons & Thomas, 2008; Khalsa et al., 2009; Likar & Raeburn, 2009; Murphy, 2004; Osborne & Kenny, 2008; Sweeney & Horan, 1982; Tarrant et al., 2010; Walker & Nordin-Bates, 2010.

Addressing causes: Ely, 1991; Emmons & Thomas, 2008; Meharg, 1988; Moors et al., 2013; Murphy, 2004; Reeve, 2015; Thayer & Lane, 2008; Thayer et al., 2012.

There would be something wrong if inaccurate information worked: Fredrickson & Barrett, 2004; Palmer et al., 2002; Sorrentino, 2013; Tugade, 2004.

Unaddressed performance problems can get worse over time: Bandura, Reese, & Adams, 1982; Boucher & Ryan, 2011; Edmondson et al., 2012; Ely, 1991; Goswami, 2008; Hinton et al., 2008; Hong, 2010b; Jalongo & Hirsh, 2010; Kenny & Osborne, 2006; Putwain, 2009; Swanson & Howell, 1966 as cited in Sena, 2012; Wigfield & Eccles, 1989; Wolfe, 1990 as cited in Boucher & Ryan, 2011; Yondem, 2007.

Unsuccessful attempts at solving performance problems cause self-esteem and confidence to plummet: Ashcraft, 2002; Assaf, 2006; Aylett, 2000; Bandura, 1983; Bandura, 1988; Bandura, Reese & Adams, 1082; Ely, 1991; Emmons & Thomas, 1998; Hong, 2010b; Likar & Raeburn, 2009; Nolen-Hoeksema et al., 2008; Putwain, 2009; Walker & Nordin-Bates, 2010; Reeve, 2015; Weisinger & Pawliw-Fry, 2015.

Many with anxiety think they are the problem: Ashcraft, 2002; Assaf, 2006; Banduraa, 1983; Bandura, 1988; Emmons & Thomas, 2008; Likar & Raeburn, 2009; Meharg, 1988; Wigfield & Eccles, 1989; Wortman & Brehm, 1975.

Performance-based problems are found every day: Abril, 2007; Abu-Radia, 2004; Ashcraft, 2002; Ashcraft & Krause, 2007; Assaf, 2006; Birenbaum & Nasser, 1994; Bloom, 2008; Gregor, 2005; Hong, 2010b; Jalongo & Hirsh, 2010; Lazaroff, 2001; Mogel, 2005; Murphy, 2004; Neimeyer, 2010; Putwain, 2009; Ryan & Andrews, 2009; Ryan & Deci, 2001; Reeve, 2015; Studer, et al., 2011; Tarrant, Leathem, & Flett, 2010; Reese, 2015; Weisinger & Pawliw-Fry, 2015.

Something is wrong with the method, not the person; it's best to get rid of the problem: Ashcraft, 2002; Bandura, 1988; Jalongo & Hirsh, 2010; Likar & Raeburn, 2009; Ortony & Clore, 1989; Palmer, Donaldson & Stough, 2002; Reeve, 2015; Taborsky, 2007; Wall, 2005.

Anxieties automatically dissipate when inner causes are deeply understood: Bandura, 1988; Likar & Raeburn, 2009; Martin & March, 2006; Palmer, Donaldson & Stough, 2002; Reeve, 2015; Tugade, Fredrickson & Barrett, 2004; Wall, 2005.

There are reasons for fear, nervousness, and/or subconscious concerns, and the mind and body naturally react: Bandura, 1988; Ely; 1991; Hong, 2010b; Meharg, 1988; Murphy, 2004; Nolen-Hoeksema et al., 2008; Osborne & Kenny, 2008; Reeve, 2015; Robertson, 2010.

There's a place for, and many ways of, managing symptoms: Boucher & Ryan, 2011; Edwards, 2009; Ely, 1991; Khalsa et al., 2009; Likar & Raeburn, 2009; Murphy, 2004; Osborne & Kenny, 2008; Sweeney & Horan, 1982; Tarrant et al., 2010; Walker & Nordin-Bates, 2010; Wall, 2005.

Get rid of fear rather than learn to deal with it: Likar & Raeburn, 2009; Martin & March, 2006; Murphy, 2004; Palmer, Donaldson & Stough, 2002; Reeve, 2015; Tugade, Fredrickson & Barrett, 2004; Weiner, 1985; Werner et al., 1987.

Concerns reduce enjoyment; play becomes work; depletion; less intrinsic interest: Deci, Koestner & Ryan, 1999; Wiechman & Gurland 2009.

Knowledge is the most powerful performance weapon: Ashcraft, 2002; Bandura, 1988; Chan, 2011; Ely, 1991; Gilman, 2012; Hong, 2010; Lazarus, 1991; Meharg, 1988; Moors et al., 2013; Murphy, 2004; Ortony & Clore, 1989; Osborn & Kenny, 2008; Putwain, 2009; Reeve, 2015; Reisenzein, 1994; Ryan & Deci, 2001.

Each person has a unique history, so the things that eliminate problems are also unique: APA, 2013; Bandura, 1988; Boucher & Ryan, 2011; Buck, 1984 as cited in Reeve, 2015; Esch, 2014; Hong, 2010b; Izard, 2007; Kenny & Osborne, 2006; Ortony & Clore, 1989; Wigfield & Eccles, 1989.

It's important to focus in the right direction: Ashcraft, 2002; Assaf, 2006; Bandura, 1988; Bloom, 2008; Birenbaum & Nasser, 1994; Chan, 2011; Cottny et al., 2006; Esch, 2014; Gregor, 2005; Hong, 2010b; Jalongo & Hirsh, 2010; Lazaroff, 2001; Lazarus, 1991;

Likar & Raeburn, 2009; Martin & March, 2006; Moors et al., 2013; Neimeyer, 2010; Ortony & Clore, 1989; Palmer, Donaldson & Stough, 2002; Putwain, 2009; Reeve, 2015; Taborsky, 2007; Tarrant, Leathem & Flett, 2010; Ryan & Deci, 2001; Sorrentino, 2013; Walker & Nordin-Bates, 2010.

The problem is deeper or it would be taken care of already: Bandura,1983, 1988; Bandura, Reese & Adams, 1982; Emmons & Thomas, 2008; Ortony & Clore 1989; Reeve, 2015. Sorrentino, 2013; Weisinger & Pawliw-Fry, 2015.

Writing is much better than just thinking: Kerka, 1989; Lenhart, Arafeh & Smith, 2008; Petranek, Corey & Black, 1992.

Subconscious and conscious brain processing makes a difference: Bandura, 1988; Buck, 1994 as cited in Reeve, 2015; Gilman, 2012; Moors et al., 2013; Lazarus, 1991; Levenson, 1999; Ortony & Clore, 1989; Panksepp, 1994 as cited in Reeve, 2015; Putwain, 2009; Reeve, 2015; Reisenzein, 1994; Ryan & Deci, 2001; Weisinger & Pawliw-Fry, 2015; Winecoff et al., 2011.

Establishing a sure core is beneficial: Ashcraft, 2002; Castillo, 2009; Chan, 2011; Edmondson et al, 2012; Emmons, & Thomas, 1998; 2008; Martin & March, 2006; Murphy, 2004; Nolen-Hoeksema et al., 2008; Palmer, Donaldson & Stough, 2002; Reeve, 2015; Ryan & Deci, 2001; Tugade, Fredrickson & Barrett, 2004; Weiner, 1985; Werner et al., 1987; Wall, 2005.

Simple things make a difference: Ashcraft, 2002; Castillo, 2009; Emmons, & Thomas, 2008; Esch, 2014; Gallwey, 1974; Gross & John, 2003; Hodgins & Knee, 2002; Johnson et al., 2012; Khalsa et al., 2009; Martin & Marsh, 2006; Ryan & Deci, 2001; Wall, 2005; Werner et al., 1987.

Chapter 3: Ready Set—Unlearn!
Everyone benefits from a thorough understanding of outcome anxiety: Emmons & Thomas, 1998; 2008; Martin & March, 2006; Murphy, 2004; Palmer, Donaldson & Stough, 2002; Putwain, 2009; Reeve, 2015; Ryan & Deci, 2001; Sweeney & Horan, 1982; Taylor, 1970 & Leffingwell, 1971 as cited in Leffingwell, 2001; Tugade, Fredrickson & Barrett, 2004; Weiner, 1985, 1986.

Understanding how anxiety affects optimal performance is critical to optimum output: Abril, 2007; Ashcraft, 2002; Aylett, 2000; Berenson, 2005; Chan, 2011; Collishaw et al., 2010; Emmons & Thomas, 2008; Fehm & Schmidt, 2006; Gallwey, 1974; Gilman, 2012; Giovanni & Csikszentmihalvi, 1996; Gregor, 2005; Haid, 1999; Hale III et al., 2009; Hamann 1982, 1985; Hamann & Gordon, 2000; Hanin & Hanina 2009; Hobson, 1996; Hong, 2010a, 2010b; Hunnicutt, 2011; Johnson et al., 2012; Kokotsaki & Davidson, 2003; LeBlanch et al., 1997; Lehrer, 1985; Lehrer & Raeburn, 2009; Lepper et al., 2005; Loyd, 2005; Petrovich, 2003; Putwain, 2009; Rae & McCambridge, 2004; Rideout, 2002; Robertson & Eisensmith, 2010; Roughan & Hadwin, 2011; Solar, 2011; Stolpa, 2004; Sweeney & Horan, 1982; Taborsky, 2007; Trolinger, 2005; Woolfolk, 2010; Zinn, McCain & Zinn, 2000.

Anxiety and flow/zone problems are learned reactions that can be revised: Ashcraft & Krause, 2007; Boucher & Ryan, 2011; Ely, 1991; Eysenck & Calvo, 1992 as cited in Goswami, 2008; Forkey, 2015; Hinton et al., 2008; Hong, 2010b; Jalongo & Hirsh, 2010; Keifer et al., 2015; Kenny & Osborne, 2006; Leffingwell, 2001; Lepper et al., 2005; Putwain, 2009; Reeve, 2015; Weaver, 2007; Wigfield & Eccles, 1989.

Early childhood and other experiences can result in ability and flow/zone limitations: Ashcraft & Krause, 2007; Boucher & Ryan, 2011; Ely, 1991; Forkey, 2015 Hong, 2010b; Kenny & Osborne, 2006; Leffingwell, 2001; Putwain, 2009; Reeve, 2015; Wigfield & Eccles, 1989.

Uncomfortable thoughts and feelings cause people to give up sooner and not reach their potential: Ashcraft, 2002; Emmons & Thomas, 2008; Forkey, 2015; Franzel et al., 2007 as cited in Jalongo & Hirsh, 2010; Hamilton et al., 2012; Isen, 2005; Isen & Reeve, 2005; Izard, 2007; Nolen-Hoeksema et al., 2008; Taylor, 1970 & Leffingwell, 1971 as cited in Leffingwell, 2001.

When thoughts and feelings are comfortable, effort is repeated, initiative persists, and things work well: Ashcraft, 2002; Bandura, 1993; 1988; Chan, 2011; Csikszentmihalyi & Nakamura, 1989; Isen, 2005; Isen & Reeve, 2005; Izard, 2007; Martin & Jackson, 2008.

Avoidance vs. approach strategies affect engagement and output: Elliot & Church, 1997; Isen, 2005; Isen & Reeve, 2005; Iwata, 1987; Izard, 2007; Forkey, 2015; Martin & Jackson, 2008; Ryan and Deci, 2000.

Knowledge and a deeper awareness of thoughts and feelings reduces problems: Bandura, 1983, 1988; Bandura, Reese, Adams, 1982; Buck, 1994 as cited in Reeve, 2015; Chan, 2011; Emmons & Thomas, 1978; Emmons & Thomas, 2008; Frijda, 2007; Gilman, 2012; Lazarus, 1991; Levenson, 1999; Moors, Ellsworth, Scherer, & Frijda, 2013; Ortony & Clore, 1989; Panksepp, 1994 as cited in Reeve, 2015; Putwain, 2009; Reeve, 2015; Reisnzein, 1994; Ryan & Deci, 2001; Sorrentino, 2013; Weisinger & Pawliw-Fry, 2015; Winecoff et al., 2011.

Performance anxiety is common across all ability levels and subjects: Abu-Radia, 2004; Ashcraft, 2004; Assaf, 2006; Bloom, 2008; Boucher & Ryan, 2011; Fehm & Schmidt, 2006; Hong, 2010a, 2010b; James, 1998 as cited in Kenny, 2005; Kirchner et al., 2008; Mogel, 2005; Murphy, 2004; Nolen-Hoeksema et al., 2008; Reeve, 2015; Ryan, 2009; Ryan & Andrews, 2009; Studer et al., 2011; Young, 2016.)

70% professional orchestra musicians (James 1998 as cited in Kenny, 2005).

Common, growing school problem (Mogel, 2005).

Many don't know they have performance anxiety: Ashcraft, 2004; Ashcraft & Krause, 2007; Bandura, 1988; Emmons & Thomas,1998; 2008.

Performance anxiety commonly limits ability and choices, reducing potential achieved: Emmons & Thomas, 2008; Hong, 2010b; Forkey, 2015; Martin & March, 2006; Murphy, 2004; Palmer, Donaldson & Stough 2002; Putwain, 2009; Reeve, 2015; Ryan & Deci, 2001; Emmons &Taylor, 1970, & Leffingwell, 1971 as cited in Leffingwell 2001.

People hide performance-based anxiety because they're embarrassed, scared, or discouraged: Ashcraft, 2002; Assaf, 2006; Brach, 2015; Ely, 1991; Emmons & Thomas, 2008; Krause, 2007; Meharg, 1988; Rosenhan & Seligman, 1984; Wortman & Brehm, 1975.

Anxiety can increase if a person perceives they aren't handling things as well as others: Nolen-Hoeksema et al., 2008; Putwain, 2009.

No one starts out with performance anxiety: Deci & Ryan, 1985; Ely, 1991; Emmons & Thomas, 2008; Kenny & Osborne, 2006; Wolfe, 1990 as cited in Boucher & Ryan, 2011.

Young children have higher cortisol levels when performing: Boucher & Ryan, 2011.

Children unabashedly bask in the joy of learning and sharing regardless of performance ability: Boyle, 2015; Deci & Ryan, 1985; Ely, 1991; Kenny & Osborne, 2006; Small, 1998; Wolfe, 1990 as cited in Boucher & Ryan, 2011.

The embrace-the-world kid is still inside: Bandura, 1988; Bandura, Reese & Adams, 1982; Berlyne, 1975; Leffingwell, 2001 ; Rogers, 1961; Small, 1998.

Anxiety usually begins in the early-to-mid elementary school years: Hong, 2010b; Wolfe, 1990 as cited in Boucher & Ryan, 2011.

Anxiety peaks in junior high: Hembree, 1988 as cited in Sena et al., 2012; Hong, 2010b; Manley & Rosemier, 1972 as cited in Wigfield & Eccles, 1989.

Adolescents are particularly vulnerable to anxiety: Abril, 2007; Ely, 1991; Sternbach, 2008.

More secure environments correlate to less anxiety; high emotion, unexpected difficulties, or unpredictable circumstances contribute to performance problems: Ashcraft, 2002; Aylett, 2000; Chirkov & Ryan, 2001; Deci & Ryan, 1985; Forkey, 2015; Hong, 2010b; Keller, 2008; Mogel, 2005; Osborn & Kenny, 2008; Reeve, 2015; Ryan & Deci, 2000; Shonkoff & Garner, 2011; Sarason et al., 1960 and Hermans et al., 1972 as cited in Wigfield & Eccles, 1989; Weaver, 2007.

Untreated, anxiety problems generally increase over time and/or remain until intervention: APA, 2013; Goswami, 2008; Forkey, 2015; Hinton et al., 2008; Hong, 2010b; Jalongo & Hirsh, 2010; Swanson & Howell, 1996 as cited in Sena et al., 2012.

Excessive guilt/blame slows progressive change: Forkey, 2015; Reeve, 2015.

Performance-based anxiety can develop from experience; even one very bad experience can instigate it: Ely, 1991; Putwain, 2009; Yehuda et al., 2016; Yondem, 2007.

Performance-based anxiety can develop from observing someone in a negative situation: Bandura, 1986 as cited in Woolfolk, 2010; Brown & Inouye, 1978 as cited in Reeve, 2015; Ely 1991; Yehuda et al., 2016.

Flow/zone problems can develop from milder situations that may not even be considered negative: Gilman, 2012; Murphy, 2004; Reeve, 2015.

A person is imprinted with the positive or negative emotion experienced when first introduced to a subject or situation: Goswami, 2008; Hinton et al., 2008; Jalongo & Hirsh, 2010; Keyes, 2007; Ryan & Deci, 2000; Young et al., 2012.

Personality plays into how anxiety presents: Cherniss & Goleman, 1998; Hamman, 1982; Hamman & Gordon, 2000; Hong, 2010b; Kenny & Osborne, 2006; Kokotsaki & Davidson, 2003.

Genetics and environment affect the anxiety: APA, 2013; Belsky & Pluess, 2009; Chakravarti & Little, 2003; Dias & Ressler, 2013; Ely, 1991; Houri-Ze'evi et al., 2016; Immler, 2018; Lamm & Jablonka, 2008; Olivares, 2016; Putwain, 2009; Rutter, Moffit & Caspi, 2005; Shonkoff & Garner, 2011; Tooby & Cosmides, 2008 as cited in Reeve, 2015; Weaver, 2007; Yondem, 2007; Yehuda et al., 2016.

Gene bar doesn't take into account personal experience, lifestyle, or ability to cope: Chakravarti & Little, 2003.

Memories, knowledge, and instincts are passed through genes: Bateson & Curley, 2013; Chakravarti & Little, 2003; Cloninger &Gillgan,1987; Davies, G., 2010; Dias & Ressler, 2018; Houri-Ze'evi et al., 2016; Immler, 2018; Lamm & Jablonka, 2008; Rutter, Moffit & Caspi, 2005; Weaver, 2007; Yehuda et al., 2016.

The effects of inherited genes can be changed: Al-Ghaili, Dias & Ressler, 2013; Immler, 2018; Weaver, 2007; Yehuda et al., 2016.

Most people have some hang-ups: Abu-Radia, 2004; Ashcraft, 2004; Assaf, 2006; Bloom, 2008; Boucher & Ryan, 2011; Cherniss & Goleman, 1998; Fehm & Schmidt, 2006; Hong, 2010; Kenny, 2005; Kirchner et al., 2008; Mogel, 2005; Murphy, 2004; Olivares, 2016; Ryan & Andrews, 2009; Studer et al., 2011; Reeve, 2015; Studer et al., 2011; Van Kemenade et al., 1995; Van Oort et al., 2009.

Some pigeon-hole their abilities: Ashcraft & Krause, 2007; Ely, 1991; Hong, 2010a, 2010b; Martin & Marsh, 2006; Osborne & Kenny, 2008; Stolpa, 2004.

People don't know competence is shaped by experiences and the environment, let alone how to decrease negative and increase positive effects: Brach, 2015; Cherniss & Goleman, 1998; Ely, 1991; Emmons & Thomas, 2008; Forkey, 2015; Hong, 2010a; Murphy, 2004; Reeve, 2015; Weaver, 2007.

When addressing anxiety, ability goes up without additional practice or instruction, and it progresses faster and higher than expected: Ashcraft, 2002; Ashcraft & Krause, 2007; Birenbaum & Nasser, 1994.

Attitude is a big factor in reversing situations: Castillo, 2009; Cherniss & Goleman, 1998; Frankl, 1960, 1975, 1985; Fredrickson & Barrett, 2004; Isen & Daubman, 1984; Isen et al., 1985; Isen & Reeve, 2005; Izard, 2007; Reeve, 2015.

Limitations handled positively develop powerful qualities: Boyle, 2005; Cohn & Fredrickson, 2009 as cited in Reeve, 2015; Frankl, 1960, 1975; Fredrickson, 1998; Isen et al., 1985; Isen & Daubman, 1984; Isen & Reeve, 2005.

Change perception of situations and self to reduce or eliminate learned negative responses: Ashcraft, 2002; Cherniss & Goleman, 1998; Ely, 1991; Emmons & Thomas, 2008; Frankl, 1960; Hong, 2010a; Murphy, 2004; Reeve, 2015.

Handel's life and the *Messiah*: Condie, 2010.

Beethoven experienced a transformation similar to Handel after going deaf: Vaillant, 2000.

Difficulties often precede success, and overcoming them can provide inspiration: China Disabled Peoples Performing Arts Group; Frankl, 1959; Infinite Flow Dance Company, 2018; Hansen, 2014, 2016; International VSA Festival Arts and Disability, 2010; Zaccardi, 2016.

Tackling limitations may provide many benefits: Ashcraft, 2002; Ashcraft & Krause, 2007; Frankl, 1959; Madsen as cited in Hansen, 2016; Hansen, 2014; Hansen, 2016; Young, 2016.

Anxiety affects performance, relationships, learning, and health; can experience improvements in these areas: Ashcraft, 2002; Berenson 2005; Berlyne, 1975; Bragge; 2006; Cizek & Burt, 2005 as cited in Salend, 2010; Edmondson et al, 2012; Emmons & Thomas, 2008; Hurrell, 1996; Jangalo & Hirsh, 2010; Jensen, 2005 as cited in Jalongo, 2010; Keyes, 2007; Likar & Raeburn, 2009; Meharg, 1988; Mogel, 2005; Mogel, 2005; Murphy, 2004;

NIOSH, n/a; Nolen-Hoeksema et al., 2008; Putwain, 2009; Reeve, 2015; Sena et al., 2012; Trolinger, 2005; Young, Wu & Menon, 2012; Zinn, McCain, Zinn, 2000.

Chapter : 4 Performance Anxiety Doesn't Exist!

Fear when performing is actually fear of the outcome: Ashcraft, 2002; Assaf, 2006; Bandura, 1983; Bandura, 1988; Bandura, Reese & Adams, 1982; Bloom, 2008; Birenbaum & Nasser, 1994; Cottny et al., 2006; Emmons & Thomas, 1998, 2008; Gregor, 2005; Jalongo & Hirsh, 2010; Lazaroff, 2001; Lazarus, 1991; McCraty et al., 2009; Moors et al., 2013; Murphy, 2004; Neimeyer, 2010; Ortony & Clore, 1989; Putwain, 2009; Reeve, 2015; Ryan & Deci, 2001; Tarrant et al., 2010; Thayer & Lane, 2008; Walker & Nordin-Bates, 2010.

Anxiety can be positive: Emmons & Thomas, 2008; Murphy, 2004, Reeve, 2015.

Mind and body react with symptoms: Ashcraft, 2002; Bloom, 2008; Ely, 1991; Emmons & Thomas, 2008; Hunnicutt & Winter, 2011; Leffingwell, 2001; Meharg, 1988; Murphy, 2004; Neimeyer, 2010; Osborne, 2008; Petrovich, 2003; Posener et al., 2000; Reeve, 2015; Robertson & Eisensmith, 2010; Sternbach, 2008; Tarrant, et al., 2010.

Anxiety only occurs when feeling incapable of successfully handling a situation: Abril, 2007; Emmons & Thomas, 2008; Jalongo & Hirsh, 2010.

Anxiety can happen before or after a performance: Emmons & Thomas, 2008; Van Kemenade et al., 1995.

Rumination: Hervas & Vazquez,2011; Neilsen et al., 2017; Nolen-Hoeksema, Wisco, & Lyubomirsky, 2008; Spasojevic & Alloy, 2001 as cited in Reeve, 2015.

Fear of not coming out okay inhibits ability: Ashcraft, 2002; Assaf, 2006; Bandura, 1983; Bandura, 1988; Bandura, Reese & Adams, 1982; Bloom, 2008; Birenbaum & Nasser, 1994; Cherniss & Goleman, 1998; Cottny et al., 2006; Gregor, 2005; Jalongo & Hirsh, 2010; Lazaroff, 2001; Lazarus, 1991; McCraty et al., 2009; Moors et al., 2013; Murphy, 2004; Neimeyer, 2010; Ortony & Clore, 1989; Putwain, 2009; Reeve, 2015; Ryan & Deci, 2001; Tarrant et al., 2010; Thayer & Lane, 2008; Walker & Nordin-Bates, 2010.

There may be concerns regarding skills: Ashcraft, 2002; Murphy, 2004; Reeve, 2015; Weisinger & Pawliw-Fry, 2015.

Pay attention to unsure feelings: Ely, 1991; Goswami, 2008; Hinton, et al., 2008; Jalongo & Hirsh, 2010; Meharg, 1988; Moors et al., 2013; Murphy, 2004; Reeve, 2015; Thayer & Lane, 2008; Thayer et al., 2012; Weisinger & Pawliw-Fry, 2015.

Primary fears consist of not feeling loved, accepted, appreciated, secure, valued, capable: Brach, 2015; Boyle, 2015; Ely, 1991; Meharg, 1988; Moors et al., 2013; Murphy, 2004; Reeve, 2015; Thayer & Lane, 2008; Thayer et al., 2012.

Can manage even if performance bombs if loved, accepted, appreciated, secure, valued, and capable; can't if not: Brach, 2015; Boyle, 2015; Castillo, 2009; Ely, 1991; Meharg, 1988; Moors et al., 2013; Murphy, 2004; Reeve, 2015; Thayer & Lane, 2008; Thayer et al., 2012.

Insecurity regarding the support of others increases outcome anxiety: Brach, 2015; Boyle, 2015; Castillo, 21009; Ely, 1991; Meharg, 1988; Moors et al., 2013; Murphy, 2004; Reeve, 2015; Thayer & Lane, 2008; Thayer et al., 2012.

There's a tendency to hide unlovable stuff: Brach, 2015; Castillo, 2009; Cherniss & Goleman, 1998; Reeve, 2015; Stevens & Smith, 2013.

Supportive disclosure is helpful: Emmons & Thomas, 1998; 2008; Putwain, 2009; Sweeney & Horan 1982.

Authentic awareness is important: Brach, 2015; Emmons & Thomas, 1998; 2008; Putwain, 2009; Reeve, 2015; Sweeney & Horan 1982.

Outcome anxiety affects health and quality of life: APA, 2013; Berlyne, 1975; Bragge, 2006; Cizek & Burt, 2005 as cited in Salend, 2010; Emmons & Thomas, 2008; Jangalo & Hirsh, 2010; Jensen, 2005 as cited in Jalongo, 2010; Keyes, 2007; Meharg, 1988; Mogel, 2005; Murphy, 2004; NIOSH, nd; Nolen-Hoeksema et al., 2008; Putwain, 2009; Reeve, 2015; Sena et al., 2012; Young, Wu & Menon, 2012.

Stress reduction and other benefits comes from steps that decrease anxiety and increase flow/zone: APA, 2013; Bandura, 1983, 1988; Berlyne, 1975; Bragge, 2006; Cizek & Burt, 2005 as cited in Salend, 2010; Emmons & Thomas, 2008; Gilman, 2012; Jangalo & Hirsh, 2010; Jensen, 2005 as cited in Jalongo, 2010; Keyes, 2007; Lazarus, 1991; McCraty et al., 2009; Meharg, 1988; Mogel, 2005; Moors, Ellsworth, Scherer & Frijda, 2013;

Murphy, 2004; Neimeyer, 2010; Nolen-Hoeksema et al., 2008; Ortony & Clore, 1989; Putwain, 2009; Reeve, 2015; Reisenzein, 1994; Ryan & Deci, 2001; Sena et al., 2012; Thayer et al., 2012; Young, Wu & Menon, 2012.

Chapter 5: The Inseparables
Understanding and managing performance anxiety is essential to performing optimally: Emmons & Thomas, 1998, 2008; Ely, 1991; McGonigal, 2013; Murphy, 2004; Osborne & Kenny, 2008; Reeve, 2015.

Anxiety management should be as well prepared as performance skills to strengthen the performer and performance: Emmons & Thomas, 1998, 2008; Ely, 1991; Goswami, 2008; Hinton, et al., 2008; Jalongo & Hirsh, 2010; Osborne & Kenny, 2008.

Personal qualities that help in some situations can hinder in others: Abril, 2007; Ely, 1991; Hammn, 1982; Hamann & Gordon, 2000; Kenny & Osborne, 2006; Kokotsaki & Davidson, 2003; Tarrant et al., 2010; Walker & Nordin-Bates, 2010; Yondem, 2007.

There are many strategies to eliminate symptoms: Boucher & Ryan, 2011; Ely 1991; Edwards, 2009; Emmons & Thomas, 1008; Kamath, 2013; Khalsa et al. 2009; Putwain, 2009; Sweeney & Horan, 1982; Tarrant, et al., 2010; Walker & Nordin-Bates, 2010.

To eliminate anxiety, management strategies must be different: Adams, 2012; Ashcraft, 2002; Emmons & Thomas, 1998, 2008; McGonigal, 2013.

The things that feel unsure in a performance are the things that were somewhat unsure in practice: Huettel et al., 2006; Kuhnen & Knutson, 2005; Paulus & Stein, 2006; Singer, Critchley, & Preuschoff, 2009 in Reeve, 2015; Sorrentino, 2013.

If effort is less productive, there are likely deeper causes involving thoughts and feelings: Ashcraft, 2002; Ashcraft & Krause, 2007; Bandura, 1983, 1988; Bloom, 2006; Ely, 1991; Emmons & Thomas, 1998; Leffingwel, 2001; Meharg, 1988; Moors et al., 2013; Murphy, 2004; Putwain, 2009; Reeve, 2015; Sorrentino, 2013; Thayer & Lane, 2008; Thayer et al., 2012.

Practice is a time to improve the quality of skills and the quality of thoughts and feelings: Adams, 2012; Ashcraft, 2002; Ashcraft & Krause, 2007; Bandura, 1983, 1988; Bloom, 2006; Ely, 1991; Emmons & Thomas, 1998; Goswami, 2008; Hinton et al., 2008; Jalongo & Hirsh, 2010; Leffingwel, 2001; Meharg, 1988; Moors et al., 2013; Murphy, 2004; Putwain, 2009; Reeve, 2015; Thayer & Lane, 2008; Thayer et al., 2012.

Thoughts and feelings are recorded in the brain with an activity: Goswami, 2008; Hinton et al., 2008; Jalongo & Hirsh, 2010; Keyes, 2007; Reeve, 2015; Ryan & Deci, 2000; Young et al., 2012.

Injuries cause physical, mental, and emotional changes: Cramer et al., 2011; Lynn, 2013; Murphy, 2004; Reeve, 2015.

Direct, indirect, unrelated psychological factors affect performance: Adams, 2012; Ashcraft, 2002; Ashcraft & Krause, 2007; Bandura, 1983, 1988; Bloom, 2006; Ely, 1991; Emmons & Thomas, 1998; Leffingwel, 2001; Meharg, 1988; Moors et al., 2013; Murphy, 2004; Putwain, 2009; Reeve, 2015; Thayer & Lane, 2008; Thayer et al., 2012.

Self-reflection is the best way to collect data; self-awareness has many benefits: Bandura, 1988; Bloom, 2006; Boucher & Ryan, 2011; Buck, 1984 as cited in Reeve, 2015; Boyle, 2015; Emmons and Thomas, 1998, 2008; Izard, 2007; Kenny & Osborne, 2006; Ortony & Clore, 1989; Wigfield & Eccles, 1989.

Unsure feelings aren't a big deal; there are ways to move forward: Augustine & Hemenover, 2009; Boyle, 2015; Brach, 2018; Gilman, 2012; McGonigal, 2013.

Performance anxiety evolves: Augustine & Hemenover, 2009; Bandura, 1988; Bloom, 2006; Boucher & Ryan, 2011; Buck, 1984 as cited in Reeve, 2015; Emmons and Thomas, 1998, 2008; Izard, 2007; Kenny & Osborne, 2006; McGonigal, 2013; Ortony & Clore, 1989; Wigfield & Eccles, 1989.

Self-awareness makes adaptation to change easier; there are always reasons for unsure feelings: Bloom, 2006; Boyle, 2015; Brach, 2018; Ely, 1991; Emmons & Thomas, 2008; Gilman, 2012; Leffingwell, 2001; McGonigal, 2013; Nolen-Hoeksema, 2012; Putwain, 2009; Reeve, 2015; Thomas, Mellalieu & Hanon, 2008). [For an excellent compilation of sport psychology stress management applicable to other fields see Thomas, Mellalieu & Hanon, 2008.]

Chapter 6: Fear Is Your Friend

Edgy fear prepares for success; adrenaline provides benefits: Ely, 1991; Emmons & Thomas, 1998; McGonigal, 2013; Murphy; 2004; Kenny 2008, as cited in Studer, et al., 2011.

In an over-edgy, out-of-control fear cycle, often there's more fear of fear than fear of performance: Bandura & Adams, 1977 as cited in Reeve, 2015; Bandura, 1983; Bandura, Reese & Adams, 1982; Murphy, 2004.

Multiple hormones are involved in a fear cycle: Giusto, Cairncross & King, 1971; McEwen, 1999; Schulkin & Rosen, 1999.

Fear is easier to manage when understood and spotted: Ely, 1991; Emmons & Thomas, 1998; Hong, 2010a; Keifer et al., 2015; McGonigal, 2013; Wall, 2005; Sarason et al 1960 and Hermans et al. 1972 as cited in Wigfield & Eccles, 1989; Schulkin & Rosen, 1999.

Adrenaline supports the person when under physical/emotional/mental stress, but prolonged stress causes problems: Ely, 1991; Harvard Health Publishing, 2018; McEwen, 1998; Niijima, 1992.

The adrenaline response system is amazing, and understanding it can help reduce stress: Ely, 1991; Emmons & Thomas, 1998; McEwen, 1998; Murphy, 2004; Reeve, 2015.

If a fear response kicked in, something caused it: Augustine & Hemenover, 2009; Boyle, 2015; Brach, 2018; Gilman, 2012; McGonigal, 2013; Sorrentino, 2013; Reeve, 2015.

Without the emotion of fear, there's less motivation: Reeve, 2015; Weiner, 1985.

Ability starts inside: McGonigal, 2013; Murphy, 2004; Reeve, 2015; Weiner, 1985.

It's important to be able to spot all types of fear: Ashcraft, 2002; Assaf, 2006; Aylett, 2000; Bandura, Reese & Adams, 1982; Birenbaum & Nasser, 1994; Boyle, 2015; Brach, 2015; Day, 2006; Dossey, 2014; Hamann, 1985; Harvard Health Publishing, 2018; Isen & Reeve, 2005; NIOSH, n/a; Petrovich, 2003; Studer et al., 2011; Tugade & Fredrickson, 2006; Van Kemenade, Van Son & Van Heesch, 1995; Weiner et al., 1987; Zinn, McCain & Zinn, 2000.

Some fear is not visible [emotion-specific patterns in the brain]: Chetham, 2017; Janik, 2008; Jensen, 2005 as cited in Jalongo, 2010; McGonigal, 2013; Reeve, 2015; Young, Wu & Menon.

Fear causes symptoms: Ashcraft, 2002; Assaf, 2006; Aylett, 2000; Bandura, Reese & Adams, 1982; Birenbaum & Nasser, 1994; Boyle, 2015; Brach, 2015; Day, 2006; Dossey, 2014; Hamann, 1985; Harvard Health Publishing, 2018; Isen & Reeve, 2005; NIOSH, n/a; Studer et al., 2011; Tugade & Fredrickson, 2006; Van Kemenade, Van Son & Van Heesch, 1995; Weiner et al., 1987; Zinn, McCain & Zinn, 2000.

It's unlikely to have either zero or all fear symptoms [anxiety is prevalent, commonly overlooked, and some types are not seen without training]: Adams, 2012; Abu-Radia, 2004; Ashcraft, 2002; Ashcraft & Krause, 2007; Assaf, 2006; Birenbaum & Nasser, 1994; Bloom, 2008; Gregor, 2005; Jalongo & Hirsh, 2010; Lazaroff, 2001; Mogel, 2005; Murphy, 2004; Neimeyer, 2010; Petrovich, 2003; Putwain, 2009; Ryan & Andrews, 2009; Ryan & Deci, 2001; Reeve, 2015; Studer, et al., 2011; Tarrant, Leathem, & Flett, 2010.

Anxiety manifests physical, mental, emotional, behavioral symptoms [these are listed together since most references list multiple types of symptoms]: Adams, 2012; Ashcraft, 2002; Assaf, 2006; Aylett, 2000; Bandura, Reese & Adams, 1982; Birenbaum & Nasser, 1994; Bloom, 2008; Boyle, 2015; Brach, 2015; Day, 2006; Dossey, 2014; Ely, 1991; Emmons & Thomas, 2008; Hamann, 1985; Harvard Health Publishing, 2018; Hunnicutt & Winter, 2011; Isen & Reeve, 2005; Leffingwell, 2001; McGonigal, 2013; Meharg, 1988; Murphy, 2004; NIOSH, n/a; Neimeyer, 2010; Osborne, 2008; Petrovich, 2003; Robertson, 2010; Sternbach, 2008; Studer et al., 2011; Tarrant, et al., 2010; Tugade & Fredrickson, 2006; Van Kemenade, Van Son & Van Heesch, 1995; Weiner et al., 1987; Zinn, McCain & Zinn, 2000.

A lack of preparation increases anxiety: Birenbaum &Nasser 1994; Bloom, 2008; Putwain, 2009; Sweeney & Horan, 1982; Walker & Nordin-Bates, 2010; Wigfield & Eccles, 1989.

Preparation can be difficult/impossible for those with anxiety [unless addressed]: Ashcraft, 2002; Birenbaum &Nasser 1994; Hinton, et al., 2008; Jalongo & Hirsh,

2010; Putwain, 2009; Reeve, 2015; Sweeney & Horan, 1982; Taborsky, 2007; Tarrant, et al, 2010; Walker & Nordin-Bates, 2010; Wigfield & Eccles, 1989; Yondem, 2007.

Ability can immediately improve without additional instruction or practice: Adams, 2012; Ashcraft, 2002; Ashcraft & Krause, 2007; Wall, 2005.

Addressing anxiety saves time: Adams, 2012; Ashcraft, 2002; Ashcraft & Krause, 2007; Nolen-Hoeksema, Wisco & Lyubomirsky, 2008; Patterson et al., 2002; Reeve, 2015; Roughan & Hadwin, 2011.

Anxiety handled improperly decreases preparation and output, and increases dropout: Ashcraft, 2002; Birenbaum & Nasser, 1994; Bradberry & Greaves, 2005; Hinton, et al., 2008; Jalongo & Hirsh, 2010; Putwain, 2009; Reeve, 2015; Sweeney & Horan, 1982; Taborsky, 2007; Tarrant, et al, 2010; Walker & Nordin-Bates, 2010; Wall, 2005; Wigfield & Eccles, 1989; Yondem, 2007.

Conscious or subconscious nervousness can hamper performers: Ashcraft, 2002; Bandura, 1988; Chan, 2011; Csikszentmihalyi & Nakamura, 1989; Isen, 2005; Isen & Reeve, 2005; Izard, 2007; Martin & Jackson, 2008.

Chapter 7: Fix Quick without Quick Fix
Negative feelings are avoided: Franzel et al., 2007 as cited in Jalongo & Hirsh, 2010; Gross & John, 2003; Hamilton et al., 2012; Isen & Reeve, 2005; Izard, 2007; Nolen-Hoeksema et al., 2008; Taylor, 1970 & Leffingwell, 1971 as cited in Leffingwell, 2001.

Negative feelings initiate protection/warning of a conscious/subconscious concern: Ashcraft, 2002; Bandura, 1988; Bradberry & Greaves, 2005; Chan, 2011; Csikszentmihalyi & Nakamura, 1989 in Reeve, 2015; Isen & Reeve, 2005; Izard, 2007; Leffingwell, 2001; Martin & Jackson, 2008; Reeve, 2015; Semin & Manstead, 1982; Tooby & Cosmides, 1990 as cited in Reeve, 2015.

Initially positive and negative emotions feel the same, and negative emotions can heal or injure: Frijda 1986 as cited in Reeve, 2015; ; Gross & John, 2003; Izard, 1989; McGonigal, 2013; Miller et al., 2003; Reeve, 2015; Semin & Manstead, 1982; Solomon, 1990; Sternbach, 2008; Tooby & Cosmides, 1990 as cited in Reeve, 2015.

The intensity of negative emotions is not always appropriate to the situation: Augustine & Hemenover, 2009; Bloom, 2008; Bradberry & Greaves, 2005; Emmons & Thomas, 2008; Gross & John, 2003; Miller et al., 2003; Nolen-Hoeksema, 2012; Murphy, 2004; Reeve, 2015; Semin & Manstead, 1982.

Fight, flight, and freeze responses, in addition to "quick fix" defense mechanisms and triggers, kick in with anxiety: Augustine & Hemenover, 2009; Bradberry & Greaves, 2005; Emmons & Thomas, 2008; Freud as cited in Reeve, 2015; Gross & John, 2003; Miller et al., 2003; Murphy, 2004; Nolen-Hoeksema, 2012; Reeve, 2015; Semin & Manstead, 1982.

Triggers are emotional responses that affect situations: Augustine & Hemenover, 2009; Bradberry & Greaves, 2005; Edmondson et al., 2012; Emmons & Thomas, 2008; Freud as cited in Reeve, 2015; Gilman, 2012; Levenson, 2011; Gross & John, 2003; Miller et al., 2003; Nolen-Hoeksema, 2012; Patriquin, et al., 2012; Reeve, 2015; Wall, 2005.

Coping responses develop in childhood; dysfunctional ones can impact for life unless addressed: Freud as cited in Reeve, 2015; Gross & John, 2003; Kail & Cavanaugh, 2016; Kohlberg, 1969 as cited in Kail & Cavanaugh, 2016.

Thinking worse of others or circumstances than is merited is a common response: Bradberry & Greaves, 2005; Chapman et al., 2009; Kohlberg, 1969 as cited in Kail & Cavanaugh, 2016; McGonigal, 2013; Narvaez, 2010; Ochsner & Gross, 2005 as cited in Reeve, 2015.

Situations can happen before brain structures are sufficiently developed to process thoughts and feelings: Cheatham, 2017; Giovanello & Schacter, 2012; Janik, 2008; Kitchener, King & DeLuca, 2006.

It is damaging to be down on others or self; rather, focus on the future: Augustine & Hemenover, 2009; Edmonson et al., 2012; Gross & John, 2003; McGonigal, 2013; Nolen-Hoeksema et al. 2008; Reeve, 2015.

Positive change requires sustained balance of patience and self-honesty: Augustine & Hemenover, 2009; Bandura, 1983, 1988; Bradberry & Greaves, 2005; Gross & John, 2003; Reeve, 2015.

Focus on present, avoid triggers, change present to improve: Belsky & Pluess, 2009; Bradberry & Greaves, 2005; Gross & John, 2003; Miller et al., 2003; Nolen-Hoeksema et al. 2008; Patriquin, et al., 2012; Wall, 2005; Weirner et al., 1987.

Learning is usually a repeating, multi-layered process: Belsky & Pluess, 2009; Brach, 2015; Gross & John, 2003; Miller et al., 2003; Wall, 2005; Weirner et al., 1987.

It's not dredging the past, it's being aware of how the past affects now: Boyle, 2015.

Sitting with negative emotion without arousal, judging, or acting is a giant step in right direction; it allows learning and evaluation: Augustine & Hemenover, 2009; Boyle, 2015; Brach, 2015; Elliot & Church, 1997; Esch, 2014; Fiennes, nd; Gross & John, 2003; Kamath, 2013; Nolen-Hoeksema et al. 2008; Wall, 2005.

What about this is too hard? [other helpful questions: What would I do differently? Why am I sad/fearful/angry/discouraged?]: Ashcraft, 2002; Boyle, 2015; Brach, 2015; Emmons & Thomas, 2008; Hobson, 1996; Sternbach, 2008.

The goal in eliminating anxiety is to resolve the underlying conscious and subconscious concerns: Ashcraft 2002; Assf, 2006; Boyle, 2015; Brach, 2015; Ely, 1991; Emmons & Thomas, 2008; Gilman, 2012; Hobson, 1996; Sternbach, 2008.

It's easier to explore than evade: Ashcraft, 2002; Augustine & Hemenover, 2009; Bradberry & Greaves, 2005; Emmost & Thomas, 2008; Gross & John, 2003.

Shifting to the underlying concern is beneficial in many types of emotional situations, not just fear: Bradberry & Greaves, 2005; Emmons & Thomas, 2008; Gross & John, 2003; Patterson, et al., 2002; Reeve, 2015.

Performance-based fear is not about performing; there's an underlying concern: Boyle, 2015; Brach, 2015; Collishaw et al., 2010; Emmons & Thomas, 1998, 2008; Hobson, 1996; Sternbach, 2008.

Instead of evading or suppressing fear, gather valuable data regarding direct, indirect, and unrelated concerns: Gross & John, 2003; Likar & Raeburn, 2009; Martin & March, 2006; Murphy, 2004; Palmer, Donaldson & Stough, 2002; Reeve, 2015; Tugade, Fredrickson & Barrett, 2004; Weiner, 1985; Werner et al., 1987.

Chapter 8: Progress!

Tracking data increases progress and motivation: Murphy, 2004; Reeve, 2015; Weisinger & Pawliw-Fry 2015.

Definitions of "record" and "pro": Farlex, 2018; Oxford Dictionary, 2018.

Core Power Pro-Launch Pad workbook: Adams, in press, anticipated 2018.

Taking things too seriously prevents serious improvement: Hansen, 2014, 2016; Nezlek & Derks, 2006; Reeve, 2015.

There's always a reason for problems, and questioning brings attention to factors: Ashcraft 2002; Assf, 2006; Boyle, 2015; Brach, 2015; Cherniss & Goleman, 1998; Ely, 1991; Emmons & Thomas, 2008; Gilman, 2012; Hobson, 1996; Sternbach, 2008.

Examining anxiety concerns makes other efforts more efficient and effective: Ashcraft & Krause, 2007; Boucher & Ryan, 2011; Cherniss & Goleman, 1998; Ely 1991; Fredrickson, 1998; Goswami, 2008; Hinton et al., 2008; ; Isen & Daubman, 1984; Isen, Johnson, Mertz & Robinson, 1985; Isen & Reeve, 2005; Wall, 2005.

Typical time needed for recording observations [based on related info]: Bawa, 1981; Cherniss & Goleman, 1998; Erismann & Kohler, n/a.

[Note: Specific *what, when, where, why* information is documented in the next chapter]

Quick, deep, VIP reflection is beneficial: Boyle, 2015; Brach, 2015; Cherniss & Goleman, 1998; Esch, 2014; Wall, 2005.

It's common to be affected by thoughts right before performing: Boucher & Ryan, 2011; Bradberry & Greaves, 2005; Castillo, 2009; Morgan, 2008; Ryan, 1998 as cited in Tabosky, 2007; Weisinger & Pawliw-Fry, 2025.

Anxiety can be high months before performing: Emmons & Thomas, 2008; Van Kemenade, et. Al., 1995 as cited in Studer, et al., 2011.

Anxiety durations can be macro, meso, and micro: Hanton & Jones, 1999a and Hanton et al., as cited in Thomas, Mellalieu & Hanton, 2008.

[Note: Specifics regarding the types of situations, people, and activities that affect performance is documented in detail next chapter]

Chapter 9: Treasure Hunt

[Note: Factors contributing to performance-based problems and flow/zone issues is documented collectively below.]

Proactively preventing problems is beneficial: Berenson, 2005; Bradberry & Greaves, 2005; Castillo, 2009; Cherniss, & Goleman, 1998; Esch, 2014; Emmons & Thomas, 2008; Likar & Raeburn, 2009; Murphy, 2004; Reeve, 2015.

Look for problematic/helpful patterns and exceptions: Bradberry & Greaves, 2005; Castillo, 2009; Cherniss, & Goleman, 1998; Esch, 2014; Emmons & Thomas, 2008; Murphy, 2004; Sorrentino, 2013.

The first things to look for are fear symptoms [see Chapter 6: Fear is your Friend for detailed symptoms and documentation].

[The following is a fairly comprehensive list of factors that can affect performance anxiety and flow/zone. This list has more factors and patterns than contained in the chapter.] High-stress situations: Collishaw, et al., 2010; Sternbach, 2008; Tarrant, et al., 2010; high stakes—like testing or tournaments: Assaf, 2006; Birenbaum & Nasser, 1994; Gregor, 2005; Putwain, 2009; changes in positive/negative emotions in practice/performance: Murphy, 2004; Cizek & Burt, 2005 and Huberty 2009 as cited in Salend, 2010; Loehr as cited in Sternbach, 2008; changes in thought clarity, concentration, and memory retrieval: Ashcraft, 2002; Ely, 1991; Jalongo & Hirsh 2010; Mogel, 2005; Putwain, 2009; Sena et al., 2012; possible imprinting: Young et al., 2012; difficulty with specific activities or skills within an activity: Ashcraft, 2002; the same/reduced ability despite practice: Ashcraft, 2002; Jalongo & Hirsh, 2010; varied motivation: Leffingwell, 2001; physical or mental health/energy fluctuation: Ashcraft, 2002; Jalongo & Hirsh, 2010; Likar & Raeburn, 2009; Trolinger, 2005; Zinn, McCain, Zinn, 2000; self-harm like eating disorders, drugs, suicidal thoughts: Mogel, 2005; feelings of increased/decreased pressure: Lazaroff, 2001; Sternbach, 2008; mental/physical weakening: Ashcraft, 2002; Bloom, Emmons & Thomas, 2008; Murphy, 2004; Walker & Nordin-Bates, 2010; positive/negative environmental changes: Sternbach, 2008; changed sense of control over a situation: Abril, 2007; Emmons & Thomas, 2008; feeling capable/incapable of success: Emmons & Thomas, 2008; Meharg, 1988; memories of experiencing or seeing successes/failures or positive/negative treatment: Ashcraft & Krause, 2007; Boucher & Ryan, 2011; Ely, 1991; Kenny & Osborne, 2006; Putwain, 2009; Wigfield & Eccles, 1989; Yondem, 2007; attitudes that something is hard: Ashcraft & Krause, 2007; cognitive perceptions of situations: Ely, 1991; Emmons & Thomas, 2008; positive or negative learned reactions: Ely, 1991; Goswami, 2008; Hinton et al., 2008; Jalongo & Hirsh, 2010; feelings of tenacity/giving up: Frenzel et al, 2007 as cited in Jalongo & Hirsh, 2010; feelings that effort will/won't make a difference: Martin & Marsh, 2006; implementation of strategy skills: Martin & Marsh, 2006; perceptions of others' expectations on you or your own expectations: Walker & Nordin-Bates, 2010; what groups are comfortable to be in/with: Schwarzer & Lange, 1983 and Schwarzer & Schwarzer, 1982 as cited in Wigfield & Eccles, 1989; an inner desire to succeed or desire not to fail: Murphy, 2004; Putwain, 2009; is the situation impromptu/well-rehearsed, public/private, high or low memory requirements, timed or untimed: Ashcraft, 2002; Haid, 1999; LeBlanc, Jin, & Obert, 1997; Putwain, 2009; Studor, et al., 2011; smile/firmness of leader, room size/temperature/lighting, arrived early/late, familiar or unfamiliar format/location/support/situation: Abril, 2007; Ely, 1991; Emmons & Thomas, 2008; Putwain, 2009; if a situation was known in advance or not: Emmons & Thomas, 2008; Van Kemenade, et. Al., 1995 as cited in Studer, et al., 2011; feelings before, during, after—particularly right before: Boucher & Ryan, 2011; Ryan, 1998, as cited in Taborsky, 2007; perceptions in relation to outcome: Osborn & Kenny, 2008; Walker & Nordin-Bates, 2010; lack of consistency—this is a big deal so look deeper for variables causing it like higher stakes, interpersonal situations, or additional stressors: Emmons & Thomas, 2008; Sternbach, 2008; sense of self-worth or disappointment/approval of self or by others: Leffingwell, 2001; confidence level and sense of control: Ely, 1991; Walker & Nordin-Bates, 2010; dysfunctional attitudes, thoughts, or perfectionism: Abril, 2007; Bloom, 2006; Ely, 1991; Tarrant, et al., 2010; Yondem, 2007; group attitude/influence: Bloom, 2008; Murphy, 2005; comments by leaders: Stolpa, 2004; cultural attitudes/background: Goetz et al., 2008 not in ref, Putwain, 2009; Whitaker et al. 2007 as cited in Salend, 2012; if you are highest or lowest in ability levels: Assf, 2006; male/female gender factors [generally female anxiety is from social approval, male is from peer evaluation: Abril, 2007; Khalsa et al., 2009; LeBlanc, et al., 1997; Rae & McCambridge, 2004; Dweck & Bush, 1976 as cited in Wigfield & Eccles, 1989; Yondem, 2007; level of experienced flow: Kirchner, et al., 2008; Lazaroff, 2001; level of fun/freedom: Kirchner et al., 2008; type of environmental structure and ability to tackle problems [big tasks with little support vs. smaller tasks with solid support, experienced/novice]: Emmons & Thomas, 2008; Jalongo & Hirsh, 2010; Leffingwell, 2001; treatment by others: DeWitt, et al., 2011; overall work load: Assaf, 2006; Lazaroff, 2001; Mogel, 2005; Small, 1998; Solar, 2011; is attention on the present rather than past/future: Ashcraft, 2002; Murphy, 2004; Osborne & Kenny, 2008; Tarrant, et al., 2010; is your focus/the environmental focus on competition or cooperation: DeWitt et al., 2011; level of mindfulness and emotional intelligence: Brach, 2015; Ruiz-Aranda, Salguero & Cabello, 2012; ability to select thoughts: Fernandez-Berrocal, Alcaide, & Extremera, 2006; Loyd, 2005; ability to select emotions: Solar, 2011; what was done well, what could be done differently: Sternbach, 2008; level of preparation: Ely, 1991; any aversion to preparation and why: Putwain, 2009; ways used to compensate for ability: Birenbaum &Nasser 1994; Wigfield & Eccles, 1989; possible desensitization [smaller things leading up to practicing simulation]: Boucher & Ryan, 2011; Ely, 1991; Tarrant, et al., 2010; Walker & Nordin-Bates, 2010; level of relaxation and strategies to achieve it: Emmons & Thomas, 2008; Khalsa et al. 2009; Sweeney & Horan, 1982; what was imagined: Emmon & Thomas, 2008; Hinton, 2008; Murphy, 2004; were neural pathways physically warmed up before execution: Emmon & Thomas, 2008; Hinton, 2008; Murphy, 2004; was negativity countered: Emmons & Thomas, 2008; were positive distractions used: Emmons & Thomas, 2008; was there a lack of arousal or working energy up: Murphy, 2004; life balance and workloads kept up: Aylett, 2000; Boyle, 2015; Brach, 2015; and level of humor: Nezlek & Derks, 2006; Reeve, 2015.

Those with highest and lowest abilities have the most anxiety: Assaf, 2006; Hong, 2010a; Osborne & Kenny, 2005; Putwain, 2009; Whitaker et al. 2007 as cited in Salend, 2012.

Awareness of thoughts/feelings improves preparation/performance, but the type of awareness matters: Ashcraft & Krause, 2007; Bradberry & Greaves, 2005; Boucher & Ryan, 2011; Boyle, 2015; Brach, 2015; Castillo, 2009; Cherniss & Goleman, 1998; Ely 1991; Fredrickson, 1998; Goswami, 2008; Hinton et al., 2008; ; Isen & Daubman, 1984; Isen et al.,1985; Isen & Reeve, 2005; Morgan, 2008; Wall, 2005 Weisinger & Pawliw-Fry, 2015.

Chapter 10: Got Your Brain?
[Note: This chapter contains original methods based on a synthesis of research and experience.]
Brain function is affected by emotion: Ashcraft, 2002; Assf, 2006; Cloninger & Gillgan, 1987; Esch, 2014; Gilman, 2012; Goswami, 2008; Hamilton et al., 2012; Hinton et al., 2008; Jakin, 2008; Jalongo & Hirsh, 2010; Martin & Jackson, 2008; McEwen, 1998; McEwen & Sapolsky, 1995; Morgan, 2008; and Young et al., 2012). [Also see kinesthetic imagery Callow & Waters, 2005; Munroe et al., 2000; Hardy & Callow, 1999; Moritz et al., 1996; Monsma & Overby, 2004 all as cited in Cumming and Ramsey, 2008.

The research influential in developing the concepts of brain shorting, crunching, fogging, and blanking: Abu-Rabia, 2004; Adams, 2012; APA, 2013; Ashcraft, 2002; Assf, 2006; Augustine & Hemenover, 2009; Aylett, 2000; Bandura, 1983, 1988; Bawa, 1981; Berlyne, 1975; Berthoud & Neuhauer, 2000; Bloom, 2008; Bragge, 2006; Chan, 2011; Chrousos & Gold, 1992; Cloninger & Gillgan, 1987; Deci & Ryan, 1085; Draganski et al., 2004; Elliot & Church, 1997; Ely, 1991; Emmons & Thomas, 1998, 2008; Esch, 2014; Etkin & Wager, 2007; Fehm & Schmidt, 2006; Fernandez-Berrocal et al., 2006; Fredrickson, 1998; Fredrickson & Barrett, 2004; Gilman, 2012; Giovanello & Schacter, 2012; Giovanni & Csikszentmihalyi, 1996; Goswami, 2008; Gross & John, 2003; Haid, 1999; Hamann, 1982, 1985; Hamilton et al., 2012; Hanin & Hanina, 2009; Hinton et al., 2008; Hedden & Gabrieli, 2004; Hodgins & Knee, 2002; Hong, 2010a; Hunnicutt, 2011; Izard, 1989, 2007; Jalongo & Hirsh, 2010; Kirchner et al., 2008; Lazaroff, 2001; Lazarus, 1991; LeBlanch et al., 1997; Lehrer, 1985; Martin & Jackson, 2008; Martin, 2006; McEwen & Sapolsky, 1995; McEwen, 1998; Murphy, 2004; Neilsen et al., 2017; Neimeyer, 2010; Nezlek, 2006; Nolen-Hoeksema, et al., 2008; Ortony & Clore, 1989; Putwain, 2009; Putwain & Best, 1911; Sorrentino, 2013; Studer et al., 2011; Tugade et al., 2004; Tugade & Fredrickson, 2006; Van

Oort et al., 2009; Wall, 2005; Weiner et al., 1987; Wortman & Brehm 1975; Young et al., 2012; Zinn et al., 2000). [Of primary interest sparking the initial development of these concepts were Ashcraft, 2002; Goswami, 2008; Hinton et al., 2008; Jalongo & Hirsh, 2010; and Young et al., 2012. Also excellent are Cheatham, 2007; Janik, 2008; and Morgan, 2008.

Chapter 11: Bring Your Brain
[See Chapter 10 for references influential in the development of these original concepts and methods.]

Chapter 12: Plan a Neuroplasticity Party!
Neuroplasticity is the brain's adaption through synapse development or pruning: Bawa, 1981; Bradberry & Greaves, 2005; Cramer et al., 2011.

Synapse changes appear within a week of intervention: Davidson & McEwen, 2012.

Evidence that the brain changes with incidental and deliberate social/emotional intervention; stress enlarges the amygdala, and shrinks the hippocampus and prefrontal cortex: Draganski et al., 2004.

Evidence that not just synapses are changed, actual grey matter is added: Gardian, 2012 [Commentary on Erismann & Kohler, flipped images 3 weeks]; Reeve, 2015; Theodore Erismann and Ivo Kohler: Erismann, n/a [video documentation of flipped images]; Stevens & Smith, 2013.

Brain structures overused in anxiety and depression can be changed with knowledge, support and effort: Bradberry & Greaves, 2005; Cloninger & Gillgan, 1987; Cramer et al., 2011; Davidson & McEwen, 2012; Draganski et al., 2004; Esch, 2014; Etkin & Wagner, 2007; Groves & Brown, 2005; Hinton et al., 2008; Jalongo & Hirsh, 2010; McEwen & Sapolsky, 1995; McEwen, 1998; McGonigal, 2013; Murphy, 2004; Neilsen et al., 2017; Paton et al., 2006; Paulus & Stein, 2006; Poirazi & Mel, 2001; Reeve, 2015; Schreurs et al., 1986; Weisinger & Pawliw-Fry, 2015; Winecoff et al., 2011; Young et al., 2012; Yuan, et al., 2011.

Level of belief affects outcome [specifically self-talk]: Araki et al., 2006 as cited in Hardy, Oliver & Tod, 2008; Oikawa, 2004 as cited in Hardy, Oliver & Tod, 2008. [For an excellent compilation of research on self-talk see Hardy, Oliver & Tod, 2008.]

Visual, aural, memory parts are different [and have to converge, code, and decode for coordinated memory]: Attwood, 1971; Cramer et al., 2011; Hassabis et al., 2007; Hinton et al., 2008.

Think one thing at a time, as multitasking is ineffective: Miller as cited in Hamilton, 2008.

Thinking negative thoughts of failing is problematic: Cumming & Ramsey, 2008; Cramer et al., 2011; Davidson & McEwen, 2012; Draganski et al., 2004; Emmons & Thomas, 2008; Hardy, Oliver & Tod, 2008; Hinton et al., 2008; Murphy, 2004; Reeve, 2015.

Addictions are maladaptive neuroplasticity: Cramer et al., 2011.

Neuroplasticity does not determine the quality support developed: Cumming & Ramsey, 2008; Cramer et al., 2011; Davidson & McEwen, 2012; Hinton et al., 2008; Reeve, 2015.

A good habit is as hard to break as a bad one: Richards, nd.

Disrupting fear, shrinking: Bandler, 2016.

Benefits of imagery, visualization, mental practice, kinesthetic imagery, etc: Attwood, 1971; Belnap, 2012; Cumming & Ramsey, 2008; Lynn, 2013; Emmons & Thomas, 2008; Lynn, 2013; Libby et al., 2007; Morgan, 2008; Murphy, 2004; Reeve, 2015. [For an excellent compilation of research on this subject see Cumming and Ramsey, 2008. The following are cited in that source:

Functions of visualization: Martin et al., 1999; Paivio, 1985. Injury recovery regarding anatomical improvement: Giacobbi et al., 2003; Hanrahan & Vergeer, 2000; Nordin & Cumming, 2005b, Driediger et al., 2006; Evans et al., 2006. Self efficacy: Sordoni et al., 2002. Motivation and intention: Gammage et al., 2000; Hausenblas et al., 1999; Rogers et al., 2001. Kinesthetic imagery: Callow & Waters, 2005; Munroe et al., 2000; Hardy & Callow, 1999; Moritz et al., 1996; Monsma & Overby, 2004; artistry (Nordin & Cumming 2005b. PETTLEP: Holmes and Collins, 2001, 2002. Replace negative thoughts: Smith et al., 2007. Vivid mental exercises affect physical reactions: Smith et al., 2007. Biofeedback shows physical/mental practice effect: Cumming et al., 2007; Callego et al., 1996; Hecker & Kaczor, 1988; Smith & Collins, 2004; Smith et al., 2003; Ehrsson et al., 2003. Overt and imagined motor activities activate similar brain structures: Ehrsson et al., 2003; Fadiga et al., 1999.]

External 3rd person/internal 1st person view: Blair et al., 1993 as cited in Cumming & Ramsey, 2008; Cumming & Ste-Marie, 2001 as cited in Cumming & Ramsey, 2008 ; Hardy & Callow, 1999 as cited in Cumming & Ramsey, 2008; Emmons & Thomas, 2008; Lynn, 2013; Libby et al., 2007.

Visualization benefits and affect on the body: [see previous several references cited in Cumming and Ramsey, 2008.]

Organist and mental practice story: Belnap, 2012; for similar benefits see also Cumming & Ramsey, 2008; Lynn, 2013, Morgan, 2008.

Chapter 13: When Not To Think

Different tasks use different parts of the brain: Bradberry & Greaves, 2005; Cloninger & Gillgan, 1987; Cramer et al., 2011; Davidson & McEwen, 2012; Draganski et al., 2004; Esch, 2014; Etkin & Wagner, 2007; Florin-Lechner et al., 1996; Groves & Brown, 2005; Hinton et al., 2008; Jalongo & Hirsh, 2010; McEwen & Sapolsky, 1995; McEwen, 1998; McGonigal, 2013; Murphy, 2004; Neilsen et al., 2017; Paton et al., 2006; Paulus & Stein, 2006; Reeve, 2015; Schreurs et al., 1986; Weisinger & Pawliw-Fry, 2015; Winecoff et al., 2011; Young et al., 2012; Yuan, et al., 2011.

Working memory can become taxed; anxiety affects memory: Ashcraft & Krause, 2007; Eysenck & Calvo, 1992; Eysenck et al., 2007; Fallon et al., 1978; Florin-Lechner et al., 1996; Holdefer & Jensen, 1985; Segal et al., 1991.

The brain performs differently under pressure: Ashcraft & Krause, 2007; Hinton et al., 2008; Holdfer & Jensen, 1985; Jalongo & Hirsh, 2010; Janik, 2008.

Tasks requiring memory or muscle memory, and automated tasks should not be shifted to the right hemisphere to the prefrontal cortex: Morgan, 2008; Murpy, 2004; Reeve, 2015; Weisinger & Pawliw-Fry, 2015.

The cause of choking is related to thinking choking only happens when you want something: Janik, 2008; Morgan, 2008; Murpy, 2005; Reeve, 2015; Wegner, 2005; Wegner et al., 1987; Weisinger & Pawliw-Fry, 2015.

Right hemisphere processing is not consciously aware, frontal lobe processing is aware: Janik, 2008; Morgan, 2008; Reeve, 2015; Weisinger & Pawliw-Fry, 2015.

Only one thing can be consciously thought of at a time: Miller, nd, as cited in Hamilton, 2008; Morgan, 2008. [It is possible to do more than one thing because of subconscious right hemisphere function; but conscious thought is singular.]

Focus on the specific task instead of internal or external distractions. Brain shifts cause problems in performance. When skills or other performance material becomes automatic, conscious thinking can focus elsewhere: Weisinger & Pawliw-Fry, 2015.

Experienced performers are better able to keep self-awareness in check during performance. The three types of awareness are internal, task, and external: Emmons & Thomas, 1998; 2008; Morgan, 2008; Weisinger & Pawliw-Fry, 2015.

The conscious mind imposes judgment and improvements: Emmons & Thomas, 1998; 2008; Morgan, 2008; Murphy, 2004; Reeve, 2015; Weisinger & Pawliw-Fry, 2015.

Practice makes permanent; perfect practice makes perfect: Watts, nd.

Squeeze a ball in the left hand or make a fist: Beckman, 2013 as cited in Weisinger & Pawliw-Fry, 2015.

Gum chewing raises test scores: Johnson, et al., 2012; Stephen & Tunney, 2004; Takeuchi, et al., 2013.

Brains need breaks: Belnap, 2012; Ericsson as cited in Schwartz, 2013; Haupt, 2014.

Chapter 14: Glucose and Grudge Busting

It's tough to have good output without good brain support: Cloninger & Gillgan, 1987; Cramer et al., 2011; Davidson & McEwen, 2012; Draganski et al., 2004; Esch, 2014; Emmons & Thomas, 1998, 2998; Etkin & Wagner, 2007; Groves & Brown, 2005; Hinton et al., 2008; Jalongo & Hirsh, 2010; McEwen & Sapolsky, 1995; McEwen, 1998; McGonigal,

2013; Murphy, 2004; Neilsen et al., 2017; Paton et al., 2006; Paulus & Stein, 2006; Reeve, 2015; Schreurs et al., 1986; Weisinger & Pawliw-Fry, 2015; Winecoff et al., 2011; Young et al., 2012; Yuan, et al., 2011.

The brain averages about 60,000 thoughts/day: Boyle, 2015.

There are 10 billion brain nerve cells, linked with 10 trillion connections. EEG electrode synaptic feedback consists of between 10 million-1 billion neurons communicating through neurotransmitters: McCraty et al., 2009.

Neurotransmitters are made from glucose. Brain pathways can't communicate without them. The brain uses 20% of the body glucose: Baumeister & Tierney, 2011 as cited in Reeve, 2015; Gailliot & Baumeister, 2007; Stephens & Tunney, 2004.

Positive things burn glucose slower and widen attention; negative things burn glucose faster and narrow attention: Bandura, 1988; Chan, 2011; Cohn & Fredrickson, 2009; Csikszentmihalyi & Nakamura, 1989; Fredrickson, 2009; Gailliot & Baumeister, 2007; Isen, 2005; Isen & Reeve, 2005; Izard, 2007; Martin & Jackson, 2008; Reeve, 2015.

Not all glucose is the same in the body: Galilliot & Baumeister, 2007; Monteiro, 2009; Reeve, 2005.

Glucose equals willpower, and it affects emotions: Baumeister & Tierney, 2011 as cited in Reeve, 2015; Gailliot & Baumeister, 2007; Reeve, 2015.

Gut bacteria affect the brain and emotions: Foster, 2013; Galland, 2014; Savignac et al., 2015; Spencer et al., 2018.

Brain mass in relation to blood support, and the effect of dehydration: Foltz & Ferrara, 2006.

A negative attitude burns glucose faster, it's beneficial to develop cheerful, informed engagement: Ashcraft, 2002; Bandura, 1988; Chan, 2011; Cohn & Fredrickson, 2009; Csikszentmihalyi & Nakamura, 1989; Fredrickson, 2009; Gailliot & Baumeister, 2007; Isen, 2005; Isen & Reeve, 2005; Izard, 2007; Martin & Jackson, 2008; Reeve, 2015. [Related, Importanceofplay.eu 2018]

There is always an ability to choose attitude: Frankl, 1959, 1985, 1960, 1975.

The brain is pre-programmed to conserve energy: Bandura, 1988; Chan, 2011; Cohn & Fredrickson, 2009; Csikszentmihalyi & Nakamura, 1989; Fredrickson, 2009; Gailliot & Baumeister, 2007; Isen, 2005; Isen & Reeve, 2005; Izard, 2007; Martin & Jackson, 2008; Reeve, 2015.

There are two basic neural pathways for learning, dependent on things like stress and negative emotion: Cheatham, 2017; Hinton et al., 2008; Holdefer & Jensen, 1985; Jolongo & Hirsh, 2010; Janik, 2008; Reeve, 2015.

A negative person can affect others: Murphy, 2004; Reeve, 2015.

Chapter 15: Heart Attacking

Thought comes from the whole body and organizes according to body responses and sensory stimuli: Bandura, 1991; Cheatham, 2017; Cramer et al., 2011; Draganski et al., 2004; Gaillot & Baumeister, 2007; Edmondson et al., 2012;Gross & John, 2003; Groves & Brown, 2005; Janik, 2008; Lawrence et al., 1995; Mauskop, 2005; Niijima, 1992; Paton, 1998; Paton et al., 2006; Reeve, 2015; Seitz, 2000; Schreurs et al., 1986.

The heart may store information that affects ability on a deep level: Berthoud & Neuhuber, 2000; Bressler et al., 1993; Francis, et al., 2016; Gilman, 2012; Hirsch & Bishop, 1081; Kamath, 2013; Langhorst et al., 1986; Lehrer et al., 2003; Matsui et al., 2018; Mauskop, 2005; McCraty et al., 1985; McCraty et al., 2009; Patriquin, et al., 2012; Raschke, 1986; Thayer et al., 2012; Thayer & Lane, 2008; Tiller, et al., 1996; Tugade & Fredrickson, 2006; Turpin, 1986.

More information transmits from the heart to brain than vice versa; the heart can anticipate and override the brain, modulate systemic activity, and produce neurotransmitters: Berthoud & Neuhuber, 2000; Bressler et al., 1993; Gilman, 2012; Hirsch & Bishop, 1081; Kamath, 2013; Langhorst et al., 1986; Lehrer et al., 2003; Matsui et al., 2018; Mauskop, 2005; McCraty et al., 1985; McCraty et al., 2009; Raschke, 1986; Thayer et al., 2012; Thayer & Lane, 2008; Tiller, et al., 1996; Tugade & Fredrickson, 2006; Turpin, 1986.

The heart rate can be used for diagnosis of anxiety/depression: Matsui, Shinba & Sun , 2018.

Heart rate used for increasing flow/zone: Gilman, 2012; McCraty et al., 1985; McCraty et al., 2009.

The heart's electrical and chemical processes are complicated and have a greater effect than realized: Berthoud & Neuhuber, 2000; Bressler et al., 1993; Edmondson et al., 2012; Gilman, 2012; Hirsch & Bishop, 1081; Kamath, 2013; Langhorst et al., 1986; Lehrer et al., 2003; Matsui et al., 2018; Mauskop, 2005; McCraty et al., 1985; McCraty et al., 2009; Raschke, 1986; Thayer et al., 2012; Thayer & Lane, 2008; Tiller, et al., 1996; Tugade & Fredrickson, 2006; Turpin, 1986.

The heart affects self-control: Tiller et al., 1996.

If the emotional regulation part of the brain is damaged, a person can't function: Harlow, 1848 as cited in Bradberry & Greaves, 2005.

Emotion is felt in the heart: Boyle, 2015; Brach, 2015; Esch, 2014; Fiennes, n/a; Kamath, 2013.

Flow/zone is affected by the heart: Berthoud & Neuhuber, 2000; Gilman, 2012; Gross, et al., 2017; McCraty et al., 1985; McCraty et al., 2009; Tiller et al., 1996.

The vagus nerve, amygdala, prefrontal cortex function, and insula, in relation to anxiety: Berthoud & Neuhuber, 2000; Cheatham, 2017; Coupland et al., 1989; Davidson & McEwen, 2012; Etkin & Wager, 2007; Groves & Brown, 2005; Hamilton et al., 2012; Janik, 2008; Keifer et al., 2015; Kitchener et al., 2006; McEwen & Sapolsky, 1995; Niijima, 1992; Paulus & Stein, 2006; Paton et al., 2006; Schulkin & Rosen, 1999; Thayer et al., 2012; Thayer & Lane, 2008; Tiller et al., 1996.

The interoceptive prediction signal, amygdala, insular activity: Paulus & Stein, 2006; Paton et al., 2006.

Vagus nerve stimulation affects putting experiences in long-term memory: Lawrence, Watking & Jarrott, 1996; Schreurs, Seeling, & Schulman 1986.

Believed level of control is more important than actual threat: Bandura, 1983; Bandura, 1988; Ely, 1991; Emmons & Thomas, 2008; McGonigal, 2013; Meharg, 1988; Paulus & Stein, 2006; Thayer et al., 2012; Weisinger & Pawliw-Fry, 2015.

The heart can be trained: Gilman, 2012; Gross et al., 2017; McCraty et al., 1985; McCraty et al., 2009; Thayer et al., 2012; Thayer & Lane, 2008; Tiller et al., 1996.

Breathing modulates the heart: Fiennes, nd; Gilman, 2012; Hirsch & Bishop, 1981; Tiller, 1996.

Teachers recognized correlation between ability and experiences, and found that ability improved with emotional healing: Ashcraft, 2002; Ashcraft & Krause, 2007; Ely, 1991; Forkey, 2015; Hong, 2010b; Kenny & Osborne, 2006; Leffingwell, 2001; Putwain, 2009; Reeve, 2015; Wigfield & Eccles, 1989.

Body function changes: Gilman, 2012; Fiennes, nd; Forkey, 2015; McCraty et al., 1985; McCraty et al., 2009; Patriquin, et al., 2012.

DNA may change and be passed on: Bateson & Curley, 2013; Chakravarti & Little, 2003; Dias & Ressler, 2013; Houri-Ze'evi et al., 2016; Immler, 2018; Lamm & Jablonka, 2008; Pinzon-Rodriguez, Bensch, Muheim, 2018; Rutter, Moffit & Caspi, 2005; Tooby & Cosmides, 2008 as cited in Reeve, 2015; Weaver, 2007.

Emotional triggers can cause heart attacks: Edmondson et al., 2012.

Psychological healing after injuries may need to take place on several levels: Boyle 2015; Brach, 2015; Davidson & McEwn, 2012; Esch, 2014; Etkin & Wagner, 2007; Fiennes, nd; Gilman, 2012; Forkey, 2015; McCraty et al., 1985; McCraty et al., 2009; Olivares, 2016; Thayer et al., 2012; Thayer & Lane, 2008; Tiller et al., 1996; Yehuda et al., 2016.

Yoga masters identify an interplay with meditation, ability, and the heart chakra, and the benefits of "clearing emotional blocks": Boyle, 2015; Brach, 2015; Esch, 2014; Fiennes, nd; Kamath, 2013; Khalsa et al., 2009.

Experiences are imbedded into tissue, memories and perhaps more: Bateson & Curley, 2013; Chakravarti & Little, 2003; Gilman, 2012; Lamm & Jablonka, 2008; McCraty et al., 1985; McCraty et al., 2009; Poirazi & Mel, 2001; Rutter, Moffit & Caspi, 2005; Tooby & Cosmides, 2008 as cited in Reeve, 2015.

Experiences appear to change the body function/tissue: Gilman, 2012; Lamm & Jablonka, 2008; McCraty et al., 1985; McCraty et al., 2009; Rutter, Moffit & Caspi, 2005. The effect of experiences appear to be removed: Fiennes, nd; Gilman, 2012; McCraty et al., 1985; McCraty et al., 2009; Thayer et al., 2012; Thayer & Lane, 2008; Tiller et al., 1996. [Related concept, Insular causes unsure feelings: Paulus & Stein, 2006.]

Small things can affect performance flow/zone: Ashcraft, 2002; Boyle, 2015; Brach, 2015; Ely, 1991; Gilman, 2012; Reeve, 2015.

An interplay is noted between trauma, the heart and lungs and chakra clearing affecting function: Fiennes, nd.

The heart can be trained for maximum ability: Fiennes, nd; Gilman, 2012; Gross, et al., 2017; Khalsa et al., 2009; McCraty et al., 1985; McCraty et al., 2009; Thayer et al., 2012; Thayer & Lane, 2008; Tiller et al., 1996.

Chapter 16: A Change of Heart

Bodies have a strong propensity toward physical and emotional homeostasis where baselines are maintained. This makes changes stressful: Cummings et al., 2002; Chrousos & Gold, 1992; Chrousos 1995; Edmondson et al., 2012; Hamilton et al., Reeve, 2015; Vaillant, 2000.

Stress affects heart and lung function: Langhorst, Schulz, & Lambertz, 1986; Raschke, 1986; Turpin, 1986 in McCarty 2009.

Respiration changes the heart and vagus nerve input; vagus nerve input changes the brain/body activity: Finnes, nd; Gilman, 2012; Groves & Brown; 2005; Hassert et al., 2004; Hirsch & Bishop, 1981; McCraty et al., 1985; McCraty et al., 2009; Raschke, 1986; Thayer et al., 2012; Thayer & Lane, 2008; Tiller et al., 1996; Turpin, 1986.

Service is beneficial: Astin, 2000; Gilman, 2012; Neumann & Chi, 1999; McCraty, 2009; McGonigal, 2013; Sax, 1997.

Yoga has physical and emotional benefits: Boyle, 2015; Brach, 2015; Fiennes, nd; Khalsa et al., 2009.

Gratitude is advocated by major religions, and is beneficial in Hinduism, Christianity, Islam, Buddhism, and Judaism: Bible, 2018; Boyle, 2015; Brach, 2015; Sood & Cupta, 2013.

The benefits of gratitude, and the benefits and mechanics of gratitude breathing: Akhtar, M. 2012; Boyle, 2015; Brach, 2015; Gilman, 2012; McCraty, 1995; McCraty, 2009; Tiller et al., 1996 as cited in McCraty, 2009.

There are long-lasting changes in the heartbeat as improvement is made: Gilman, 2012; McCraty et al., 1985; McCraty et al., 2009; Raschke, 1986; Thayer et al., 2012; Thayer & Lane, 2008; Tiller et al. 1996; Turpin, 1986.

There can be physical healing of traumatic experiences: Boyle, 2015; Brach, 2015; Gilman, 2012.

Emotion referred to as energy states: Boyle, 2015; Brach, 2015; Gilman, 2012; Matsui, Shinba, & Sun 2018.

Athletes and teams use heart biofeedback, possible electromagnetic field interaction: Gilman, 2012.

Choir heart beats in synchronized: Vickhoff, 2013.

An audience affects performers [and interpersonal action affects performance]: Le Blanch et al, 1997; Murphy, 2004; Reeve, 2015; Vickhoff, 2013.

Chapter 17: Culture Shock!

Cultural comparison: Small, 1998 [insightful, since prior to significant internet]

Technology has positive and negative effects: Cherniss & Goleman, 1998; Cottyn et al., 2006; Deci et al., 1999; Dossey, 2014; Elliot & Church, 1997; Fairburn & Harrison, 2003; Gilman, 2012; McGonigal, 2013; NIOSH; Natarajan, 2018.

"New normal" stress has negative physiological effects, and it impacts psychological and sociological function: Chrousos & Kino, 2015; Cottyn et al., 2006; Dossey, 2014; McEwen, 1998; McEwen & Sapolsky, 1995; Yuan et al., 2013.

Better than kings, time, machines and resources to grow: Richards, nd.

Information overload and addictions cause damage: Dossey, 2014; Herman, 2016 as cited in Natarajan, 2018; Yuan, et al., 2013.

Brain structure changes with information overload: Yuan, Qin, Wang et al. 2011.

Digital overload terms: Dossey, 2014; Natarajan, 2018.

Too much information is addictive, causes stress, and reduces brain function and grey matter in a way similar to addiction: Chaetham, 2017; Dossey, 2014; Janik, 2008; Chousos & gold, 1992; Davidson & McEwen, 2012; McEwen & Sapolsky, 1995; Yuan et al., 2011.

Roger Bannister's four-minute mile: First Four Minute Mile, 2018.

It's the perception of stressful situations that determines if they cause damage or invigorate: Deci & Ryan, 1985; McGonigal, 2013; Murphy, 2004; Posener, 2000; Reeve, 2015; Weiner et al., 1987.

Pressure is a choice; a person can learn to release pressure: Bandura, 1988; Bandura et al., 1982; Boyle, 2015; Brach, 2015; Castillo, 2009; Cherniss & Goleman, 1998; Esch, 2014; Fernandez-Berrocal et al., 2006; Fiennes, nd; Frankl, 1975; Harvard Health Publishing, 2018; Hurrell & Murphy, 1996; McCraty et al., 2009; McGonigal, 2013; Palmer et al., 2002; Patterson et al., 2002; Ruiz-Aranda et al., 2012; Wall, 2005; Weisinger & Pawliw-Fry, 2015; Young, 2016.

Chapter 18: Stop Trying to Get It Right
[See previous chapters for related references, particularly how perceptions affect stress and ability.]

Chapter 19: Appearance Anxiety
Most of the concepts in this chapter have been previously documented, however the word use may be different. These notes help clarify documentation: Anxiety clouds judgment—thinking changes with anxiety; there is no right way—see perfectionism and avoidance behavior; unreal expectations—see social media effects; joy is missed—see effects of anxiety; reasonable solutions—see perfectionism.

The Princess Diaries example: Houston, Chase, Iscovich, & Marshall, 2001.

Edited muffins picture alters perceptions: Stevenson, 2017.

Authentic impossible w/o core concerns, including being okay appearing weak: Frankl, 1985, 1960, 1975; Fredrickson & Barrett, 2004. [See also inner resiliency, self-efficacy, self-determination.]

Smile about hair: Richards, nd.

Some products little value or quality: Richards,1997.

Time, money, energy resources: Richards, nd.

Anxiety eats resources: Ramsey, 2018.

Chapter 20: Emo Safety
Ability to maintain emotional safety for self and others is emotional IQ; it's the greatest predictor of success: Bandura, 1988; Berenson, 2005; Bradberry & Greaves, 2005; Bradley et al., 2010; Chan, 2011; Cherniss & Goleman, 1998; Emmons & Thomas, 2008; Fernandez-Berrocal, Alcaide, & Extremera, 2006; Fredrickson & Barrett, 2004; Grieve, 2013; Gross, 2003; Gross et al., 2017; Kirchner et al., 2008; Lazaroff, 2001; Likar & Raeburn, 2009; Loyd, 2005; Palmer, Donaldson & Stough, 2002; Patterson et al., 2002; Ruiz-Aranda, Salguero & Cabello, 2012; Taylor, 1970 & Leffingwell, 1971 as cited in Leffingwell 2001; Wall, 2005; Weisinger & Pawliw-Fry, 2015.

A person is vulnerable when performing: Bandura, 1991; Cizek & Burt, 2005 as cited in Salend, 2010; Emmons & Thomas, 2008; Gilman, 2012; Jangalo & Hirsh, 2010; Meharg, 1988; Mogel, 2005; Murphy, 2004; Nolen-Hoeksema et al., 2008; Putwain, 2009; Putwain & Best, 2011; Reeve, 2015; Sena et al., 2012.

Anxiety flow/zone concerns are not just about a performance but about emotional safety: Adams et al., 2005; Bandura, 1988; Bandura, 1991; Berenson, 2005; Bradberry & Fincham, 1990; Bradberry & Greaves, 2005; Bradley et al., 2010; Chan, 2011; Cherniss & Goleman, 1998; Emmons & Thomas, 2008; Fernandez-Berrocal et al., 2006; Hoover & Olson, 2000; Palmer et al., 2002; Patterson et al., 2002; Ruiz-Aranda et al., 2012; Taylor, 1970 & Leffingwell, 1971 as cited in Leffingwell 2001; Weisinger & Pawliw-Fry, 2015.

Emotional safety is not optional; people are driven to get it and get a little wacky without it: Adams et al., 2005; APA, 2013; Ashcraft, 2002; Bjorkqvist et al., 1992; Bjorkqvist et al., 2000; Brown & Richardson, 1996; Franzel et al., 2007 as cited in Jalongo & Hirsh, 2010; Freud 1946 as cited in Reeve, 2015; Hamilton et al., 2012; Hoover & Olson, 2000; Isen, 2005; Isen & Reeve, 2005; Izard, 2007; Nichols, 1996; Nolen-Hoeksema et al., 2008; Taylor, 1970 & Leffingwell, 1971 as cited in Leffingwell, 2001; Posener et al., 2000; Slavich, et al., 2010; Vaillant, 2000; Weiner et al., 1991.

Emotional wounds are real and can be felt; there are reasons for emotional pain: Adams, et al., 2005; Bradbury & Fincham, 1990; Brendtro, 2001; Hoover & Olson, 2000;

Nichols, 1996; Slavic et al., 2010; Ten Boom 1974 as cited in Worthington, 1998; Weiner et al., 1991; Worthington, 1998.

There are two ways to get emotional safety, manipulation and respect: Austin et al., 2007; Bandura, 1991, 2001; Bradbury & Fincham, 1990; Brendtro, 2001; Green et al., 1996; Grieve & Mahar, 2010; Grieve & Panebianco, 2013; Hoover & Olson, 2000; Levenson et al., 1995; Nichols, 1996; Richardson & Green, 1999; Richardson & Green, 2003; Richardson & Brown, 2006.

Kissing up and prejudice are forms of manipulation for position [affected by subconscious preferences]: Brendtro, 2001; Evans, 2002; Greenwald et al., 2003; Greenwald et al., 2009; Weiner et al., 1991; Worthington, 1998.

Manipulation trips up competent people: Levenson et al., 1995; Weiner et al., 1991; Worthington, 1998.

Artistry vs. manipulation [artistry is confident competence, manipulation is a form of aggression to feel more confident]: Bandura, 1983, 1988, 2001; Emmons & Thomas, 1998; 2008; Murphy, 2004; Weiner et al., 1991; Worthington, 1998.

Kind manipulation [see "kissing up"].

It's important to disclose carefully to good support; this is different than suppression: Brach, 2015; Brendtro, 2001; Boyel, 2015; Emmons & Thomas, 1998, 2008.

Chapter 21: Intrinsic vs. Extrinsic Worth

[Note: There is a difference between intrinsic/extrinsic motivation and intrinsic/extrinsic worth. The author believes that they are almost always connected and bases research support upon this premise. Others have called intrinsic worth "true self esteem" and extrinsic worth "contingent self-esteem" (Deci & Ryan, 1995). Additionally, this author believes that intrinsic vs. extrinsic factors strongly influence a traumatic/low road versus transformational/high road brain processing difference when learning (Cheatham, 2017; Janik, 2008). The author's conclusions are based on observation, case studies, and research synthesis.]

Focus on intrinsic worth and motivation allows for greater optimal wellbeing, application, creativity, quality learning, and motivation: Cheatham, 2017; Deci & Ryan, 1985, 1995; Janik, 2008; Murphy, 2004; Reeve, 2015; Ryan & Deci, 2000; Ryan, 1982; Vansteenkiste et al., 2006.

Focus on extrinsic worth and motivation decreases motivation, engagement, and internal motivation; what was play becomes work, and there are hidden costs: Cheatham, 2017; Deci & Ryan, 1995; Deci et al., 1999; Emmons & Thomas, 1998, 2008; Hoover & Olson, 2000; Janik, 2008; Murphy, 2004; Lepper & Greene, 1978; Plant & Ryan, 1985; Putwain, 2009; Ryan, 1982; Vansteenkiste et al., 2006; Wiechman & Gurland, 2009.

Extrinsic worth is based on comparisons [ego involvement]: Deci & Ryan, 1995; Nichols, 1996; Plant & Ryan, 1985; Ryan, 1982; Vansteenkiste et al., 2006.

Society emphasizes extrinsic worth: Deci & Ryan, 1995; Lepper et al., 2005; Reeve, 2015.

Focusing on extrinsic worth is a cause of outcome anxiety [when there are internal evaluations, comparisons, and detrimental self-awareness]: Deci & Ryan, 1987, 1995; Plant & Ryan, 1985; Ryan, 1982; Reeve, 2015.

Extrinsic worth is insatiable; it leads to subconscious insecurity, and it's difficult to manage without greater understanding of it: Deci & Ryan, 1995; Nichols, 1996; Ryan, 1982.

Research shows there is more focus, enjoyment, and motivation focusing on intrinsic worth rather than extrinsic positioning: Deci & Ryan, 1995; Nichols, 1996; Ryan, 1982.

Intrinsic motivation can influence and pass on to others : Hatfield, E., Cacioppo, J. T., Rapson, R. L. 1993, and Oatley & Duncan 1994, as cited in Reeve, 2015; Nichols, 1996.

Focusing on intrinsic worth enhances ability and increases positive relationships: Black & Deci, 2000; Chirkov & Ryan, 2001; Ryan, 1982.

Focusing on intrinsic worth engages a higher brain function [lower fear factor]: Cheatham, 2017; Hinton, et al., Janik, 2008.

The cello story and comments by Professor Bruce Walker: Walker, 2018.

Chapter 22: THE Best vs. MY Best
[See previous chapter documentation; THE Best correlates with Extrinsic Worth, MY Best correlates with Intrinsic Worth.]
Societal changes and emphasis on competition: Assaf, 2006; Cottyn et al., 2006; Deci et al., 1999; Nichols, 1996; Small, 1998.
For some, a fear of looking stupid can prevent effort; for others, effort may only extend through obtaining a reward. [Ego involvement affects effort]: Murphy, 2004; Plant & Ryan, 1985; Sorrentino, 2013; Reeve, 2015.
There can be unthinkable actions toward self and others: Adams et al., 2005; Ely 1991; Fairburn & Harrison, 2003; Hoover & Olson, 2000; Lehrer, 1987; Murphy, 2004; Nolen-Hoeksema et al., 2008; Reeve, 2015; Stevens & Smith, 2013; Taborsky, 2007.
How and why honors are achieved [to prove worth]: Bandura, 1988; Deci & Ryan, 1995; Murphy, 2004; Plant & Ryan, 1985; Reeve, 2015; Ryan, 1982; Vansteenkiste et al., 2006.
Self-esteem is based on what internal thoughts: Deci & Ryan, 1985, 1995; Murphy, 2004; Plant & Ryan, 1985; Reeve, 2015; Ryan & Deci, 2000; Ryan, 1982; Sorrentino, 2013; Vansteenkiste et al., 2006.
Olympic interviews: Hansen, 2014, 2016; Zaccardi, 2014.

Chapter 23: Subtle Bullying
[Note: The author distinguishes between overt and subtle bullying in terms of degree of aggression. Most literature on aggression contains both overt and subtle types, usually listed together.]
Types and effects of bullying [also called aggression]: Bandura, 1991, 2001; Bjorkqvist et al., 1992; Bjorkqvist et al., 2000; Brendtro, 2001; Brown & Richardson, 1996; Collishaw et al., 2010; Del Gaizo & Falkenbach, 2008; Green et al., 1996; Greenwald, 1996; Greenwald et al., 2003; Grieve & Mahar, 2010; Grieve & Panebianco, 2013; Groves & Brown, 2005; Lagerspetz et al., 1988; Levenson et al., 1995; Miller et al., 2003; Nichols, 1996; Niemiec & Ryan, 2009; Olweus, 1996; Richardson & Green, 1999, 2003; Richardson & Brown, 2006.
Emotional abuse solicitation: Brendtro, 2001; Nichols, 1996; Olweus, 1996; Richardson & Green, 1999, 2003; Richardson & Brown, 2006.
Subtle bullying is damaging to both the abuser and victim: Brendtro, 2001; Biali, 2013; Hoover & Olson, 2000; Nichols, 1996; Olweus, 1996.
No one can relax in an environment with subtle bullying; emotional safety based on manipulation is not secure: Brendtro, 2001; Gibbs, Potter, Goldstein, & Brendtro, 1998; Nichols, 1996; Olweus, 1996; Ryan & Deci, 1989, 2000, 2001; Vansteenkiste et al., 2006; Van Oort et al., 2009; Weiner, 1985; Weiner et al., 1987.
Subtle bullying results in emotional and physical injuries [injuries that are stress-related, as opposed to inflicted]: Brendtro, 2001;Nichols, 1996; Tugade et al., 2004; Vaillant, 2000.
Racism, sexism, and appearance anxiety is damaging: Nichols, 1996, Reeve, 2015, Richardson et al., 2003; Richardson & Brown, 2006.
Ability is affected by bullying, but resiliency can lessen the effect: Brendtro, 2001; Nichols, 1996; Olweus, 1996; Sorrentino, 2013.
The characterization of abusers, users, enablers, and choosers [original concepts built on previous concepts]: AA, 1994; Adams, 2018; Cloud & Townsend; Olweus, 1996.
Abusers walk on; enablers are walked on; users join or remain silent—a form of abusing. General concepts supported in: Brendtro, 2001; Nichols, 1996; Olweus, 1996; Sorrentino, 2013.
It can be painful to recognize bullying: Brendtro, 2001; Biali, 2013; Evans, 2002; Nichols, 1996; Olweus, 1996.
Past bullying triggers can affect future situations [see triggers].

Chapter 24: Choose Respect
[Note: the bulk of boundary information is original: Adams, 2018.]
Be respectful 100% of the time: Brendtro, 2001; Dillon, 1997; Nichols, 1996; Olweus, 1996.
Respect and trust are different: Brown, 2015; Dillon, 1997.

Emotional wounds are real: Adams, 2018.

Every person benefits from understanding boundaries: Adams, 2018; Biali, 2013; Cleantis, 2017; Cloud & Townsend, 1992; Worthington, 1998.

Boundary and manipulation clarifications: Adams, 2018; Cloud & Towsend.

Boundaries become noticed when respect is lacking: Biali, 2013.

Chapter 25: Strong and Squeaky Clean

[Note: many chapter concepts are original synthesis based on previously documented concepts: Adams, 2018.]

There's no such thing as losing focus: Morgan, 2008.

Thought suppression, "white bear" research: Wegner et al., 1987.

Negative self-talk is emotional abuse, and forms of self-bullying, self-consciousness [see also ego involvement; control; autonomic thoughts]: Adams, 2018; Boyel, 2015; Brach, 2015; Cleantis, 2017; Deci & Ryan, 1985, 1987; Hardy, Oliver & Tod, 2008; Reeve, 2015.

Benefits of admitting wrongdoing: Weiner et al., 1991.

There is no giving joy, peace, or strength without having them: Meyer, nd as cited in Cleantis, 2017.

Cleaning the street [see related, previous chapters and inner congruency/reduction of cognitive dissonance]: Harmon-Jones & Mills, 1999 as cited in Reeve, 2015; Reeve, 2015.

Chapter 26: Fail... and Other Smart Things

[Note: many chapter concepts are supported previously or are original concepts based on research synthesis and experience.]

Thoughts and info on failure: Smith, 2018; Hansen 2014, 2016; Fail Forward, 2018.

Information on Edison: quora.com, nd.

Information on muscle failure training: Williamson, 2018.

Never perform; always practice: Emmons & Thomas, 1998; 2008; Goldsberry, 2017.

Retain performance power: Goldsberry, 2017.

Perspective is altered by telling Stories: Castillo, 2009. [See also cognitive dissonance resolution.]

How and why is affected by motivation: Reeve, 2015 [see also perfectionism]

Changing perspectives, or reframing, enhances progress: [see previous similar concepts]

The importance of life balance: Boyle, 2015; Brach, 2015; Cleantis, 2017.

The affect of food, water, and allergies on performing: Cummings et al., 2002; Foltz & Ferrara, 2006.

Take emotion down a notch [see previous affect of anxiety on brain function.]

How to handle embarrassment: Harris, 2001; Keltner, 1995 as cited in Reeve, 2015.

Direct attention to what can be affected: Bandura, 1983, 1988, 1991, 2001; Reeve, 2015.

Procrastination and perfectionism: [see previous chapters]

The 20% 80% rule: Urban, 2016.

Time things [see timing and initiating effort; note that timing tests or similar things can slow ability significantly so practicing timed tests prior helps reduce anxiety and increase test scores (Hill & Eaton 1977 as cited in Wigfield & Eccles, 1989). Timing to reduce the drag of initiating task engagement is always helpful.]

Break jobs into small tasks: Adams, 2012; Leffingwell, 2001; Salend, 2010; Wigfield & Eccles, 1989.

Five seconds to success [see initiating effort]

Good habits hard to break: Richards, nd. [see also neuroplasticity]

The importance of play and rejuvenation: Cleantis, 2017; Importanceofplay.eu, 2018; Iyer as cited in Haupt, 2014; Lepper & Green, 1975; Lepper et al., 2005; Whitebread, 2012 as cited in Cleantis, 2017.

Support yourself [see also intrinsic motivation]: Boyle, 2015; Brach, 2015; Cleantis, 2017.

Distractions are eliminated by treating practice as performance; thought is diverted elsewhere and performance anxiety is managed: [see previous chapters on neuroplasticity and the brain]

Performance Quality 75% of performance: Margetts, 2012.

Sport event, don't quit; learn: Castillo, 2018.

Chapter 27: Core Integrity

[Chapter concepts are either previously documented, documented below, or are original concepts based research synthesis and experience.]

Defining core integrity: [see congruency and cognitive dissonance]

Concepts on power: Smith, 1981.

Trust your practice, practice your trust: Emmons & Thomas, 1998; 2008.

Share rather than compare: Boyle, 2015; Brach, 2015; Brown, 2011.

The benefits of banishing control: Boyle, 2015; Brach, 2015; Brown, 2011; Murphy, 2004; Reeve, 2015.

The benefits of vulnerability: Boyle, 2015; Brach, 2015; Brown, 2011.

Engineering and integrity definitions: Oxford, 2008

Addictions and dysfunctional self-care can be changed: AA, 1994; Ingjaldsson, et al., 2003.

Chapter 28: Effective Leadership

[Chapter concepts are either previously documented, documented below, or are original concepts based on research synthesis and experience. See also Appendix C.]

The many problems associated with anxiety: Ashcraft, 2002; Birenbaum & Nasser, 1994; Collishaw, et al, 2010; Leffingwell, 2001; Mogel, 2005; Sena, et al., 2012; Tobias, 1980 as cited in Birenbaum & Nasser, 1994.

Little things matter, questions, comments, team anxiety log: Dodson, 2018 [see also previous similar concepts].

Anxiety weeds people out of a field: Hong, 2010; Yong et al., 2010.

Judging increases problems: Reeve, 2015; Richards, 2017 [see also assessment, empathy].

Problems becoming burnt out: Assaf, 2006; Day, Kington, Stobart, & Samons, 2006 [see also grudges and affects of stress].

Positive change is initially stressful [see baselines].

Sense the energy of a task [see kinesthetic imagery and thought construction]

Fear is contagious: Assaf, 2006; Bloom, 2008; Putwain, 2009; Putwain & Best, 2011; Reeve, 2015.

Leadership methods and emotional climates vary, like my approach between these students: Murphy, 2004; Reeve, 2015 [see also other concept documentation such as brain function, intrinsic worth, motivations]

References

AA (1994). *The Twelve Steps*. RPI Publishing, Inc.

Abril, C. R. (2007). I have a voice but I just can't sing: a narrative investigation of singing and social anxiety. *Music Education Research*, 9(1), 1-15.

Abu-Rabia, S. (2004). Teachers' role, learners' gender differences, and foreign language among seventh-grade students studying English. *Psychology*, 24(5), 722-732.

Adams, M.R. (2012). Educational Anxieties: Combining subject anxieties to improve anxiety management through educator training (unpublished thesis). Eastern Oregon University.

Adams, M.R. (2018). The difference between boundaries and manipulation (unpublished manuscript).

Adams, M.R. (in press). *Core Power Pro-Launch Pad*. [Anticipated 2018, Workbook companion to *Boost Core Power and Bust Anxiety*.]

Adams, M. R. (nd). *Just Respect*. [Manuscript in press, anticipated early 2019. Quotes used by permission.]

Adams, J. Rodham, K., Gavin, J. (2005). Investigating the "self" in deliberate self-harm. *Qualitative Health Research*, 15(10).

Akhtar, M. (2012). *Positive psychology for overcoming depression: Self-help strategies for happiness, inner strength and well-being*. London: Watkins Publishing.

Al-Ghaili, H. (nd). *Memories can pass between generations through DNA*. Retrieved from https://www.facebook.com/ScienceNaturePage/videos/1319435594855362/ [See also the references to this documentary.]

Al-Ghaili, H. (nd). *Your "Second Brain" is In Your Gut*.
Retrieved from www.facebook.com/ScienceNaturePage/videos/329301501157551/ [See also the references to this documentary.]

American Psychiatric Association [APA] (2013). *Diagnostic and statistical manual of mental disorders* (5th ed.). Arlington, VA: American Psychiatric Publishing.

Andrus, C. (2015). *The emotional edge: Discover your inner age, ignite your hidden strengths, and reroute misdirected fear to live your fullest*. New York: Harmony.

Ashcraft, M. H. (2002). Math anxiety: Personal, educational, and cognitive consequences. *Current Directions in Psychological Science*, 11(5), 181-185.

Ashcraft, M. G., & Krause, J. A. (2007). Working memory, math performance, and math anxiety. *Psychonomic Bulletin & Review*, 14(2), 243-248.

Assaf, L. (2006). One reading specialist's response to high-stakes testing pressures. *The Reading Teacher*, 60(2), 159-167.

Astin, A. W., Vogelgesang, L. J., Ikeda, E. K., Yee, J. A. (2000). How service learning affects students. *Higher Education*. Paper 144.

Atwood, G. (1971). An experimental study of visual imagination and memory. *Cognitive Psychology*, 2(3), 290-299. doi: 10.1016/0010-0285(71)90015-6

Augustine, A. A., Hemenover, S. H. (2009). On the relative effectiveness of affect regulation strategies: A meta-analysis. *Cognition and Emotion*, 23(6), 1181-1220. doi: 10.1080/02699930802396556

Austin, E. J., Farrelly, D., Black, C., Moore, H. (2007). Emotional intelligence, Machiavellianism and emotional manipulation: Does EI have a dark side? *Personality and Individual Differences*, 43, 179-189.

Aylett, A. (2000). Setting: Does it have to be a negative experience? *Support for learning*, 15(1), 41-45.

Bandler, R. (2016). Retrieved from richardbandler.com

Bandura, A. (1983). Self-efficacy determinants of anticipated fears and calamities. *Journal of Personality and Social Psychology, 452*, 464-469.

Bandura, A. (1988). Self-efficacy conception of anxiety. *Anxiety Research*, 1, 77-98. doi: 10.1080/10615808808248222

Bandura, A. (1991). Social cognitive theory of moral thought and action. In W. M. Kurtines & J. L. Gewirtz (Eds.), *Handbook of moral behavior and development*, Vol. 1 (pp. 45–103). Hillsdale, NJ: Erlbaum.

Bandura, A. (2001). Social cognitive theory: An agentic perspective. *Annual Review of Psychology, 52*(1), 26.

Bandura, A., Reese, L., & Adams, N. E. (1982). Microanalysis of action and fear arousal as a function of differential levels of perceived self-efficacy. *Journal of Personality and Social Psychology*, 43(1), 5-21. doi: 10.1037/0022-3514.43.1.5

Bateson, P. Curley, J. (2013). Developmental approaches to behavioral biology. *Nova Acta Leopoldina NF111*, Nr. 380, 89-110.

Bawa, P. (1981) Neural development in children: A neurophysiological study. *Electroencephalography and Clinical Neurophysiology*, 52(4), 249-256. doi: 10.1016/0013-4694(81)90054-7

Belnap, P. (2012, August). Lecture, International Organ Workshop, Brigham Young University, Provo, UT.

Belsky, J., Pluess, M. (2009). Beyond diathesis stress: Differential susceptibility to environmental influences. *Psychological Bulletin, 135(6)*, 885-908. doi: 10.1037/a0017376

Berenson, G. (2005). Health promotion in school of music. *American Music Teacher*, 54(6), 103-104.

Berlyne, D. E., (1975). Behaviorism? Cognitive theory? Humanistic psychology? To Hull with them all. *Canadian Psychological Review/Psychologie, 16(2)*, 69-80. doi: 10.1037/h0081798

Berthoud, H., & Neuhuber, W. L. (2000). Functional anatomy of the afferent vagal system. Autonomic Neuroscience, 85, 1–17.

Biali, S., (2013, April 30). If you set a boundary, expect to deal with anger. *Psychology Today*. Retrieved from www.psychologytoday.com

Bible (2018). [King James Bible] www.kingjamesbibleonline.org

Bible (2018). [King James Bible] www.mormon.org

Birenbaum, M., Nasser, F. (1994). On the relationship between test anxiety and test performance. *Measurement & Evaluation in Counseling & Development, 27*(1), 293.

Bjorkqvist, K. Lagerspertz, K. M. J., Kaukiainen, A. (1992). Do girls manipulate and boys fight? Developmental trends in regard to direct and indirect aggression. *Aggressive Behavior,* 18, 117-127.

Bjorkqvist, K., Osterman, K., Kaukiainen, A. (2000). Social intelligence – empathy + aggression? *Aggression and Violent Behavior,* 5(2), 191-200. doi: 10.1016/S1359-1789(98)00029-9

Bloom, A. (2008, May 30). When exam nerves turn to anger. *The Times Educational Supplement*, 4790.

Boucher, H. & Ryan, C. (2011). Performance stress and the very young musician. *Journal of Research in Music Education*, 58(4), 329-345.

Boyle, S. (2015). *The Four Gifts of Anxiety: Embrace the Power of Your Anxiety and Transform Your Life*. Avon, MA: Adams Media.

Brach, T. (2015). The RAIN of self-compassion. (Dec. 16, 2015). Retrieved from https://www.tarabrach.com/

Bradberry, T., Greaves, J. (2005). *The emotional intelligence quick book: Everything you need to know to put your EQ to work*. New York, NY: Fireside.

Bradbury, T. N., Fincham, F. D. (1990). Attributions in marriage: review and critique. Psychological Bulletin, 107, 3–33.

Bradley, R. T., McCraty, R., Atkinson, M., Tomasino, D., Daugherty, A., Arguelles, L. (2010). Emotion self-regulation, psychophysiological coherence, and test anxiety: results from an experiment using electrophysiological measures. *Applied Psychophysiol Biofeedback*, 35, 261-283.

Bragge, P. (2006). Performing arts medicine-past, present, and future. *Victorian Journal of Music Education*, 6-14.

Brendtro, L. K. (2001). Worse than sticks and stones: Lessons from research on ridicule. *Reclaiming Children and Youth*, 10(1), 47-49.

Bressler, S. L, Coppola, R., & Nakamura, R. (1993). Episodic multiregional cortical coherence at multiple frequencies during visual task performance. *Nature*, 366(6451), 153-156.

Brown, B. (2011). Shame perfectionism and embracing wholehearted living. Excepted from *The Gifts of Imperfection*. *Iris; Charlottesville*, 61(Fall), 12-16, 1.

Brown, B. (2015). *Daring Greatly: How the courage to be vulnerable transforms the way we live, love, parent, and lead*. New York, NY: Gotham Books.

Brown L. G., Richardson, D. S. (1996). How do friendship, indirect, and direct aggression relate? *Aggressive Behavior*, 22, 81-85. doi: 10.1002/(SICI)1098-2337(1996)22:23.0.CO;2-X

Castillo, B., (2009). *Self Coaching 101: Use your mind—don't let it use you*. Lexington, KY: Castillo.

Castillo, B. (2018). https://thelifecoachschool.com/podcasts

Chakravarti, A., Little, P. (2003, Jan 23). Nature, nurture and human disease. *Nature Publishing Group* 421, pp. 412-414.

Chan, K. O. L. (2011, May). Affective concepts in music performance education: An Einsteinian approach (doctoral thesis). University of Western Australia: Education.

Chapman, H. A., Kim, D. A., Susskid, J. M., Anderson, A. K. (2009). In bad taste: Evidence for the oral origins of moral disgust. *Science*, 323(5918), 1222-1226. doi: 10.1126/science.1165565

Cheatham, M. J. (2017). Train with the Brain in Mind: Neuroscience education as a force multiplier. *InterAgency Journal*, 8(4), 82-91.

Cherniss, C. & Goleman, D. (1998, October 7). Bringing Emotional Intelligence to the Workplace (a technical report). *The Consortium for Research on Emotional Intelligence in Organization*.

China Disabled Peoples Performing Arts Group. https://www.facebook.com/greatbigstory/videos/1792571651045260/

Chirkov, V. I., & Ryan, R. M. (2001). Parent and teacher autonomy-support I Russian and U.S. adolescents: Common effects on well-being and academic motivation. *Journal of Cross Cultural Psychology*, 32, 618-635.

Chrousos, G. P. (1995). The hypothalamic-pituitary-adrenal axis and immune-mediated inflammation. *The New England Journal of Medicine* 332, 1351-1363. doi: 10.1056/NEJM199505183322008

Chrousos G. P. Gold, P. W. (1992). The concepts of stress and stress system disorders: overview of physical and behavioral homeostasis. *Journal of the American Medical Association*, 267, 1244-52. doi:10.1001/jama.1992.03480090092034

Chrousos, G. P., Kino, T. (2005) Interactive functional specificity of the stress and immune responses: The Ying, the yang, and the defense against 2 major classes of bacteria. *The Journal of Infectious Diseases,* 192(4) 551-555. doi: 10.1086/432135

Cleantis, T. (2017). *An Invitation to Self-Care.* Center City, MN: Hazelden.

Cloninger, C. R., Gillgan, S. B. (1987). Neurogenetic mechanisms of learning: A phylogenetic perspective. *Journal of Psychiatric Research,* 21(4), 457-472. doi: 10.1016/0022-3956(87)90094-X

Cloud, J., Townsend, J. (1992). *Boundaries: when to say yes, how to say no, to take control of your life.* Grand Rapids, Michigan: Zondervan.

Collishaw, S., Maughan, B,; Natarajan, L., & Pickles, A. (2010). Trends in adolescent emotional problems in England: a comparison of two national cohorts twenty years apart. *Journal of Child Psychology & Psychiatry,* 51(8), 885-894.

Condie, S. J, (2010, December). Handel and the Gift of Messiah. *Ensign.*

Cottyn, J., De Clercq, D., Pannier, J., Crombez, G., & Lenoir M. (2006). The measurement of competitive anxiety during balance beam performance in gymnasts. *Journal of Sports Sciences,* 24(2), 157-164.

Coupland, R. E., Parker, T. L., Kesse, W. K., & Mohamed, A. A. (1989). The innervation of the adrenal gland. III: Vagal innervation. Journal of Anatomy, 163, 173–181.

Cramer, S. C., Sur, Mriganka, Dobkin, R. H., O'Brien, C., et al., (2011). Harnessing neuroplasticity for clinical applications. *Brain: a Journal of Neurology,* 134(6), 1591-1609. doi: 10.1093/brain/awr039

Cumming, J., Ramsey, R. (2008). Imagery interventions in sport. *Advances in Applied Sport Psychology: A Review.* S. D. Mellalieu, S. Hanton (Eds.) Routledge: New York, NY.

Cummings, D. E., Weigle, D. S., Frayo, R. S., Breen, P. A., Ma, M. K.,, Dellinger, E. P., et al. (2002). Plasma ghrelin levels after diet-induced weight loss or gastric bypass surgery. *New England Journal of Medicine,* 346, 1623-1630.

Davidson, R. J., McEwen, R. S. (2012). Social influences on neuroplasticity: stress and interventions to promote well-being. *Nature Neuroscience,* 15, 689-695.

Davis, G. (2010) Captivating behavior: mouse models, experimental genetics and reductionist returns in the neurosciences. *The Sociological Review.* 58(1), 53-72. doi: 10.1111/j.1467-954X.2010.01911.x

Day, C., Kington, A., Stobart, G., & Samons, P. (2006). The personal and professional selves of teachers: stable and unstable identities. *British Educational Research Journal*, 32(4), 601-616.

Deci, E. L., Ryan, R. M. (1985). The general causality orientations scale: Self-determination in personality. *Journal of research in personality, 19(2)*, 109-134. doi: 10.1016/0092-6566(85)90023-6

Deci, E. L., Ryan, R. M. (1995). Human Anatomy. In M. H. Kernis (Ed.) *Efficacy, Agency, and Self-Esteem*. New York, NY: Springer Science+Business Media.

Deci E. L., Koestner, R., Ryan, R. M. (1999). A meta-analytic review of experiments examining the effects of extrinsic rewards on intrinsic motivation. *Psychological Bulletin, 125*, 627-668.

Del Gaizo, A., & Falkenbach, D.M. (2008). Primary and secondary psychopathic-traits and their relationship to perception and experience of emotion. *Personality and Individual Differences, 45*, 206-212.

Dias, B. G., Ressler, K. J. (2013). Parental olfactory experience influences behavior and neural structure in subsequent generations. *Nature Neuroscience, 17*, 89-96. Retrieved from https://www.nature.com

Dillon, R. S. (1997). Self-respect: Moral, emotional, political. *Ethics, 107*, 226-249.

Dodson, S. (2018). Correspondence. Pasco, WA.

Domesticviolence.org (2015). http://domesticviolence.org/personalized-safety-plan/

Dossey, L. (Ed.) (2014). FOMO, digital dementia, and our dangerous experiment. *The Journal of Science and Healing, 10(2)*, 69-73. Retrieved from https://doi.org/10.1016/j.explore.2013.12.008 [lists many angles of information overload]

Draganski, B., Gaser, C., Busch, V., Schuierer, G., Bogdahn, U., May, A. (2004, Jan. 22). Neuroplasticity: Changes in grey matter induced by training. *Nature International Journal of Science, 427*, 311-312.

Edmondson, D., Newman, J. D., Whang, W., Davidson, K. W. (2012) Emotional triggers in myocardial infarction: do they matter? *European Heart Journal, 34(4)*, 300-306. doi: 10.1093/eurheartj/ehs398

Edwards, J. (2009). Physical activity and test anxiety. *School Science & Mathematics, 109(1)* 5-6.

Elliot, A. J., Church, M. A. (1997). A hierarchical model of approach and avoidance achievement motivation. *Journal of Personality and Social Psychology, 72(1)*, 218-232.

Ely, M. C. (1991). Stop performance anxiety! *Music Educators Journal, 78*(2), 35-39.

Emmons, S., Thomas, A. (1998). *Power Performance for Singers*. New York: Oxford University.

Emmons, S., Thomas, A. (2008). Understanding performance anxiety. *Journal of Singing*, 64(4), 461-465.

Erismann, T. (nd). Erismann and Kohler: Inversion Goggles [documentary]. University of Innsbruck: posted by BioMotionLab. Retrieved from www.youtube.com/watch?v=jKUVpBJalNQ

Esch, Tt. (2014). The neurobiology of meditation and mindfulness. In S. Schmidt & H. Walach (Eds.), *Meditation—Neuroscientific approaches and philosophical implication* (pp. 153-173). New York: Springer.

Etkin, A., Wager, T.D. (2007). Functional neuroimaging of anxiety: a meta-analysis of emotional processing in PTSD, social anxiety disorder, and specific phobia. *American Journal of Psychiatry*, 164, 1476–1488.

Evans, P. (2002). *Controlling People*. Adams Media Corp: Avon, MA

Eysenck, M. W., Calvo, M. G. (1992). Anxiety and performance: The processing efficiency theory. *Cognition and Emotion*, 6(6), 409-434. doi: 10.1080/02699939208409696

Eysenck, M. W., Derakshan, N., Santo, R., Calvo, M. G. (2007). Anxiety and cognitive performance: attentional control theory. *Emotion*, 7(2), 336-343. doi: 10.1080/02699939208409696

Fail Forward (2018). Fail Forward – Best 2018 Motivational Video [filmstrip]. Posted by InspireDiscipline. Retrieved from https://www.youtube.com/watch?v=lHkbo1LZWLU

Fairburn, C. G., Harrison, P. J. (2003). Eating disorders. *The Lancet,* 361(9355) 407-416.

Farlex, (2018). The Free Dictionary. Retrieved from www.thefreedictionary.com

Fehm, L, & Schmidt, K. (2006). Performance anxiety in gifted adolescent musicians. *Journal of Anxiety Disorders*, 20(1), 98-109.

Fernandez-Berrocal, P., Alcaide, R., & Extremera, N. (2006). The role of emotional intelligence in anxiety and depression among adolescents. *Individual Differences Research, 4(1),* 16-27.

Fiennes, M. (nd). Kundalini Yoga with Maya Fiennes: A Journey through the Chakras. Retrieved from www.bodyinbalance.tv.

First Four Minute Mile (2018). Retrieved from https://www.history.com/this-day-in-history/first-four-minute-mile

Florin-Lechner, S. M., Druhan, J. P., Aston-Jones, G., & Valentino, R. J. (1996). Enhanced norepinephrine release in prefrontal cortex with burst stimulation of the locus coeruleus. *Brain Research*, 742, 89–97.

Foltz, B. D., Ferrara, J. (2006). Dehydration's hidden symptoms. Excerpts from *The Secrets of Superior Hydration.* Retrieved from *http://www.kokopelliswellness.com/wordpress/DehydrationHiddenSymptoms.pdf*

Forkey, H. (2015). Medical effects of trauma: A guide for lawyers. Child Law practice, 34:7. American Bar Association. Retrieved from https://www.americanbar.org/content/dam/aba/administrative/child_law/clp/vol34/july15.authcheckdam.pdf

Foster, J. A. (2018). Gut feelings: Bacteria and the Brain. *Cerebrum* July-Aug, www.ncbi.nlm.nih.gov/pmc/articles/PMC3788166/ [Good reference resource for the gut-brain axis impact.]

Francis, H. M., Fisher, A., Rushby, J. A., McDonald, S. (2016). Reduced heart rate variability in chronic severe traumatic brain injury: Association with impaired emotional and social functioning, and potential for treatment using biofeedback. *Neuropsychological Rehabilitation, 26*(1), 103-125. doi: 10.1080/09602011.2014.1003246

Frankl, V. E. (1959; 1985). *Man's Search for Meaning.* Beacon Press.

Frankl, V. E. (1960). Paradoxical intention: A logotherapeutic technique. *American Journal of Psychotherapy, 14,* 520-535.

Frankl, V. E. (1975) Paradoxical intention and dereflection. *Psychotherapy: Theory, Research & Practice, 12*(3), 226-237.

Fredrickson, B. L. (1998). What good are positive emotions? *Review of General Psychology, 2*(3), 300-319. dx.doi: 10.1037/1089-2680.2.3.300

Fredrickson, B. L., Barrett, L. F (2004). Psychological resilience and positive emotional granularity: Examining the benefits of positive emotions on coping and health. *Journal of Personality, 72(6),* 1161-1190. doi: 10.1111/j.1467-6494.2004.00294.x

Frijda, N. H. (2007). *The laws of emotion.* Mahwah, NJ: Erlbaum.

Gaillot, M. T., Baumeister, R. F. (2007). The psychology of willpower: linking blood glucose to self-control. *Personality and Social Psychology Review, 11,* 303-327. doi: 10.1177/1088868307303030

Galland, L. (2014). The gut microbiome and the brain. *Journal of Medicinal Food* 17(2), 1261-1272 Doi: 10.1089jmf.2014.7000

Gallwey, W. T. (1974). *The Inner Game of Tennis.* New York, NY: Random House and Bantam Book.

Gardian (2012, November 12). Experiments show we quickly adjust to seeing everything upside-down. *The Guardian.* Retrieved from www.theguardian.com/education/2012/nov/12/improbable-research-seeing-upside-down [Theodore Erismann and Ivo Kohler research with glasses].

Gibbs, J., Potter, G., Goldstein, A., & Brendtro, L. (1998). How EQUIP programs help youth change. *Reclaiming Children and Youth, 7,* 117-124.

Gilman, S. G. (2012, Jan. 28). Get to the heart of the Matter by Harnessing the Power of the Zone for Peak Performance. California Southern University, guest lecture series Jan. 28, 2012. Retrieved from calsouthern.edu/content/events/21012-get-to-the-heart-of-the-matter-by-harnessing-the-power-of-the-zone-for-peak-performance

Giovanello, K. S., Schacter, D. L. (2012). Reduced specificity of hippocampal and posterior ventrolateral prefrontal activity during relational retrieval in normal aging. *Journal of Cognitive Neuroscience*, 24, 159-170. doi: 10.1152.jocn_a_00113

Giovanni, B. M., Csikszentmihalyi, M. (1996, June). The effect of perceived challenges and skills on the quality of subjective experience. *Journal of Personality*. doi: 10.1111/j.1467-6494.1996.tb00512.x

Giusto, E. L., Cairncross, K., King, M. G. (1971). Hormonal influences on fear-motivated responses. *Psychological Bulletin,* 75(6), 432-444.

Goldsberry, R. E. (2017). [Master Class guest lecture]. Presented at Brigham Young University, Provo, UT.

Goswami, U. (2008). Principles of learning, implications for teaching: a cognitive neuroscience perspective. *Journal of Philosophy of Education*, 42(3-4), 381-399.

Green, L. R., Richardson, D. R., Lago, T. (1996). How do friendship, indirect, and direct aggression relate? *Aggressive Behavior,* 22, 81-86. doi: 10.1002/(SICI)1098-2337(1996)22:23.0.CO;2-X

Greenwald, A. G., Nosek, B. A., Banaji, M. R. (2003). Understanding and using the Implicit Association Test: I. An improved scoring algorithm. *Journal of Personality and Social Psychology*, 85(2), 197-216. dx.doi.org.proxy1.calsouthern.edu/10.1037/h0087889

Greenwald, A. G., Poehlman, T. A., Uhlmann, E. L., Banaji, M. R. (2009). Understanding and using the Implicit Association Test: III. Meta-analysis of predictive validity. *Journal of Personality and Social Psychology,* 97(1), 17-41.

Gregor, A. (2005). Examination anxiety: live with it, control it or make it work for you? *School Psychology International*, 26, 617.

Grieve, R., Mahar, D. P. (2010). The emotional manipulation-psychopathy nexus: Relationships with emotional intelligence, alexithymia, and ethical position. *Personality and Individual Differences,* 48(8), 945-950. Retrieved from https://eprints.qut.edu.au/

Grieve, R., Panebianco, L. (2013) Assessing the role of aggression, empathy, and self-serving cognitive distortions in train emotional manipulation. *Australian Journal of Psychology,* 65(2), 79-88.

Gross, J. J., John, O. P. (2003). Individual differences in two emotion regulation processes: Implications for affect, relationships, and well-being.

Journal of Personality and Social Psychology, 85(2), 348-362. doi: 10.1037/0022-3514.85.2.348

Gross, M. J., Hall, R., Bringer, J. D., Cook, C. J., Kilduff, L. P., Shearer, D. A. (2017). Resonant frequency training in elite sport: A case study example. *Journal of Sport Psychology in Action,* 8(3). doi: 10.1080/21520704.2017.1287797

Groves, D. A., Brown, V. J. (2005). Vagal nerve stimulation: A review of its applications and potential mechanisms that mediate its clinical effects. Neuroscience and Biobehavioral Reviews, 29(3), 493-500.

Haid, K. (1999). Coping with performance anxiety. *Teaching Music,* 7(1), 40-60.

Hale III, W. W., Raaijmakers, Q. A. W., Muris, P., Van Hoof, A., & Meeus, W. H. J., (2009). One factor or two parallel processes? Comorbidity and development of adolescent anxiety and depressive disorder symptoms. *Journal of Child Psychology and Psychiatry,* 50(10), 1218-1226.

Hamann, D. L., (1982). An assessment of anxiety in instrumental and vocal performances. *Journal of Research in Music Education,* 30(2), 77-90.

Hamann, D. L. (1985). The other side of stage fright. *Music Educators Journal,* 71(8), 26-28.

Hamann, D. L., Gordon, d. G. (2000). Burnout. *Music Educators Journal,* 87(3), 34.

Hamilton, J. (2008, October 2). Think you're multitasking? Think again. National Public Radio's *Morning Edition.* Retrieved from www.npr.org/templates/story/

Hamilton, J. P., Etkin, A., Furman, D. J., Lemus, M. G., Johnson, R. F., Gotlib, I. H. (2012). Functional neuroimaging of major depressive disorder: A meta-analysis and new integration of baseline activation and neural response data. *American Journal of Psychiatry,* 169(7), 693-703.

Hanin Y., & Hanina M. (2009). Optimization of performance in top-level athletes: an action- focused coping approach. *International Journal of Sports Science & Coaching,* 4(1), 47-58.

Hansen, Kate (2014, January). Broken, not beaten. *BYU Magazine.* Retrieved from https://www.youtube.com/watch?v=DMpqHi2Z7lg

Hansen, Kate (2016, May). How failure got me to the Olympics. [TEDxBYU]. Retrieved from https://www.youtube.com/watch?v=B056xz8Ztlk

Hardy, J. Oliver, E., Tod, D. (2008). A framework for the study and application of self-talk within sport. *Advances in Applied Sport Psychology: A Review.* S. D. Mellalieu, S. Hanton (Eds.) Routledge: New York, NY.

Harris, C. R. (2001). Cardiovascular responses of embarrassment and effects of emotional suppression in a social setting. *Journal of Personality and Social Psychology,* 81(5), 886-897. doi: 10.10371//0022-3514.81.5.886

Harvard Health Publishing (2018, May 1) Understanding the stress response: Chronic activation of this survival mechanism impairs health. Harvard Medical School. Retrieved from www.health.harvard.edu/staying-healthy/

Hassabis, D., Kumaran, D., Maguire, E. A. (2007). Using imagination to understand the neural basis of episodic memory. *Journal of Neuroscience,* 27(52), 14365-14374. doi: 10.1523/JNEUROSCI.4549-07.2007

Hassert, D. L., Miyashita, T., & Williams, C. L. (2004). The effects of peripheral vagal nerve stimulation at a memory-modulating intensity on norepinephrine output in the basolateral amygdala. *Behavioral Neuroscience,* 118(1), 79-88.

Haupt, J., (2014). The art of doing nothing. [interview with Pico Iyer]. *Psychology Today.* Retrieved from www.psychologytoday.com/blog/one-true-thing/201411/pico-iyer-the-art-doing-nothing.

Hinton, C., Miyamoto, K., & Dilla-Chiesa, B. (2008). Brain research, learning and emotions: implications for education and research, policy and practice. *European Journal of Education,* 43(1), 87-103.

Hirsch, J. A., & Bishop, B. (1981). Respiratory sinus arrhythmia in humans: How breathing pattern modulates heart rate. *American Journal of Physiology,* 241 (4), H620-H629.

Hedden, T., Gabrieli, J. D. E. (2004). Insights into the ageing mind: a view from cognitive neuroscience. *Nature reviews Neuroscience,* 5, 87-97. Retrieved from www.nature.com/articles/nrn1323

Hobson, S. M. (1996). Test anxiety: rain or shine! *Elementary School Guidance & Counseling,* 30(4), 316-318.

Hodgins, H. S., & Knee, C. R. (2002). The integrating self and conscious experience. In E. L. Deci & R. M. Ryan (Eds.) *Handbook of self-determination* (pp. 65-86). Rochester, NY: University of Rochester Press.

Holdefer, R. N., & Jensen, R. A. (1985). The effects of peripheral d-amphetamine, 4-OH amphetamine, and epinephrine on maintained discharge in the locus coeruleus with reference to the modulation of learning and memory by these substances. Brain Research, 417, 108– 117. doi: 10.1016/0006-8993(87)90184-3

Hong, Z-R. (2010a). Effects of a collaborative science intervention on high achieving students' learning anxiety and attitudes towards science. *International Journal of Science Education,* 32(15), 1971-1988. doi: 10.1080/09500690903229304

Hong, Z-R. (2010b). An investigation of students' personality traits and attitudes toward science. *International Journal of Science Education,* 33(7), 1001-1028. doi: 10.1080/09500693.2010.524949

Hoover, J., & Olson, G. (2000). Sticks and stones may break their bones: Teasing as bullying. *Reclaiming Children and Youth*, 9, 87-91.

Houri-Ze'evi, L. et al (2016). A Tunable Mechanism Determines the Duration of the Transgenerational Small RNA Inheritance in *C. elegans*. *Cell* 165(1) 88-99 doi.org/10.1016/j.cell.2016.02.057 [Also cited in *US National Library of Medicine National Institutes of Health NCBI*. Mar 24; 165(1):88-99, doi: 10.1016/j.cell.2016.02.057.]

Houston, W., Chase, D., Iscovich, M. (Producers) & Marshall, G. (Director). (2001). *The Princess Diaries* [Motion Picture]. United States: Walt Disney Pictures.

Hunnicutt, H., Winter, S. (2011). Musical performance anxiety: adapting psychotherapy techniques of desensitization to the voice studio, part 1. *Journal of Singing*, 67(3) 331-336.

Hurrell, J. J., Murphy, L. R., (1996). Occupational stress intervention. *American Journal of Industrial Medicine*, *29(4)*, 338-341. doi: 10.1002/(SICI)1097-0274(199604)29:4<338::AID-AJIM11>3.0.CO;2-2

Immler, S. (2018, September). The sperm factor: Paternal impact beyond genes. *Heredity (Edinb)*, 121(3), 239-247. doi: 10.1038/s41437-018-0111-0. Retrieved from https://ueaeprints.uea.ac.uk/67487/

Importanceofplay.eu (2018). [Articles on the importance of play.]

Infinite Flow Dance Company (2018). Retrieved from http://www.infiniteflowdance.org/home

Ingjaldsson, J. T., Thaeyer, J. F., Laberg, J. C. (2003). Craving for alcohol and pre-attentive processing of alcohol stimuli. *International Journal of Psychophysiology*, 49(1), 29-39. doi: 10.1016/S0167-8760(03)00075-8

International VSA Festival Arts and Disability (2010, June 6-12). Retrieved from http://www.prweb.com/releases/2010/05/prweb3979414.htm and https://www.youtube.com/watch?v=hvxKKIzup78

Isen, A. M. Daubman, K. A. (1984). The influence of affect on categorization. *Journal of Personality and Social Psychology*, 47(6), 1206-1217.

Isen, A. M., Johnson, M. M., Mertz, E., Robison, G. F. (1985). The influence of positive affect on the unusualness of word associations. *Journal of Personality and Social Psychology*, 48(6), p. 1413-1426.

Isen, A. M., Reeve, J. (2005). The influence of positive affect on intrinsic and extrinsic motivation: Facilitating enjoyment of play, responsible work behavior, and self-control. *Motivation and Emotion,* 29(4), 295-323. doi: 10.1007/s11031-006-9019-8

Iwata, B. A. (1987). Negative reinforcement in applied behavior analysis: an emerging technology. *Journal of Applied Behavior Analysis,* 20(4), 361-378.

Izard, C. E. (1989). The structure and functions of emotions: Implications for cognition, motivation, and personality. In I. S. Cohen (Ed.), *The G. Stanley Hall lecture series: Vol. 9. The G. Stanley Hall lecture series* (pp. 39-73). Washington, DC, US: American Psychological Association. http://dx.doi.org/10.1037/10090-002

Izard, C. E. (2007). Basic emotions, natural kinds, emotion schemas, and a new paradigm. *Perspectives on Psychological Science, 2,* 260-280.

Janik, D. S. (2008). What every language teacher should know about the brain. *From brawn to brain: Strong signals in foreign language education.* [Proceedings of the ViKiPeda-2007 Conference in Helsinki, May 21–22, 2007, published 2008]. Retrieved from http://www.helsinki.fi/~tella/290.pdf#page=11

Jalongo, M., & Hirsh, R. (2010). Understanding reading anxiety: New insights from neuroscience. *Early Childhood Education Journal, 37,* 431-435.

Johnston, C. A., Tyler, C., Stansberry, S. A., Moreno, J. P., Foreyt, J. P. (2012). Brief report: gum chewing affects standardized math scores in adolescents [Abstract]. *Journal of Adolescence, 35*(2), 455-459.

Kail, R. V., Cavanaugh, J. C. *Human Development: A Life-Span View (7th Ed).* Cengage Learning: Boston, MA.

Kamath, C. (2013). Analysis of heart rate variability signal during meditation using deterministic-chaotic quantifiers. *Journal of Medical Engineering & Technology, 37*(7), 436-448. doi: 10.3109/03091902.2013.828106

Keifer, Jr., O. P., Hurt, R. C., Ressler, K. J., Marvar, P. J. (2015). The physiology of fear: Reconceptualizing the role of the central amygdala in fear learning. *Physiology, 30,* 389-401. doi: 10.1152/physiol.00058.2014

Keller, J. (2008). On the development of self-regulatory focus: The role of parenting styles. *European Journal of Social Psychology, 38,* 3354-364. doi: 10.1002/ejsp.460

Kenny, D. T. (2005). A systematic review of treatments for music performance anxiety. *Anxiety, Stress, and Coping, 18*(3), 183-208.

Kenny, D. T., Osborne, M. S. (2006). Music performance anxiety: new insights from young musicians. *Advances in Cognitive Psychology, 2*(2-3), 103-112.

Kerka, S. (1989). Journal Writing and Adult Learning. *ERIC Digest No. 174.* Retrieved from https://www.ericdigests.org/1997-2/journal.htm

Keyes, C. L. M. (2007). Promoting and protecting mental health as flourishing: A complementary strategy for improving national mental health. *American Psychologist, 62*(2), 95-108.

Kitchener, L. S., King, P. M., & DeLuca, S. (2006). Development of reflective judgment in adulthood. In C. Hoare (Ed.), *Handbook of adult development and learning* (pp. 73-98). New York: Oxford University Press.

Khalsa, S., Shorter, S., Cope, S., Wyshak, G., Sklar, E. (2009). Yoga ameliorates performance anxiety and mood disturbance in young professional musicians. *Applied Psychophysiol Biofeedback*, 34, 279-289.

Kirchner, J., Bloom, A., Skutnick-Henley, P. (2008). The relationship between performance anxiety and flow. *Medical Problems of Performing Artists*, 23, 59-65.

Kokotsaki, D., Davidson, J. W. (2003). Investigating musical performance anxiety among music college singing students: a quantitative analysis. *Music Educator Research*, 5(1), 45-59.

Lagerspetz, K.M.J., Bjorkqvist, K., Peltonen, T. (1988). Is indirect aggression typical of females? Gender differences in aggressiveness in 11- to 12- year-old children. *Aggressive Behavior*, 14, 403-414.

Lamm, E. & Jablonka, E. (2008). The nurture of nature: Hereditary plasticity in evolution. *Philosophical Psychology*, 21(3), 305-319. doi: 10.1080/09515080802170093

Langhorst, P., Schulz, G., & Lambertz, M. (1986). Integrative control mechanisms for cardiorespiratory and somatomotor functions in the reticular formation of the lower brain stem. In P. Grossman, K. H. L. Janssen, & D. Vaitl (Eds.), *Cardiorespiratory and cardiosomatic psychophysiology* (pp. 9-39). New York, NY: Plenum Press.

Lawrence, Watking & Jarrott, 1995 Lawrence, A. J., Watkins, D., & Jarrott, B. (1995). Visualization of beta-adrenoreceptor binding sites on human inferior vagal ganglia and their axonal transport along the rat vagus nerve. *Journal of Hypertension*, 13, 631–635.

Lazaroff, E. (2001). Performance and motivation in dance education. *Arts Education Policy Review*, 103(2), 23-29.

Lazarus, R. S. (1991). Progress on a cognitive-motivational-relational theory of emotion. *American Psychologist*. 46(8), 819-834.

LeBlanc, A., Jin, Y. C., & Obert, M. (1997.) Effect of Audience on Music Performance Anxiety. *Journal of Research in Music Education*, 45(3), 480-496.

Leffingwell, R. J. (2001). Misbehavior in the classroom—anxiety, a possible cause. *Education*, 97(4), 360-363.

Lenhart, A., Arafeh, S., Smith, A. (2008). Writing, technology and teens. Pew Internet & American Life Project website: http://pewinternet.org. Retrieved from heeps://eric.ed.gov/?id_ED524313

Lehrer, P. M. (1985). Psychological approaches to the management of tension in performance. *Journal of Research in Music Education*, 35(3), 143-153.

Lehrer, P. M. (1987). A review of the approaches to the management of tension and stage fright in music performance. *Journal of Research in Music Education*, 35(3), 143-153.

Lehrer, P. M, Vaschillo, E., Vaschillo, B., Lu, S. E., Eckberg, D. L., Edelberg, R., . . . Hamer, R. M. (2003). Heart rate variability biofeedback increases baroreflex gain and peak expiratory flow. *Psychosomatic Medicine*, 65 (5), 796-805.

Lepper, M. R., & Greene, D. (1975). Turning play into work: Effects of adult surveillance and extrinsic rewards on children's intrinsic motivation. *Journal of Personality and Social Psychology*, 31, 479-486.

Lepper, M. R., Corpus, J. H., Iyengar, S. S. (2005). Intrinsic and extrinsic motivational orientations in the classroom: Age differences and academic correlates. *Journal of Educational Psychology*, 97(2), 184-196. dx.doi.org.proxy1.calsouthern.edu/10.1037/0022-0663.97.2.184

Levenson, R. W. (2011). Basic emotion questions. *Emotion Review*, 3(4), 378-386. doi: 10.1177/1754073911410743

Levenson, M.R., Kiehl, K.A. & Fitzpatrick, C.M. (1995). Assessing psychopathic attributes in a noninstitutionalized population. *Journal of Personality and Social Psychology*, 68, 151-159.

Libby, L. K., Schaeffer, E. M., Eibach, R. P. (2007). Visual perspective in mental imagery affects self-perception and behavior. *Psychological Science*, 18(3).

Likar, A.,& Raeburn, S. (2009, Spring). Performance anxiety: a resource guide. *Flutist Quarterly*, 32.

Loyd, B. D. (2005). The effects of reality therapy/choice theory principles on high school students' perception of needs satisfaction and behavioral change. *International Journal of Reality Therapy*, 25(1), 5-9.

Lynn, K. (2013). Dance and imagery—the link between movement and imagination. *Journal of Physical Education, Recreation and Dance*, 61(2), 17. doi: 10.1080/07303084.1990.10606434

Margetts, L. (2012, August). [Lecture, International Organ Workshop]. Presented at Brigham Young University, Provo, UT.

Martin A. J., Jackson, S. A. (2008). Brief approaches to assessing task absorption and enhanced subjective experience: Examining 'short' and 'core' flow in diverse performance domains. *Motivation and Emotion*, 32(3), 141-157.

Martin, A. J., March H. W. (2006). Academic resilience and its psychological and educational correlates: a construct validity approach. *Psychology in the Schools*, 43(3), 267-281.

Matsui, T., Shinba, T., & Sun, G. (2018). The development of a novel high-prevision major depressive disorder screening system using transient autonomic responses induced by dual mental tasks. *Journal of Medical Engineering & Technology*, 42(2). doi: 10.1080/03091902.2018.1435744

Mauskop, A. (2005). Vagus nerve stimulation relieves chronic refractory migraine and cluster headaches. Cephalalgia, 25 (2), 82-86.

McCraty, R., Atkinson, M., Tomasino, D, Bradley, R. T. (2009). The Coherent Heart, Heart-Brain Interactions, Psychophysiological Coherence, and the Emergency of System-Wide Order. Integral Review website: http://www.integral-review.org/issues/

McCraty, R., Atkinson, M., Tiller, W. A., Rein, G., & Watkins, A. D. (1995). The effects of emotions on short-term heart rate variability using power spectrum analysis. *American Journal of Cardiology*, 76 (14), 1089-1093.

McEwen, B.S. (1998). Stress, adaptation, and disease. Allostasis and allostatic load. *Ann. N. Y. Acad. Sci.* 840, 33–44.

McEwen, B. S. Sapolsky, R. M., (1995). Stress and cognitive function. *Current Opinion in Neurobiology*, 5(2), 205-216. doi: 10.1016/0959-4388(95)80028-X

McEwen, B. S. (1999). Lifelong effects of hormones on brain development: Relationship to health and disease. In L. A. Schmidt & J. Schulkin (Eds.), *Series in affective science. Extreme fear, shyness, and social phobia: Origins, biological mechanisms, and clinical outcomes* (pp. 173-192). New York, NY, US: Oxford University Press. doi: 10.1093/acprof:oso/9780195118872.003.0010

McGonigal, K. (2013). How to make stress your friend. [Published TED Sept 4, 2013, presented June 2013]. Retrieved from https://video.search.yahoo.com/search/video?fr=mcafee&p=how+to+make+stress+your+friend+McGonigal#id=51&vid=c6f9e96536eac48e731de7fa41621e22&action=click

Meharg, S. S. (1988). Help for the anxious performer. *Music Educators Journal*, 75(2), 34-37.

Miller, N. Pedersen, W. C. Earleywine M. et al. (2003). A theoretical model of triggered displaced aggression. *Personality and social psychology Review, 7(1),* 75-97 doi: 10.1207/S15327957PSPR0701_5

Mogel, W. (2005). The oy, oy, oy, show. *Independent School*, 65(1) 22-26.

Monteiro, C. A. (2009). Nutrition and health. The issue is not food, nor nutrients, so much as processing. *Public Health Nutrition,* 12(5), 729-31. doi: 10.1017/S1368980009005291

Moors, A. Ellsworth, P. C., Scherer, I. R. & Frijda, N. G. (2013). Appraisal theories of emotion: State of the art and future development. *Emotion Reviews*, 5, 119-124.

Morgan, A. (2008). Attention in sport. *Advances in Applied sport Psychology.* S. D. Mellalieu, S. Hanton (Eds.) Routledge: New York, NY.

Murphy, S. (Ed.).(2004). *The Sport Psychology Handbook*. Champaign, IL: Human Kinetics.

Narvaez, D. (2010). The embodied dynamism of oral becoming: Reply to Haidt (2010). *Perspective on Psychological Science* 5(2) 1815-186 DOI: 10.1177/1745691610362353

Natarajan, S. (2018, March). The digital downpour: Combating information overload. *The Costco Connection*, 29.

National Domestic Violence Hotline (nd). Retrieved from http://www.thehotline.org

National Institute for Occupational Safety and Health [NIOSH] (n/a). *Stress...at work*. Publication No. 99-101. https://www.cdc.gov/niosh/docs/99-101/pdfs/99-101.pdf

Neilsen, C., Studer, R. K. Hildebradt, H., Nater, U. M., Wild, P., Danuser, B., Gomez, P. (2017). The relationship between music performance anxiety, subjective performance quality and post-event rumination among music students. *Psychology of Music*, 46(1). doi: 10.1177/0305735617706539

Neimeyer, R. (2010). Symptoms and significance: constructivist contributions to the treatment of performance anxiety. *Journal of Constructivist Psychology*, 23, 42-46.

Neumann, J. K., Chi, D. S. (1999) Relationship of church giving to immunological and TxPA Stress Response. *Journal of Psychology & Theology*, 27(1), 43-51.

Nezlek, J. B. & Derks, P. (2006). Use of humor as a coping mechanism, psychological adjustment, and social interaction. *International Journal of Humor Research*, 14(4). doi: 10.1515/humr.2001.011

Nichols, P. (1996). Lessons on lookism. *Reclaiming Children and Youth*, 5, 118-122.

Niemiec, C. P., Ryan, R. M. (2009). Autonomy, competence, and relatedness in the classroom: Applying self-determination theory to educational practice. *Theory and research in education*, 7(2), 133-144. doi: 10.1177/1477878509104318

Niijima, A. (1992). Electrophysiological study on the innervation of the adrenal gland in the rat. *Journal of the Autonomic Nervous System*, 41, 87–92.

Nolen-Hoeksema, S., Wisco, B. E., Lyubomirsky, S. (2008). Rethinking rumination. *Perspectives in Psychological Science*, 3, 400-424.

Olivares, J.-L. (2016, May 13). Memories can be inherited, and scientists might have just figured out how: How our experiences get passed down to our children. *Futurism*. Retrieved from https://www.sciencealert.com/

Olweus, D. (1996). Bully/victim problems at school: Facts and effective intervention. *Reclaiming Children and Youth*, 5, 15-21.

Olympic interviews, (2014). [Televised interviews, author observed].

Ortony, A., & Clore, G. L. (1989). Emotion, mood, and conscious awareness. *Cognition and Emotion*, 3, 125-137.

Osborne, M. S., Kenny, D. T. (2005). Development and validation of a music performance anxiety inventory for gifted adolescent musicians. *Journal of Anxiety Disorders*, 19(7), 725-751.

Osborne, M. S. & Kenny, D. T. (2008). The role of sensitizing experiences in music performance anxiety in adolescent musicians. *Psychology of Music*, 36(4), 447-462.

Oxford (2008). Oxford Dictionaries. Oxford University Press. Retrieved from www.oxforddictionaries.com

Palmer, B., Donaldson, C., Stough, C. (2002). Emotional intelligence and life satisfaction. *Personality and Individual Differences, 33*, 1009-1100. doi: 10.1016/S0191-8869(01)00215-X

Paton, J. F. R. (1998). Convergence properties of solitary tract neurons synaptically driven by cardiac vagal receptors in the mouse. Journal of Physiology, 508, 237–252.

Paton, J. J., Belova, M. A., Morrison, S. E., Salzman, C. D. (2006). The primate amygdala represents the positive and negative value of visual stimuli during learning. *Nature, 439*, 865-870.

Patriquin, M. A., Wilson, L. C., Kelleher, S. A., Scarpa, A. (2001). Psychophysiological reactivity to abust-related stimuli in sexually revictimized women. *Journal of Aggression, Maltreatment & Trauma, 21(7)*. doi: 10.1080/10926771.2012.690835

Patterson, K., Grenny, J., McMillian, R., Switzler, A. (2002). *Crucial Conversations: Tools for talking when stakes are high.* New York: McGraw-Hill.

Paulus, M. P., Stein, M. B. (2006). An insular view of anxiety. *Biological psychiatry: A Journal of Psychiatric Neuroscience and Therapeutics*, 60(4), 383-387. doi: 10.1016/j.biopsych.2006.03.042

Petranek, C. F., Corey, S., Black, R. (1992). Three levels of learning on simulations: Participating, debriefing, and journal writing. *Simulation & Gaming, 23(2)*, 174-185. doi: 10.1177/1046878192232005

Petrovich, A. (2003). Performance anxiety: how teachers can help. *American Music Teacher*, 53(3), 24-27.

Pipher, M. (1996). When girls become bullies. *Reclaiming Children and Youth*, 5(1),34.

Plant, R., Ryan, R. M. (1985). Intrinsic motivation and the effects of self-consciousness, self-awareness, and ego-involvement: An investigation of internally controlling styles. *Journal of Personality, 53*, 435–449.

Poirazi, P., Mel, B. W., (2001). Impact of active dendrites and structural plasticity on the memory capacity of neural tissue. *Neuron* 29(3), 779-796.

REFERENCES

Posener, J. A., DeBattista, C., Williams, G. H. et al. (2000). 24-hour monitoring of cortisol and corticotropin secretion in psychotic and nonpsychotic major depression. *Archives of General Psychiatry* 57, 755-760.

Putwain, D. W. (2009). Situated and contextual features of test anxiety in UK adolescent students. *School Psychology International*, 30, 56.

Putwain, D. W. and Best, N. (2011). Fear appeals in the primary classroom: effects on test anxiety and test grade. *Learning & Individual Differences*, 21(5), 580-584.

Quora (nd). How many times did Thomas Alva Edison fail exactly? Retrieved from https://www.quora.com/

Rae, G., McCambridge, K. (2004). Correlates of performance anxiety in practical music exams. *Psychology of Music*, 32(4), 432-439.

Ramsey, D. (2018). Retrieved from Daveramsey.com

Raschke, F. (1986). Coordination in the circulatory and respiratory systems. In L. Rensing, U. an der Heiden, & M. C. Mackey (Eds.), *Temporal disorder in human oscillatory systems* (pp. 152-158). Berlin Springer-Verlag.

Reeve, J. (2015). *Understanding Motivation and Emotion* (6th ed.). Hoboken, NJ: Wiley.

Reisenzein, R.(1994). Pleasure-arousal theory and the intensity of emotions. *Journal of Personality and Social Psychology,* 67, 525-539.

Richards, A. (nd). Personal interview. Clinton, MD.

Richards, C. (2017). Personal interview. Pocatello, ID.

Richards, J. (1997). Personal interview. Manassas, VA.

Richardson, D. R., Green, L. R. (1999). Social sanction and threat explanations of gender affects on direct and indirect aggression. *Aggressive Behavior* 25(6), 425-434. doi: 10.1002/(SICI)1098-2337(1999)25:6<425::AID-AB3>3.0.CO;2-W

Richardson, D. S., Green, L. R. (2003). Defining direct and indirect aggression: The Richardson Conflict Response Questionnaire. *International Review of Social Psychology*, 16(2), 11–30.

Richardson, D. S., Brown, L. G. (2006). Direct and indirect aggression: Relationships as social context. *Journal of Applied Social Psychology* 36(10), 2492-2508, doi: 10.1111/j.0021-9029.2006.00114.x [direct—confront, indirect—through others]

Rideout, Roger R. (2002). Psychology and music education since 1950. *Music educators Journal,* Sept., 33-37.

Robertson, D. U., Eisensmith, K. E. (2010). Teaching students about performance anxiety. *Music Educators Journal*, 00274321, 97(2).

Rogers, C. R. (1961). *On becoming a person*. Boston: Houghton Mifflin.

Roughan, L., Hadwin, J. A. (2011). The impact of working memory training in young people with social, emotional, and behavioral difficulties. *Learning and Individual Differences*, 21(6), 759-764.

Ruiz-Aranda, D., Salguero, J. M., Cabello, R., (2012). Can an emotional intelligence program improve adolescents' psychosocial adjustment? Results from the INTEMO project. *Social Behavior and Personality*, 40(8), 1373-1380.

Rutter, M., Moffitt, T. E., Caspi, A. (2005). Gene-environment interplay and psychopathology: Multiple varieties but real effects. *Journal of Child Psychology and Psychiatry, 47(3-4)*, 226-261. doi: 10.1111/j.1469-7610.2005.01557.x

Ryan, R. M. (1982). Control and information in the intrapersonal sphere: An extension of cognitive evaluation theory. *Journal of Personality and Social Psychology, 43*, 450–461.

Ryan, C., Andrews, N. (2009). An investigation into the choral singer's experience of music performance anxiety. *Journal of Research in Music Education*, 57(2), 108-126.

Ryan, R. M., Deci, E. L. (1989). Bridging the research traditions of task/ego involvement and intrinsic/extrinsic motivation: Comment on Butler (1987). *Journal of Educational Psychology* 81(2), 265-268. dx.doi.org.proxy1.calsouthern.edu/10.1037/0022-0663.81.2.265

Ryan R. M. & Deci, E. L. (2000). Intrinsic motivations: Classic definitions and new directions. *Contemporary Educational Psychology, 25, 54-67.*

Ryan, R. M., & Deci, E. L. (2001). On happiness and human potentials: A review of research on hedonic and eudaimonic well-being. *Annual Review of Psychology, 52*, 141-166.

Salend, S. J. (2012). Teaching students not to sweat the test. *Phi Delta Kappan*, 93(6), 20-25.

Savignac, H. M., Tramullas, M., Kiely, B., Dinan, T. G., Cryan, J. F. (2015). Bifidobacteria modulate cognitive processes in an anxious mouse strain. *Behav Brain Research* 287:59-72 doi:10.1016/j.bbr.2015.01.044.

Sax, L. (1997). The benefits of service: Evidence from Undergraduates. *Higher Education. Paper 38.*

Schreurs, J., Seelig, T., & Schulman, H. (1986). Beta 2-adrenergic receptors on peripheral nerves. *Journal of Neurochemistry*, 46, 294–296.

Schulkin, J., Rosen, J. B. (1999).Neuroendocrine regulation of fear and anxiety. In L. A. Schmidt & J. Schulkin (Eds.), *Series in affective science. Extreme fear, shyness, and social phobia: Origins, biological mechanisms, and clinical outcomes* (pp. 173-192). New York, NY, US: Oxford University. doi: 10.1093/acprof:oso/9780195118872.003.0009

Schwartz, (2013, February 9). Relax! You'll Be More Productive. *New York Times*. Retrieved from http://www.nytimes.com/

Segal, M., Markram, H., & Richter-Levin, G. (1991). Actions of norepinephrine in the rat hippocampus. *Progress in Brain Research*, 88, 323–330, doi: 10.1016/S0079-6123(08)63819-4

Seitz, J.A. (2000). The bodily basis of thought. *New Ideas in Psychology*, 18(1), 23-40. doi: 10.1016/S0732-118X(99)00035-5

Sena, J.D.W., Lowe, P.A., & Lee, S.W. (2012). Significant predictors of test anxiety among students with and without learning disabilities. *Journal of Learning Disabilities*, 40(4), 360-376.

Shonkoff, J. P., Garner, A. S. (2011). The lifelong effects of early childhood adversity and toxic stress. *Pediatrics* 129(1), 232-246 doi:10.1542/peds.2011-2663

Slavich, G. M., Way, B. M., Eisenberger, N. I., & Taylor, S. E. (2010). Neural sensitivity to social rejection is associated with inflammatory responses to social stress. Cousins Center for Psychoneuroimmunology and Department of Psychology, University of California, Los Angeles, Ca. doi.org/10.1073/pnas.1009164107

Small, C. (1998). *Musicking: the meanings of performing and listening (pp.208-219)*. Hanover, New Hampshire: Hanover Wesleyan University Press.

Smith, J. (1981). Section 121. *Doctrine & Covenants*. Salt Lake City, UT: Corp. of Pres.

Smith, W. (2018). [filmstrip]. Posted by Goalcast. Retrieved from https://www.youtube.com/watch?v=r1Gy5YjBMvk

Solar, E. (2011). Prove them wrong. *Teaching exceptional children*, 44(1), 40-45.

Sood, S. Gupta, R. (2012). A study of gratitude and well being among adolescents. *Journal of Humanities and Social Science*, 3(5), 35-38.

Sorrentino, R. M. (2013). Looking for B = f (P, E): The exception still forms the rule. *Motivation and Emotion*, 37(1), 4-13.

Spencer, N. J. Hibberd, T. J., Travis, L.....Sorsensen, J. (2018). Identification of a rhythmic firing pattern in the enteric nervous system that generates rhythmic electrical activity in smooth muscle. *Journal of Neuroscience* 38(24) 5507-5522. Doi.org/10.1523/JNEUROSCI.3489-17.2018

Stephens, R. Tunney, R. J. (2004). Role of glucose in chewing gum-related facilitation of cognitive function. *Appetite*, 43(2), 211-213.

Sternbach, D. J. (2008). Stress in the lives of music students. *Music Educators Journal*, 94(3).

Stevens, P. Smith, R. L. (2013). *Substance Abuse Counseling* (5th ed.). Upper Saddle River, NJ: Pearson.

Stevenson, G. E. (2017, October). Spiritual Eclipse. *Ensign.*

Stolpa, J. M. (2004). Math and writing anxieties. *Phi Kappa Phi Forum,* 84(3), 3-5.

Studer, R., Gomez, P. Hildebrandt, H., Arial, M., Danuser, B. (2011). Stage fright: its experience as a problem and coping with it. *International Archives of Occupational & Environmental Health,* 84(7), 761-771.

Sweeney, G. A., & Horan, J. J. (1982). Separate and combined effects of cue-controlled relaxation and cognitive restructuring in the treatment of musical performance anxiety. *Journal of Counseling Psychology,* 29(5), 486-497.

Taborsky, C. (2007). Musical performance anxiety: a review of literature. *Update,* (2), 15-25.

Takeuchi, N., Ekuni, D., Tomofuji, T., Morti, M. (2018). Relationship between masticatory performance and heart rate variability: A pilot study. *Acta Odontological Scandinavica,* 71(3-4), doi: 10.3109/00016357.2012.734403

Tarrant, R., Leathem, J., Flett, R. (2010). What have sport and music performance taught us about test anxiety? *Psychology Journal,* 7(2), 67-77.

Thayer, J. F., Ahs, F., Fredrikson, M., Sollers III, J. J., Wager, T. D. (2012) A meta-analysis of heart rate variability and neuroimaging studies: Implications for heart rate variability as a marker of stress and health. *Neuroscience and Biobehavioral Reviews,* 36, 747-756.

Thayer, J. F., Lane, R. D. (2008). Claude Bernard and the heart-brain connection: Further elaboration of a model of neurovisceral integration. *Neuroscience & Biobehavioral Reviews,* 33(2), 81-88. doi: 10.1016/j.neubiorev.2008.08.004

Thomas, O., Mellalieu, S. D., Hanton, S. (2008). Stress management in applied sport psychology. In S. D. Mellalieu, S. Hanton (Eds.), *Advances in Applied Sport Psychology: A Review.* New York, NY: Routledge.

Tiller, W. A., McCraty, R., & Atkinson, M. (1996). Cardiac coherence: A new, non-invasive measure of autonomic nervous system order. *Alternative Therapies in Health and Medicine,* 2(1), 52-65.

Trolinger, V. (2005). Performing arts medicine and music education: what do we really need to know? *Music Educators Journal,* 92(2), 41.

Tsujimoto, S. (2008). The prefrontal cortex, functional neural development during early childhood. *The Neuroscientist* 14(4), 345-358. doi: 10.1177/1073858408316002

Tugade, M. M., Fredrickson, B. L., Barrett, L. F. (2004). Psychological resilience and positive emotion granularity: Examining the benefits of positive emotions on coping and health. *Journal of Applied Psychology,* 71, 1161-1190. doi: 10.1111/j.1467-6494.2004.00294.x

Tugade, M. M., Fredrickson, B. L. (2006). Regulation of positive emotions: Emotion regulation strategies that promote resilience. *Journal Of Happiness Studies.* 8(3), 311-333.

Turpin, G. (1986). Cardiac-respiratory integration: Implications for the analysis and interpretation of phasic cardiac responses. In P. Grossman, K. H. L. Janssen, & D. Vaitl (Eds.), *Cardiorespiratory and cardiosomatic psychophysiology* (pp.139-155). New York, NY: Plenum Press.

Turpin, G. (1986). Cardiac-respiratory integration: Implications for the analysis and interpretation of phasic cardiac responses. In P. Grossman, K. H. L. Janssen, & D. Vaitl (Eds.), *Cardiorespiratory and cardiosomatic psychophysiology* (pp.139-155). New York, NY: Plenum Press.

Urban, Tim (2016). Inside the mind of a master procrastinator. [*TED Talks*]. Retrieved from https://www.ted.com/talks/tim_urban_inside_the_mind_of_a_master_procrastinator

Vaillant, G. E. (2000). Adaptive mental mechanisms: Their role in a positive psychology. *American Psychologist,* 55, 89-98.

Van Kemenade J.F.L.M., Van Son M. J. M., Van Heesch N. C. (1995). Performance anxiety among professional musicians in symphonic orchestras: a self-report study. *Psychological Reports,* 77(2), 555-562. doi: 10.2466/pr0.1995.77.2.555

Van Oort, F. V. A., Greaves-Lord, K., Verhulst, F. C., Ormel, J., & Huizink, A. C. (2009). The developmental course of anxiety symptoms during adolescence: the TRAILS study. *Journal of Child Psychology and Psychiatry,* 50(10), 1209-1217.

Vansteenkiste, M. Matos, Lens, W., Soenes, B. (2006). Understanding the impact of intrinsic versus extrinsic goal framing on exercise performance: The conflicting role of task and ego involvement. *Psychology of Sport and Exercise,* 8(5), 771-794. doi: 10.1016/j.psychsport.2006.04.006

Walker, B. (2018). Personal interview June; Associate Professor of Music, Columbia Basin College, Pasco, WA; Christmas Community concert, Dec. 2015, Pasco, WA.

Walker, I. J., & Nordin-Bates, S. M. (2010). Performance anxiety experiences of professional ballet dancers: the importance of control. *Journal of Dance Medicine & Science,* 14(4), 133.

Wall, R. B. (2005). Tai Chi and mindfulness-based stress reduction in a Boston public middle school. *Pediatric Health Care,* 19(4), 230-237. doi: 10.1016/j.pedhc.2005.02.006

Watts, Ardean (nd). [Lecture]. Presented at the University of Utah.

Weaver, I. C. (2007). Epigenetic programming by maternal behavior and pharmacological intervention. Nature versus nurture: let's call the whole thing off. *Epigenetics* 2(1): 22-8. Eupb 2007 Jan 15. [Also cited in Pub-Med.gov

https://www.ncbi.nlm.nih.gov/pubmed/17965624?dopt=Abstract&holding=npg]

Wegne, D. M., Schneider, D. J., Carter, S. R., White, T. L. (1987). Paradoxical effects of thought suppression. *Journal of Personality and Social Psychology*, 53(1), 5-13. dx.doi.org.proxy1.calsouthern.edu/10.1037/0022-3514.53.1.5

Weiner, B. (1985). An attributional theory of achievement, motivation, and emotion. *Psychological Review, 92(4)*, 548-573.

Weiner, B., Frieze, I., Kukla, A., Reed, L., Rest, S., & Rosenbaum, R. M. (1987). Perceiving the causes of success and failure. In E. E. Jones, D. E. Kanouse, H. H. Kelley, R. E. Nisbett, S. Valins, & B. Weiner (Eds.), *Attribution: Perceiving the causes of behavior* (pp. 95-120). Hillsdale, NJ, US: Lawrence Erlbaum Associates, Inc.

Weiner, B., Graham, S., Peter, O. and Zmuidinas, M. (1991). Public confessions and forgiveness. *Journal of Personality*, 59, 263–312.

Weisinger, H., & Pawliw-Fry (2015). *Performing Under Pressure: The science of doing your best when it matters most*. New York, NY: Crown Business.

Wiechman, B. M. Gurland, S. T. (2009). What happens during the free-choice period? Evidence of a polarizing effect of extrinsic rewards on intrinsic motivation. *Journal of Research in Personality, 125(6)*, 627-668. doi: 10.1016/j.jrp.2009.03.008

Wigfield, A., Eccles, J. S. (1989). Test anxiety in elementary and secondary school students. *Educational Psychologist*, 24(2), 159-183.

Williamson, J. (2018). What is Muscle Failure? *Bodybuilding*, 16. Retrieved from http://www.healthguidance.org/

Winecoff, A., LaBar, K. S., Madden D. J., Cabeza, R., Huettel, S. A. (2011). Cognitive and neural contributors to emotion regulation in aging. *Social Cognitive and Affective Neuroscience,* 6, 165-176. doi: 10.1093/scan/nsq030

Woolfolk, A. (2010*). Educational Psychology*. Columbus, Ohio: Merrill.

Worthington, Jr. E. J. (1998). An empathy-humility-commitment model of forgiveness applied within family dyads. *Journal of Family Therapy*, 20, 59-76. doi: 10.1111/1467-6427.00068

Wortman, C. B., Brehm, J. W. (1975). Responses to Uncontrollable Outcomes: An Integration of Reactance Theory and the Learned helplessness model. *Advances in Experimental Social Psychology*, 8, 277-336, doi: 10.1016/S0065-2601(08)60253-1

Yehuda, R., Daskalakis, N. P., Bierer, L. M. Bader, H. N. Klengel T., Holsboer, F., Binder, E. B. (2016). Holocaust Exposure Induced Intergenerational

Effects on *FKBP5* Methylation. *Biological Psychiatry: A Journal of Psychiatric Neuroscience and Therapeutics*, 80(5), 372-380. doi: 10.1016/j.biopsych.2015.08.005

Yondem, Z. (2007). Performance anxiety, dysfunctional attitudes and gender in university music students. *Social Behavior and Personality*, 35(10), 1415-1426.

Young, C. B., Wu, S. S., & Menon, V. (2012). The neurodevelopmental basis of math anxiety. *Psychological Science*, 23, 492.

Young, S. (2016). *QB: My Life Behind the Spiral*. Boston, MA: Houghton Mifflin Harcourt.

Yuan, K., Qin, W. Wang, G. et al. (2011, June 3). Microstructure abnormalities in adolescents with internet addiction disorder. *PLoS ONE*. Retrieved from http://www.plosone.org/

Zaccardi, Nick (2016, February 10). Kate Hansen retires from luge, eyes Running of the Bulls. Retrieved from https://olympics.nbcsports.com/

Zinn, M., McCain, C., Zinn, M. (2000). Musical performance anxiety and the high risk model of threat perception. *Medical Problems of Performing Artists*, 15, 69-71.

Acknowledgements

My thanks to those I learned from and those who contributed ideas and support during this project. This book has been rewritten several times as the scope widened from performance anxiety, to all educational anxieties, to outcome anxiety. New insights and research was added in the process, increasing the breadth and depth. In such a lengthy project it is always a concern that someone will be missed in the acknowledgements. If this has happened, I hope it is brought to my attention.

Special thanks to Dr. Bart Adams for his patience, ideas, and technical assistance. Special thanks also to James Adams, Michelle Adams, Sherie Christensen, Karen McNeff, Brian Adams, Julie Howald, Carolyn Richards, Ara Richards, James C. Richards and JaNae Richards for their expertise, sustained assistance and encouragement.

Thanks also to Alison Parker for editorial supervision, Kamryn Brockbank for illustrations, Teresa Lynn Anderson of Ann Lynn Photography, and Lauren Healy, Chris Morabito, and Steve Harrison's team at Bradey Communications for publicity. Thanks to my students and the things I learned from them. Thanks also for support and feedback from Lynn Belnap, Dr. Linda Margetts, Christine Riesenweber, Ben Walley, Spring McGiffin, Associate Professor Bruce Walker, Michelle Maughan, Dr. Sharlene Milner, Sarah Dodson, Mattie Lybbert, Pat Hagan, Chad Haertling, Sandy Humphreys and Matt Yoshioka.

Special thanks to Claudia Wilson, Crystal Field, Chanda Hunt, Ann Perry, Dawn Goodrich, Kathryn Burton, Tiah Peterson, Dylan Clemons, Patty Case, Melinda Gill, Jenna Lake, Jennifer Buckner, Jeanie Lemens, Hayley Lemens, The Honorable Gordon Smith, Sharon Smith, Kenny Steward, Evan Lake, Eadie Jordan, Dennis Waite, Penni Waite, Maxine Patterson, Cherish Lloyd, Cody Fielding, Diane Bricker, Deanna Lambson, Garnet Olsen, Lily Ann Gwillam, Dr. Sushma Hirani, Vanessa Orellana and Jasleen Orellana.

Thanks also to Trent Christensen, Emily Adams, Mathew McNeff, and Carl Howald, V, Annette Garcia, Bill Whitehead, Lori Keeler, Ruth Anderson, Valerie Howarth, Leslie Nufer, LaNea Adams, Lee Richards, Linda Dodson, Dr. Mark Baker, Alan Richards, Mark Richards, Sharon Richards, Valerie Richards, Ken Nufer, Joseph Keeler, Mike Anderson, Vicki Gerlach, Dr. Alan Howarth, Brett Gerlach, Joe Keeler, Dr. Karl Richards, and Diane Whitehead.

Thanks also to teachers, collogues, friends, and those I learned from: Mack Wilberg, Dr. Parley Belnap, Stephen R. Covey, Leo Richards, Lilly Richards, Bertha Reader Richards, Scott Sintay, Dennis Wilson, Nancy Wilson, Clayne Robinson, Alan Fielding, Ed Austin, Val Lindsay, Dan McNeff, Evelyn McNeff, Mike Akagi, Dr. Steve Lamb, Randy Boothe, Wade Hunsaker, Laura Hunsaker, Dee Winterton, Dennis Hamilton, Linda Hamilton, Tanya Wildbill, Marlene Stringer, Dan Leonard, Liz Leonard, Stan Cullimore, Navratils, Makalya Walker, Devon Jennings, Richard Jennings, Cindy Jennings, Pat Debenham, Jon Mitchell, Mindy Mitchell, Matt Montgomery, Melanie Contor, Barbara Montgomery, Lisa Foust, Terry Murry, Carolyn Hafen, Donald Cook, Cathy Muller, Garnet Olsen, Anny Welch, Carol Fairbanks, Irene Hendrickson, David Long, Sarah Yoshioka,

Emily Castleton, Brad Henderson, Bruce Zimmerman, Amber Henderson, Brett Amidan, James Persinger, Joan Persinger, Harry Beach, Louise Beach, Sharon Brown, Steve Muller, Kelly Brown, Linda Hardy, Marianne Larsen, Dr. Steve Neal, Tom Spackman, Beth Harrison, David Behrmann, Margaret Behrmann, Susan Neal, Mindy Davis, Sheila Holman, Julie Humphreys, Tom Humphreys, Estela Christensen, Ellis Christensen, Wendlers, Nanette Heidtman, Steven Merrill, Sue Nelson, Debra Merrill, Lester Belliston, Leona Belliston, Dan Primus, Jodi Primus, Dr. Margaret Mayer, Forths, Robert Pratt, Gundersons, Ruth Pratt, Shurtzs, Carolyn Mayer, Sonia Gerber, Myrna Van Cleave, Chris Baugh, Dr. Mike Megehee, Tony Justice, Jill Megehee, Phyllis Peterson, Dr. Todd Oyama, Laurel Pettey, Skillmans, Mandy Oyama, Cameron Howald, Debra Preston, Carla Arnold, Carol Redfield, Dave Pettey, Kedric Preston, Kathy Turner, Ken Johnson, Wendels, Bobbi Justice, Faith Pullen, Brittney Paul, Liz Nirschl, Carl Howald,IV, Julie Howald I, Janice Ballard, Var Rigby, Roberta Windham, Megan Rigby, Hunsakers, Andy Cary, Dr. Russell Harrison, Emily Muller-Cary, Angie Ford, Emily Ford, Mindi Sell, Jay Sell, Janet Sell, Brook Black, Royers, Debra Branson, Curtis Severe, Gerry Redfield, Debbie Severe, Laura Montgomery, Joel Rogo, Debra Rogo, Jessie Stragey, Margie Lamb, Burchams, Stoddards, Verla Walters, Beth Schademan, Shirley Blessinger, Craig Contor, Rachel Mohlman, Barbara Montgomery, John Remington, Haguewoods, Carol Gadaire, Paul Gadaire, Kent Jacobson, John Ashcraft, , Dr. Jason Walker, Hubbards, Alesha Walker, Tina Unrau, Colleen Smith, Patty Nelson, Dave Miller, The Honorable Jeff Bostwick, Mary Bostwick, Deanne Fielding, Chris Jones, Prestons, Carol Fairbanks, Therese Wendler, Melvin Crawford, Thomas Young, Todd Anderson, Dr. Andy Hyatt, Jannet Haddock, Carla Hyatt, Gaye Duffin, Dr. Mike Duffin, Bruce Zimmerman, Jo Latimer, Manuel Fernandez, Lori Zimmerman, Holly Harty, Brian Chambers, Roland Butler, Chaneux Chambers, Stephanie Jack, Marsha Carter.

Special thanks also to the Oregon Music Teachers Association; NYC FD support, cooperation, and commendation; RG Studios; Hale Center Theatre; LA East Studios; BYU International Organ Workshop; Brigham Young University, particularly the dance, music, theater, and education departments; Dance Educators of America; Utah Department of Education; Blue Mountain Community College, particularly the music and theater departments; Oregon East Symphony; Columbia Basin Community College, particularly the psychology and music departments; the Church of Jesus Christ of Latter-Day Saints; the Presbyterian Church; the University of Utah, particularly the dance, music and theater departments; American Mothers, Inc.; Eastern Oregon University, particularly the education, music departments and library research; USA military support for NOK; the Washington Music Teachers Association; Oregon Department of Education; California Southern University, particularly the psychology department and library research; and the Music Teachers National Association.

About the Author

Mariann Richards Adams is an internationally featured anxiety expert with experience in radio and TV. She is the author of two books and numerous articles. She presents lectures for professional organizations, universities, conferences, and businesses, as well as providing private anxiety coaching and teaching. Her masters degree was from Eastern Oregon University in music, theater, dance (PE) education, specializing in educational and performance anxieties. Her PhD studies are currently at California Southern University in clinical psychology, specializing in anxiety. Her first teaching was as an assistant to Stephen R. Covey. She now has decades of experience as a teacher, choreographer, musician, and theater director; has performed in the majority of states in the USA; and was a member of the acclaimed Young Ambassadors. She wrote and directed a celebration in Old Town San Diego for the LA Olympics, and a historical play for the Mayo Clinic centennial celebrations. A CD that her family created has been distributed throughout the United States to the families of fallen US military. She created a multi-specialty surgery center, two non-profits, and A+ Performing Arts. She is the recipient of the Oregon Mother of Achievement, NYC FD Commendation, and the BYU Alumni Distinguished Service Award. Her greatest joy is as a wife and mother to her wonderful children and delightful grandchildren. She loves to bicycle along the Columbia River and paddle board.

Made in the USA
Columbia, SC
05 February 2019